"It brings back all the allure of E.T. Hill creates and nurtures a likable character, young Danny Chase, because he's real. . . . A story to dream with."

— *The Book Reader*

AN OTTER CREEK BOOK

"This book had a good pace and the storyline was never boring. Overall, I liked it, because it dealt with an issue of changing past events or leaving the present as it is. Also, it's about how a new kid can beat the meanest of bully's, while making the best of friends. *The Magic Bicycle* is definitely a thumbs up kinda book and one I would say, 'parents, buy for your kids!'"

— *Mercury Register*

"Readers will identify with Danny, sympathize with his moral dilemma, and enjoy watching him wrestle with the tough choices that come with his magic bicycle powers."

— *Booklist* (American Library Association)

"Danny, 13, and his talking cat travel from Texas through time and space on a magical shape-changing bicycle given to him by an alien that he rescued. His quest is to consult famous thinkers (Socrates, Franklin, Einstein) and others about the wisdom of time travel and changing the past."

— *School Library Journal*

"*The Magic Bicycle* may not be an instant classic, but it is a bit deeper and more thought-provoking than many of the young adult titles being published today."

— Science Fiction SF Site

". . . a delightful story for the young as well as the young-in-spirit. The book encourages the use of imagination to deal with everyday problems. *The Magic Bicycle* is a little *Wrinkle in Time* and a little *Jonathan Livingston Seagull* with some *Calvin and Hobbes* mixed in."

— *The Tahoe Tribune*

"Everyone should read this book for the sheer pleasure it invokes. It even has a talking cat."

— E

"The best book I ever read!"

D1082517

PRAISE FOR THE MAGIC BICYCLE

". . .I didn't engage until he (Danny) began time traveling, but from then on, I was hooked. I certainly think there is an audience for this—aliens, time-travel, hint of romance with a cool girl, bullies who are put in their places—great stuff for early teens.
— Kathy Heinden, Master Teacher Provo, UT

"Incredibly imaginative. I was struck how so many ages could appreciate this piece of creative genius. I am 40 and liked it. A 14-year-old would love it."
— Keith Bissell, Toronto Canada

"I recommend this book to people who like adventure and travel. My favorite character is Murg, the calico cat. Once I started I couldn't put it down until I had read the entire book."
— Stephanie Zivkovic, Orange Park, Fl

"I felt like I was there with him as he won the bike race, as he got chased down to the haunted house and as he soared through the air. I love Murg and the alien Kah-lay-dee, with his blue hair and form changing."
— Ines Pacheco, Indianapolis, IN

Alien Encounter

Danny tumbled head over heels as he crashed down the stairs, each step biting into his body as he bounced. He tucked, covering his head, and hoped to survive the fall. His feet rebounded off the bannister, and he cartwheeled over the edge of the stairway into the pitch-dark basement.

Danny's fall ended abruptly. An old battered mattress had cushioned his fall. Something warm brushed lightly against his leg. "I'll live, Murg," Danny groaned.

When he opened his eyes, he was shocked to be staring at himself. An exact double of himself! Crimson and azure light flashed through the boarded windows of the basement and splayed about the room, illuminating his twin.

"I'm outta here!" Jumping to his feet, Danny conked his head on the underside of the steps. Stars filled his vision, falling across his double's face. Its expression had changed from imitating his surprise to capturing his pain. "Who . . . *what* are you?"

"Greetings, I am Kah-laye-dee, a stranger to your planet." Danny was amazed. Not a word had touched his ears; the alien's lips had never moved. He'd heard the words in his head.

His double's form and features began to change, no longer mimicking Danny. Kay-laye-dee's skin now gleamed with a bronze hue, and the alien grew thinner, although its head remained the same size, now looking overly large. Its flaming red curls disappeared, replaced by short blue hair that stood straight up, reminding Danny of a classmate. The alien's nose lengthened and flattened, spreading even wider. Its-his eyes were still blue, but now glowed from deep within the tall, recessed sockets of his elongated face.

Thin lips curled as the skinny being smiled. With a glowing hand, the alien reached out to touch him.

ADDITIONAL PRAISE

"The author may have been targeting 'young adults' but I found plenty in it for us 'older adults'."
—Jean Augello, Allentown, PA

"I read TMB in a very short time. Not because I am a fast reader, but because I couldn't wait to find out what happened next! This book is always entertaining and thought provoking...I am 37 years old, and all I can say is that if this is a children's book, pass me the Ovaltine!"
—Derek Fisher, Burbank,CA

"I cannot tell you how much I'm enjoying *The Magic Bicycle*. It's like I've gone back in time to when I was twelve or so, and would read all night, just couldn't put the book away. Bill will entertain people for years to come. He is a marvel."
—Shirley Butler, Green Cove Springs, FL

"I've read thousands of books, and I read best selling, well-known authors of lots of genres. The three of your books that I have read could easily be on the best seller lists, based on quality. I think they would make great movies."
—Terry Swindell, Terrell, TX

"*The Magic Bicycle* is not only an exciting yarn, but behind the action moral lessons can be identified. I couldn't put it down, so drawn was I to all the characters and the unfolding story."
—Anna Triponel, Paris, France

The Magic Bicycle

–William Hill–

OTTER CREEK PRESS, INC.
FLORIDA

The Magic Bicycle

by William Hill

Copyright © 1998 by William Hill

ISBN 1-890611-00-X (softcover)
ISBN 1-890611-07-7 (hardcover)
Library of Congress Card Number: 9766907
Retail Price: $13.95 (trade softcover)
$15.95 (Canada)
$22.95 (hardcover)
$27.95 (Canada)

All inquiries should be addressed to:

Otter Creek Press, Inc.
P.O. Box 416
Doctors Inlet, FL 32030-0416
(904)264-0465
(800)326-4809

Interior Design: Betsy Lampe
Cover Art: Mandy Davis and Rod Volkmar

First Printing 1998

Printed in the United States of America

To my family.

Dedicated to Mom, Dad, my wife Kat, sister Lynne
and nephew Evan, who never stopped believing
in my powers of imagination.

Titles by William Hill

Fiction for the Young in Spirit
The Magic Bicycle
The Magic Bicycle II: Stealing Time

Young Adult
The Vampire Hunters

Fiction
Dawn of the Vampire
Vampire's Kiss
California Ghosting
*Hunting Spirit Bear**
*The Wizard Sword**
*Dragons Counsel**

*forthcoming

I wish to thank those who made the *Magic Bicycle* possible and the best it could be.

My father and mother for supporting my efforts. My wife Kat for keeping the faith, even when my own was waning.

Volunteer proofreaders, especially my sister Lynne, nephew Evan, Dr. Steve, Jon Thatcher, Susan Spencer, Laura Dzek, Laura Brennan and my dad.

Contents

Chapter One – The Chase 13
Chapter Two – A Strange Encounter 23
Chapter Three – The Switchout 37
Chapter Four – The Magic Bicycle 51
Chapter Five – The Challenge 67
Chapter Six – Magical Transformation 77
Chapter Seven – Practice, Day One 85
Chapter Eight – Changing Terrain 97
Chapter Nine – Race Day 111
Chapter Ten – Rewards 123
Chapter Eleven – Backpedaling In Time 131
Chapter Twelve – Back To The Future 143
Chapter Thirteen – School Friends 151
Chapter Fourteen – Old Friends 163
Chapter Fifteen – Way Back 175
Chapter Sixteen – Socratic Method 187
Chapter Seventeen – Founding Father 199
Chapter Eighteen – The Visionary 209
Chapter Nineteen – Relativity 217
Chapter Twenty – Days Before Yesterday 231
Chapter Twenty-One – Gretchen and Sarah 243
Chapter Twenty-Two – Stolen 255

Chapter Twenty-Three — Friends In Need 263
Chapter Twenty-Four — Red-Handed 275
Chapter Twenty-Five — Redemption 283
Chapter Twenty-Six — Changing Time 291
Chapter Twenty-Seven — Second Chances 305

Selection from *Vampire Hunters* 311
Selection from *California Ghosting* 319
About the Author 326

Chapter One

The Chase

*B*eneath darkly overcast Texas skies, Danny Chase bicycled through the flat neighborhood of tract homes, each looking similar to the one before and the one after. Danny's thin shoulders were slumped, and his freckled face had settled in a haggard expression.

Danny sighed heavily, wishing life might be as easy as delivering the evening edition of the *Star Telegram*. At least with a paper route, you started with directions and knew your way around after a while. His life seemed to be changing all the time, usually for the worse.

Danny's front tire hit a rock that shot away, and the bicycle hopped awkwardly. Murg hissed a warning to be more careful.

His backseat driver and companion was a calico cat sitting

on the carrier above the back wheel. Her fur was covered with splashes and patches of orange, white and black. Murg appeared very bored, her green eyes almost closed. Delivering papers was a familiar routine for her.

Murg was short for Murgitroid. Since his sister Sarah's death, the calico had insisted on riding with Danny wherever he went, except to school. Danny thought it strange that Murg wanted to tag along, rain or shine, but he no longer tried to leave the cat behind. It was unhealthy; Danny had the scars to prove it. Sarah had definitely spoiled her. Or maybe Murg was lonely and just too feline to admit it. Danny knew how she felt; he missed Mom and Sarah, too.

A quick glance skyward made Danny frown. The thunder-clouds had an ominous greenish glow about them. A burst of wind almost stopped the bicycle, so Danny bore down, grinding away against the strong headwind. When a drop of rain struck his ear, Danny groaned.

He hated delivering papers in a downpour. Danny wanted to turn around and go home, but he'd made a commitment to deliver these papers. And he believed in finishing things he'd started. Danny heard a warning meow from behind him and said, "I know it's going to rain, Murg. We're almost done."

A strong gust of wind tried to steal Danny's baseball cap, but he caught it before it flew free. Murg murmured her ap-proval and meowed. "You're right. We'd better hurry or we'll get dumped on. What a great way to start October."

The sky was dark; the puffy white clouds having been pushed away by an assault of gray-black thunderheads. "Maybe we'll be lucky for once, and it'll wait until we're finished." Knowing he'd been born under a black cloud, Danny had come prepared; Murg was sitting atop his poncho.

Danny picked up the pace, then sighed heavily as he sent another Friday edition spinning. He wouldn't be surprised if it dumped on them. Maybe even hailed. Why shouldn't it? Everything else had been dumped on them.

As Danny released his final paper, a gust of wind caught it. It bounced along one of the steps, then careened off a potted plant. The planter teetered on the edge, then fell, shattering when it landed on a rock in the flower bed below.

"Murg, I'm cursed! I just know it!" Danny climbed off his bicycle, then put down the kickstand. He wanted to just leave and get home before the rain, but if he didn't tell Mrs. Wilson, and she called his father, Danny would be in big trouble. No more video games. And no more comics. Dad would call it appropriate punishment for being irresponsible. As he walked to the front porch, Danny wondered why being responsible always seemed like a punishment.

Danny knocked on the door and waited. No one answered. Staring at his reflection in the storm door, he wondered what to do and noticed that he needed a haircut. Mom had usually taken care of his wild locks; his red hair was sticking out from under his cap in all directions. There were circles under his brown eyes, and his too-freckled nose was running. He admitted he didn't look very healthy. He hoped he wasn't catching a cold. Danny absolutely abhorred being ill.

After a second knock and more waiting, Danny concluded no one was home. Mrs. Wilson couldn't really blame the broken planter on him, he thought. But with his recent luck, they'd have the front yard under camera surveillance.

With another heavy sigh, Danny got out his pad of paper and scribbled a quick note, promising to bring Mrs. Wilson a new pot soon. He left the note inside the screen door.

As Danny returned to his bicycle, two huge drops of rain splattered on the bill of his cap. They were followed by a third, then a fourth. The rain was falling sporadically but threatened to do more.

"Let's get home!" Danny donned his rain gear, then jumped onto his bicycle. He arranged the back of his poncho so Murg would be protected, then took off. Raindrops as big as marbles splattered loudly all around him.

Even during the worst of storms, his father refused to drive Danny. His dad claimed that handling adversity fostered maturity. If so, Danny thought, he should be an old man by now. Maybe being older would help. Danny snapped the poncho together and began riding.

His father and he saw eye to eye on very little nowadays. With each passing day, since the death of his mother and sister, his dad had grown more stern and distant. He hadn't always been this way. Not long ago, there had been better times; the ten speed he rode was proof of them.

He had been unable to afford a new bicycle, so his father had agreed to help him build one from used parts. Laughing, getting greasy, and having a wonderful time, they'd scoured junk yards and garage sales.

The handlebars with black striping and the pedals had come from a dump in Myrtle Beach, South Carolina. Then they'd moved. The scratched and faded red frame they'd found in Indianapolis. The seat he'd bought at a garage sale. The toe clips they'd found on a twisted bike abandoned on the side of the road. Later, they had discovered a better chain in an "antique yard" in Fallon, Nevada. The original tires had been a gift from a friend of his dad's. Danny had purchased new tires with his allowance.

When they'd gotten everything together, it had taken a long weekend to get his cycle into perfect shape – or at least as close as they could with used parts. This last spring, his father had helped him repaint it fire-engine red, and they'd put new wraps on the ten speed's handlebars.

Danny's wan smile disappeared, and he wiped away a tear. Like the weather, times had a way of changing when you least expected it. Thunder cracked loudly, and the sky seemed to rip open, the rain falling in buckets.

Danny was thinking that things couldn't get any worse until he heard the shout, "There he is! Get 'em!"

"Oh, no!" Danny cried as he glanced down the street. The sight of the three boys made Danny peddle furiously. He figured Spike was probably still hot about the lunch bag trick and had brought his brother, Rocky, and his friend, Hank, along to help him exact revenge. All three of them were huge and played football on the junior high team.

"You're dead, Chase!" Spike yelled.

Spike would pound him, again, Danny thought. But would they hurt Murg? Spurred on, Danny struggled to increase his speed against the powerful winds. A moan from Murg and a glance told Danny the three brutes were gaining on him.

With a bright flash and crack of thunder, the rain grew heavier. The wind gusted, whipping the rain about in sheets, and hammering Danny and his pursuers.

Danny hoped the storm would force the trio to quit, but he doubted it; it wasn't his fate. Anger was a powerful motivator, and Spike was very mad. Well, at least if he got pounded this time, Danny thought, it would be for something he'd done. That would be a change.

Murg expressed a pitiful meow. She hated getting wet.

Danny swung left and rode down a gentle hill. Leaning forward over the handlebars, he tried to gain extra speed. For a moment, the trick worked, and Danny pulled away. Hard splattering droplets struck his face, nearly blinding him. Why did this always happen to him? Danny wondered. Sarah had never had these kind of problems.

Danny turned left down another street, gaining a tail wind. It lashed at his back, but like a helping hand, pushed him ahead even faster. He swung right, down a steep hill, the black pavement blurring below him. Danny's knuckles were white, a death grip on the handlebars. If he slipped and fell, which would be worse? The fall? Or the beating? Sometimes he was sorry he had such a vivid imagination.

Glancing over his shoulder, Danny noticed that his pursuers had disappeared. "All right! We've lost them! This day might not be so bad after all."

The calico sounded doubtful.

Taking note of his surroundings, Danny realized he was nearing the end of the housing development. Many of the homes were still under construction, surrounded by stacks of brick and piles of lumber. The paved road ended not far ahead, continuing on as a dirt trail.

Danny looked at a mostly completed house, noticed the dry porch and said, "Hey, Murg, we can hide there until the rain stops!" Murg agreed. "After dark, we can sneak back to the house. Spike and his pals will be tired of searching for us by then."

There was a piercing whistle, followed by a distant crash that didn't sound like thunder but was accompanied by a bright flash of light. It seemed to radiate from the ground, instead of the sky downward. Did he feel the earth shake? "I wonder what that was?" Water ran down his neck, then his back, and he shivered. "Let's get out of this!"

While hiding on the covered porch, Danny's thoughts became morose. Thirteen years — and especially the last four months — had taught Danny that people were either born under a lucky star or below a black cloud that shadowed them wherever they went. Danny fell into the latter category. Maybe it was because he was redheaded. He'd heard things about redheaded stepchildren, although he wasn't a stepchild.

Watching the rain and the past few months made it easy for him to relate to the expression — when it rains, it pours — except that the saying implied there was sunshine sometimes. When had it started? The crumbling of his world . . . He had no trouble pinpointing it: last July in Germany.

Just prior to the car accident that had killed his sister and mother, Danny had argued with his mom. He was sure that her anger had distracted her; otherwise, she might have avoided the truck that had hit them. The pain of their absence was as sharp and fresh as if it had just happened yesterday.

The next day he'd forgotten to supervise the family dog, and Prince had been run over by a car. Shortly after the funeral, his dad had requested a transfer, and they had quickly left Germany for Carswell Air Force Base outside Ft. Worth, Texas.

As usual, there were relocation problems. Danny didn't fit in at school and had trouble making friends. After arriving at a new place, another stop, he always felt lucky if he was able to make even one new friend. Sometimes, Danny never met anyone with whom to share secrets, dreams, and laughter. He sorely missed Gretchen who was back in Germany. Besides Murg . . . and Sarah, Gretchen was his best friend.

Danny had tried hard to fit in, but after a month or so of repeated failures, he had finally given up. It was too tiring to pretend he was someone he was not. Besides, he was accustomed to being an outcast.

Spike Blocker – the football stud and resident thug in Danny's grade – had picked on him every day for nearly a month. At first, Spike and his buddies had just stolen his lunch, his money or his favorite pen. Recently, Spike had gotten physical. Danny was still aching from yesterday's pounding.

In years past, his mom had always talked with his teachers, but his dad refused to help him. He thought it was time for Danny to stand up for himself – to be a man. His dad believed that sometimes things needed to be settled with your fists. Danny didn't. He thought there had to be better ways to settle differences than by beating on someone.

Danny smiled with sudden satisfaction. And there was! This time he'd fixed Spike; today he'd filled his lunch bag with a surprise from Murg's litter box! Danny chuckled. Maybe, just maybe, everything wasn't going wrong after all. Spike had desperately tried to catch him after school, but Danny had given him the slip, sneaking out a different door than usual and racing away on his bicycle. Spike would be simmering all weekend!

Danny noticed it was dark and figured the three thugs had probably given up searching for him by now. "Let's go, Murg," Danny told the calico. As Danny rolled his bicycle to the dirt driveway, Murg caterwauled. Danny snapped to attention, looking right, then left.

"There he is! Now we got 'em!" Spike yelled. Riders were racing out from behind the two houses ahead. Fear surged through Danny, and he threw all his remaining energy into the ride. He made a quick right turn and headed down a badly paved road.

"Thanks for the warning," Danny breathed to Murg.

The rain continued to blind him, and the unfinished houses were a blur as Danny peddled frantically by them. Water spun off his wheels, creating a trailing spout. Danny heard splashes close behind and envisioned the awful things they might do to him. What if they carried lassos? And was it wise to use a Tazer – one of those shocking devices the police used – if it was raining?

Danny rounded the corner and suddenly came to a dead end. His eyes widened briefly, and his thoughts whirled. "Hang on!" he told Murg. Wishing he had an off road bicycle with fat tires, Danny turned off the road and down a dirt trail.

As the ground grew muddier, Danny's progress slowed. Sticky hands seemed to grab at his tires. Danny tried peddling faster, but his legs were beginning to fail him. Each breath grew more ragged, and his wet poncho clung to him, becoming more restrictive.

Danny glanced over his shoulder. The threesome had followed, but they were having even more trouble. Hank suddenly fell, the back wheel slipping out from under him. Spike almost crashed as he twisted his bicycle in an attempt to miss his downed companion.

"There's hope, Murg!" Danny cried. He wished that he

was big and strong, so he could stop, face them, and demand they leave him alone. If they didn't, then he would show them. Oh, well, Danny sighed, he wasn't big and strong, but he could probably lose them in the woods ahead.

Without slowing, Danny turned off the muddy trail, sailing over the lip and plunging into the trees. The heavy grass pulled at his tires and branches struck him, tearing his poncho. Murg let out a caterwaul and wrapped herself around the carrier. A big limb slammed into Danny, almost knocking the wind from him and nearly ripping him off the bike.

The storm had darkened the woods, and Danny could barely see, but he didn't slow down. Spike would be furious with Danny if he caught him now; no one gave Spike a hard time, especially a wimp like Danny Chase. His hat flew off before he could grab it.

Danny suddenly shot out of the trees and through a wide gap in a dilapidated fence. Before he knew what was happening, he was plummeting down a steep hill. Danny tried to brake, but his bicycle slid across the tall grass and weeds as if they were greased. Murg wailed miserably. "I'm trying!" Danny yelled.

Away from the protection of the trees, the rain struck Danny again. The storm had intensified, rain fired downward like bullets. They stung Danny all over, especially his face. He was having trouble seeing.

When Danny braked, the bicycle twisted sideways, almost getting away from him before he could right it. As his speed continued to increase, all he could do was hang on. Lightning flashed and thunder cracked harshly. Out of the corner of his eye Danny saw several old buildings; one looked like a barn or a stable.

Ahead, he thought he saw a large dark shape jutting into the night. The lightning flashed again. A huge tower loomed before him! Behind it was an old house, a mansion of some kind.

Another flare of lightning illuminated his surroundings. An

empty swimming pool was immediately ahead of him. At its nearest end, a blue-tiled tower led to a high dive. If he slid into the concrete pit, he was as good as dead.

Wait, Danny suddenly thought, there weren't any houses out here, except. . . . The hair on his neck rose, his skin seemed to crawl, and his eyes widened as the source of Danny's fear shifted. Spike and crashing into the concrete pit suddenly became a secondary worry. This was the House of Blue Lights!

"It's a haunted house!" Danny cried to Murg. Danny tried to brake again, but they continued unchecked downhill at an increasingly uncontrollable pace, slipping and sliding as though drawn toward the house and the dark maw of its pool.

When the hill bottomed out, Danny twisted the handlebars. The bike responded reluctantly, sliding to the right, then it struck something. Rearing like a bronco, the bicycle threw Danny and Murg. The calico wailed forlornly as she sailed airborne.

The bicycle bounced across the concrete porch, hit something, then careened away from the dark maw and crashed into the diving tower with the sound of crumpling metal.

Danny landed hard, lying dazed. His head throbbed, and in the driving rain and darkness, the world was a misty blur. His fear encouraged him to keep going; he had to find his bike and get out of here! The House of Blue Lights was bad news; ghosts haunted this place!

When the lightning flashed, he spotted his bicycle near the diving tower. Danny crawled toward it but became disoriented. His head was whirling around, and he saw spots dancing before his eyes. A light suddenly flashed from a window of the haunted house and a bluish radiance washed over the yard, engulfing Danny. It brightened, then grew dimmer and dimmer until only darkness remained.

Chapter Two

A Strange Encounter

Something sandpapery rubbed against Danny's cheek. And wet, he concluded through the hammering pain in his head. Heavy. There was a weight on his chest which Danny couldn't identify. It seemed to make his bones and muscles ache even more. Danny opened his bleary eyes, then quickly shut them as his face was splattered by raindrops.

In the near darkness, he'd glimpsed a dripping ball of matted black, white and orange fur. "Good kitty," Danny said as he stroked the soggy calico. Murg meowed miserably. Danny carefully opened his eyes. She looked more like a strangely colored otter than a cat.

Danny heard the distant grumble of thunder and wondered how long he'd been unconscious. The rain had nearly stopped, it was little more than a drizzle now.

Suddenly, Danny remembered where he was lying – in the yard of the House of Blue Lights – and sat up very quickly. Before passing out, he'd been engulfed by that strange light!

Murg jumped to the ground and looked back at Danny. Her expression was one of extreme annoyance, but Danny didn't care. His head was spinning with what he'd heard about this place.

The kids at school told wild stories about the strange things they'd seen at the haunted, gray stone mansion. The whole household had died from poisoning, and no one had lived there since. The kids claimed the poisoning had somehow embalmed the bodies and caused them to radiate a blue glow.

To this day, the glowing bodies wandered about the house like zombies, and their tortured spirits hovered around them, trying to recapture the life they'd once known. All they needed was extra life – a young boy or girl – to jump start them, and they would live again!

Danny shuddered. It was a creepy but impossible story. Then he thought about the blue light. Had that been his imagination? And if it hadn't been, how had he been affected? He didn't feel compelled to enter the house, or feel anything else, besides throbbing pain.

Something slammed within the mansion, riveting Danny's eyes to the three-story gray stone building. The day had grown even darker as if the sun were setting somewhere behind the stormfront, making it difficult for Danny to see much of the house beyond the empty pool.

A patchwork of gray and heavy shadows, the mammoth structure was imposing – almost like a contemporary castle. There was only one door in sight, and it stood directly before him atop cracked concrete steps. A bitter wind kicked up, howling through the broken windows of the House of Blue Lights. Shutters banged open and closed, as if people were trying to get out, but the ghosts wouldn't allow it.

All this place needed was gargoyles, Danny thought as he looked up at the roof. It was not guarded by any stone statues as far as he could see, but there did seem to be a bell tower or observatory atop the roof. A strong wind gusted again, rattling the loosely hanging gutters.

The more Danny observed the house, the more frightened he became. Strange rattles and moans emanated from the mansion. Gray paint appeared to flake off like dead skin being shed. Danny vowed to stay as far away from the place as possible. But did the zombies or ghosts ever leave the house? Chase people? "Let's grab my bike and get out of here," he muttered.

Murg murmured affirmatively.

Danny struggled to his knees, then to his feet, fighting off the waves of dizziness and the rocketing pain from his left ankle. Unable to withstand the pain, he collapsed. Danny gingerly touched his ankle; it was swollen to the size of a softball. Was it broken? That would be just his luck. But he couldn't stay here.

Danny couldn't quite remember what had happened to his bicycle but knew it lay somewhere ahead. He thought he could see the bicycle's tracks, so he followed them, crawling toward the pool through the weed-filled garden surrounding the swimming area.

Murg followed cautiously.

As Danny reached the concrete maw of the empty pool, he suddenly remembered what had happened to his bike. In the storm-dimmed twilight, he could make out the twisted frame against the base of the diving tower.

A door slammed somewhere close by and Danny jumped, his gaze shooting to the back porch. The awning was long gone, twisted metal sticking out of the stone like broken bones. The black wrought iron railing was leaning, ready at any moment to slip free from the crumbling cement. A strong wind swirled around the yard, and the door suddenly opened. Like the loose shutters, it swung wildly on its hinges, making an awful screeching noise. Then the door suddenly remained open as if inviting him inside.

Danny averted his eyes and kept crawling. He resolved to stay focused on retrieving his mangled bicycle. Just looking at it made him want to scream; he felt he'd lost a loyal friend. The front tire looked flat; and the wheel was bent double, spokes sticking out in every direction. The rest of the bicycle wasn't in any better shape; the handlebars were crooked, and the frame was warped.

Danny sighed. It was totaled. Totaled! And he was a long way from home. He was certain his father would be angry now. Danny didn't have any way to deliver the morning or evening papers except on foot . . . and that would take forever, even if he could walk tomorrow, which seemed doubtful right now. His foot throbbed and ached as though something alive was trying to chew its way to the surface.

A rustling movement and the swish of bushes somewhere behind Danny yanked him from his melancholy thoughts. Murg meowed quietly, sounding concerned. Now Danny could hear faint voices carrying from the woods. Were Spike and his friends still looking for him? Spike must really be mad. For some reason, that made Danny smile.

He peered into the dark forest, searching for signs of the threesome but saw nothing. Then he heard the sharp snap of a stick. Danny wished he were brave but knew he wasn't. Flight was best, except that he couldn't walk, let alone run on his ankle. "What should we do, Murg?" Danny asked. As he picked up his bicycle, it scraped against the concrete.

The noises in the woods halted for a moment, then the voices sounded excited. "I found something!"

Danny swore. His hat!

He wouldn't be beaten by Spike again, but the only alternative was . . . He couldn't believe what he was thinking, but then Spike and his friends would never think to look for a wimp in the House of Blue Lights. Well, he'd show them. He wasn't chicken!

Danny leaned against his mangled bicycle, using it for support as he staggered to the backporch steps. The bike squeaked and squealed as metal protested, but there wasn't anything he could do about it. If they found his bicycle, they might enter the house looking for him. The voices were now shouting and getting closer. Someone had found his trail. Still inviting, the door was open.

Danny used the shaky railing to drag himself and his bicycle up the steps. By the time he reached the door, his head was pounding like a drum, his back and arms were afire, and his ankle pulsed painfully as if ready to explode. He'd bitten his lip several times already trying to stay quiet. It was bleeding.

Danny paused at the open door. Although he was frightened by the thought of entering the haunted house, he was even more scared of Spike and company. If he'd had friends of his own, Danny thought, he wouldn't have to run and hide all the time. He could stand proudly against Spike and his pals.

Hearing, "Hey! I think we're getting close," spurred Danny forward. Leaning against his bicycle, he guided it inside.

Murg meowed, paused, then entered the mansion.

Danny quietly closed the door and jammed his ten-speed under the knob.

Exhausted, he collapsed against the wall, then slid slowly to the floor. He was sitting in what might have once been a laundry room. Wallpaper drooped from the walls, making them seem fuzzy-lined, and rotting hoses could have been dead snakes strewn across the floor.

Danny put his head in his hands. Why did these things always happen to him? He never caused any trouble, and he never bothered anybody. He just wanted to be left alone. Was that too much to ask?

Noticing he had blood on his hands, Danny touched his forehead, finding a cut atop a very large bump. By the size of the lump, he wasn't surprised that he was dizzy, or that his vision was sometimes doubled. Danny quickly took stock of his other injuries, finding numerous bruises and scratches to go along with his swollen ankle. "I'm a mess."

A creaking sound, followed by a bump and a hushed groan made Murg's ears perk up.

Danny twisted around and looked down a long corridor covered with threadbare carpet. In his imagination, the holes in the walls became the homes of amputated hands with long yellow fingernails.

Danny grabbed hold of his thoughts and forced himself to be calm. Nothing moved in the darkness, and the shadows remained still. All was quiet once more, except for a gusting wind that shook the house, rattling its gutters and shutters. Strung like a taut wire, Danny waited.

It seemed that the time between now and his next breath took forever, but he heard something again. Another series of sounds like tiny footsteps echoed from down the hallway. Danny looked at Murg who was staring in the direction of the sound. After a moment, the calico relaxed and began licking her paws. Danny wished he had a flashlight.

Until Danny heard voices, he'd forgotten about Spike. "Hey, look! I found more tracks!" It sounded like Hank.

"Follow 'em! I'm gonna kick the crap outta Chase!" Danny recognized Spike's voice.

"Strange looking tracks. They lead to the House of Blue Lights."

"Well, keep following 'em."

"I don't like this place," Hank said. "The tracks go up the steps and into the house."

Danny could hear them very clearly now. They were standing at the steps, looking up at the door.

Danny could picture the trio. Square-faced with jutting jaws, Spike and Rocky were brothers, dark, hairy behemoths with massive arms the size of railroad ties and legs like tree trunks. Spike was taller, heavier and was already growing a mustache. His eyes were set close together, giving him a deranged look. Hank was another Cro-Magnon with a prominent forehead and broken nose that hooked left. Hank was always perspiring, so his glasses were probably fogged.

"Chase is a wimp. He wouldn't go in there," Rocky said.

"Maybe. But look at the tracks. Come on," Spike grumbled.

Hank stammered something Danny couldn't understand.

"Hey, you chicken, Hank-bud? Come on. This place isn't haunted. I've . . . "

As if on cue, a golden light appeared, rolling down the hallway and washing over Danny. He was suddenly warm, and his fear was swept away. The glow faded from the laundry room, but farther down the hall a faint beam was still cast low across the floor. Danny felt drawn toward the light.

Those outside did not. "What was that?" Rocky cried.

"Not haunted, huh? Let's get out of here!" Hank yelled.

It sounded as if they were leaving in a hurry. Danny smiled. Maybe he was brave after all. That or foolhardy, he thought. As if he were receiving advice from two different people, he was of two minds on investigating the light.

He should stay put; he was in a haunted house, after all, and supernatural beasts lurked nearby. On the other hand, his curiosity was cajoling, telling him that something wondrous was occurring, and that he must go investigate.

Murg rubbed against his leg as if reinforcing the latter thought.

Danny hoped his companion would hiss and puff if they approached something dangerous. That sounded like he'd already made a decision. Surely such a beautiful radiance wouldn't bring him harm.

With one hand against the wall for support, Danny quietly moved across the laundry room and headed down the hallway. Water dripped from him as he limped, and his sneakers didn't sneak very well, squishing with every step.

The gleaming light flashed again, washing over him as it changed from golden to pink, then receded, rolling away along the hallway floor as if a carpet to guide his way. Danny bravely followed. The light was coming from behind a door not far ahead. Slivers of radiance leaked out from the edges and the top, but most of the light spilled from under the door.

Quietly mewing, Murg rubbed against it.

Danny hesitated, then reached for the doorknob. He trusted Murg's senses. Cats knew things that people didn't – or so Sarah had told him.

As Danny touched the knob, the light suddenly disappeared, leaving him in what seemed to be total darkness. Danny sensed something was close by. He was frightened, but his curiosity compelled him to investigate.

Murg rubbed against his leg, encouraging him. At least he wasn't facing this alone. Murg lightly scratched at the door.

Wishing the calico could open the door for him, Danny turned the knob. His head pounded mightily and his mouth went dry as he pulled the door toward him.

In the darkness, Danny thought he could see steps heading down. "No way! I'm not going down there!" Danny whispered to Murg.

Despite his words, Danny hung onto the doorjamb and leaned forward. Red and blue lights suddenly whirled all about him. Danny was startled but didn't lose his grip. He'd expected the lights to come from below, but they came from behind him. Danny twisted around. Out the window at the end of the hallway, a kaleidoscope of lights flashed along the yard, the fence and the woods surrounding the mansion. Had the police arrived? He hadn't heard any sirens. And why would they be looking for him?

Suddenly, the old door frame crumbled. Danny lost his balance, tumbling forward. "Hey!"

Danny rolled head over heels as he crashed down the stairs. Each step biting into him as he bounced. He covered up as best he could and hoped he survived. His feet rebounded off the bannister and sent him cartwheeling over the edge of the stairway.

Danny landed on an old tattered mattress that cushioned his impact. Something warm brushed against him. "I'll live, Murg," Danny groaned. When he opened his eyes, he was shocked to be staring at himself. Crimson and azure light flashed through the boarded windows of the basement and splayed about the room, illuminating his double.

Taken aback, Danny gasped. He'd always wanted a friend just like himself, but . . . What was going on here? He was out of here! Jumping to his feet to flee, Danny conked his head on the edge of the steps. Stars seemed to fill his vision, falling across his double's face. Its expression had changed from imitating his surprise to capturing his pain.

Danny immediately sat, pressing his hands against his throbbing head. "Who . . . what are you?" Danny whispered.

Words sounded inside Danny's head, "Greetings, I am Kahlaye-dee, a stranger to your planet."

Danny was amazed. Not a word had touched his ears. The alien's lips had never moved.

His double smiled and reached for him.

Although amazed, Danny still managed to duck but almost blacked out from the sudden movement.

Murg rubbed against his double's leg.

"You traitor!" Danny whispered harshly.

Before Danny could duck a second time, his double touched him, and a pink light enveloped them.

The alien contact sent a warm tingling feeling throughout Danny. His aches slowly faded away, and his vision improved so that he could see clearly. Slack-jawed, he couldn't believe his eyes.

His double's features were changing, no longer mimicking Danny. The shapeshifter's form shrunk, becoming thinner, but its head stayed the same size. Its flaming red curls disappeared, now replaced by short blue hair that stood straight, reminding Danny of a classmate with a mohawk. Its skin had lost its fleshy color and now gleamed with a bronze hue. The stranger's nose had lengthened, flattened and spread wide. Its – or maybe his – eyes were still blue but now glowed from deep within the tall, recessed sockets of his elongated face. Thin lips curled as the skinny being smiled.

The pink glow darkened, and the healing current strengthened. As it washed over and through Danny, it reminded him of drinking hot chocolate on a bitterly cold day, except the sensation affected his entire body. Danny touched his forehead and discovered his cut had healed. Amazing! The lump was receding; in a few moments, only smooth skin remained.

Danny smiled broadly, then careful of the stairs, stood to test his ankle. It was fine! A miracle! And his father had said there were no such things! Danny felt wonderfully renewed and invigorated; even his depression had departed. The only reminders of his desperate flight were his soggy and tattered clothing.

When the pink globe faded away, a dim golden light remained around the shapeshifter. The stranger was dressed in a white jumpsuit that was ripped and tattered, reminding Danny of his own attire. Despite the dirt and grass stains, Danny could still make out a pair of interlocked pyramids within several circles where the pocket should be. The stranger wore boots but no gloves. Its hands were palmless with four long, skinny fingers and no nails.

Words sounded inside Danny's head, "Greetings, young Terran, I am Kah-laye-dee, a Cor-ror-o'lan and visitor to your world."

"Uh, hello," Danny stammered, again amazed. "Please to meet you, Kaw-lee . . . uh . . . dah."

Again, Danny 'heard', "Kah-laye-dee."

The stranger from somewhere else picked up Murg and began stroking the calico, who purred contentedly.

"Wow! You have a real tongue-twister for a name. If you even know what a tongue is – since you don't speak," Danny finished lamely. "I'm Danny Chase." The words Daw-nee Chez sounded inside Danny's head, and he laughed. "Thanks for helping me, Kah-lee-dee. I feel great! How'd you do that?" Kah-laye-dee shrugged, then held up a finger and blew on it. Danny laughed again, and the stranger from elsewhere smiled. "Can you talk?"

"I do not know your language, so Kah-laye-dee talks to you with his mind, sending thoughts telepathically." The spike-haired stranger pointed to his very prominent forehead.

"Uh, no offense, but I'm really bad with foreign languages. I don't know why. I shouldn't be. I've had lots of practice. How about if I call you Kalyde?" Danny asked. Kah-laye-dee nodded.

Outside, car doors slammed. The sound seemed to echo through the basement like a bell tolling. There was a lot of jabbering, several people talking at once against a background of radios attuned to different stations. With a sad and fearful expression, Kah-laye-dee looked up the steps.

Danny had a sinking feeling. He thought he knew what his newfound friend was thinking. They were looking for him, and the place was surrounded. "Why are they chasing you?" Danny asked.

"Kah-laye . . . Ka-lyde is different. Kal . . . I am not from here. A foreigner, you might say."

Not meaning to do so, Danny laughed. Embarrassed by his outbreak, he placed a hand over his mouth, then said, "It sounds like we have a lot in common. I'm being chased too. When they caught up with me, I ran in here."

"They want something from Kalyde . . . from me. Information. Data. Maybe. Run tests. Absolutely."

Upstairs, there was a crashing as if the back door were being battered open. Danny remembered that his bicycle had been jammed under the knob. There was a metallic squeal, followed by cursing and footsteps moving above them. "Oh, no!" Danny quietly exclaimed. "My coming here gave you away! And now they'll find you!" Danny was appalled. This time his bad luck would harm someone else.

Kah-laye-dee shrugged.

For the first time, Danny thought that Kalyde appeared exhausted, maybe even resigned to his fate. In all the pain, surprise, and then excitement, Danny hadn't noticed Kalyde's drooping eyelids and sagging shoulders. How could I be so ungrateful? Danny wondered. Kalyde had befriended him, and since Kalyde had helped him, surely Danny could return the favor. Besides, he told himself, who knows what awful experiments might be performed on his new friend. Danny had seen the X-FILES. He knew what tests they might run on aliens. He couldn't let that happen to Kalyde. But what could he do?

Upstairs, someone ascended to the second floor. Several voices spoke to each other as more people entered the House of Blue Lights. "What's this bicycle doing in here?" somebody asked.

"It was blocking the door," another responded. "And there are wet footprints all over the hallway."

"Human?"

"Yes, sir."

Danny suddenly smiled deviously. He had an idea. No, a flash of brilliance! "Hey, Kalyde, why don't you be me for a while? My bicycle will support your story."

Kalyde's expression brightened, then suddenly became sad once more.

"You can look like me . . . Oh, that's right. Even if I tell you my story, you can't speak my language. Hey! You could point to your throat and claim that you're injured. Naw, then they'd take you to the hospital, and you'd be in trouble all over again. Jeez, I wish there was a way to help. And I thought I'd had a great idea," Danny finished dejectedly.

"There is a way, friend Daw-nee," Kalyde's thoughts danced in Danny's head, "but it can be very, very dangerous. You might be harmed."

Danny swallowed heavily, made a decision, then said, "Tell me." Footsteps approached the door. "Quickly!"

"I can touch your mind and absorb what you know. Learn your language quickly. Then I would seem normal to those hunting for me. It only takes seconds but be warned, in the touching of the minds, sometimes things can go wrong." Kalyde spread his thin arms wide in a helpless gesture. "Danny, you might become more intelligent, or possibly less, maybe even mindless. Some have lost certain memories. Others have gained new ones."

"Oh," was all Danny could say. It sounded really dangerous, and he'd just met Kalyde, but then Kalyde had healed him right after they'd met.

What to do? What would Dad do? Danny scowled. What would Mom or Sarah have done? Danny knew. He wasn't going to let down his new friend. "Go for it!" Danny whispered hoarsely.

With fingers spread, Kalyde placed one hand on Danny's forehead. Then the alien put his other fingers against his own head. Immediately, Danny felt a tugging sensation. For a moment, he thought he was going to black out, but then his senses expanded, stretching beyond flesh – stretching beyond the confines of the basement and into space.

At first, Danny was disoriented, then he realized he was aboard a spacecraft. Was this past or present? All around were members of Kah-laye-dee's race, adults and children alike . . . Cor-ror-o'lans. Something was wrong. They were scurrying about, their expressions concerned. The young ones appeared on the verge of panicking. The lighting which seemed to surround the ship dimmed, then went out. The craft began spinning awkwardly, then it shuddered mightily, throwing Danny to the floor.

Looking down at himself, Danny saw he was a Cor-ror-o'lan. Maybe he was Kalyde. Hands helped him into a transparent capsule of some kind, then the door was slammed shut. Through the window of his capsule, he watched others get into the clear eggs. Then with a lurch, he was launched into space – no, the sky! Earth's sky!

Just as suddenly, Danny was elsewhere. Somewhere familiar. The heavens were green-black, and it looked like rain. Danny tossed the last paper. It collided with Mrs. Wilson's planter, breaking it. He left a note. There was a shout. He rode fast – faster. Spike followed. Heavy rain – racing through it. Panting. Drenched. Free? No, surprised. Muddy road . . . forest . . . darkness . . . trees, then he was out of control. Speeding. Crashing . . . Light.

Danny opened his eyes, staring into Kalyde's glowing azure orbs. Thoughts raced between them, and they both smiled.

Footsteps again moved toward the basement door. "Ya know, I think this place has a basement," they heard.

"Goodbye, Danny," Kalyde said. Not only did the alien sound like Danny, but he looked like him, again, including his prior head injury. The jumpsuit was gone, replaced by Danny's torn clothing. "And thanks." Kalyde grabbed a loose 2 x 4 board and bounded up the steps.

As the door was pulled open, Kalyde/Danny burst through it, knocking over a man. "Not anymore, Spike! I won't let you guys beat me again!" the shape-changed Cor-ror-o'lan screamed.

As the startled officer collapsed, Kalyde/Danny ran down the hall – swinging the 2 x 4.

Chapter Three

The Switchout

*L*istening to the shouting, the hurried footsteps, and the shuffling above, Danny smiled nervously. As if on cue, his headache returned abruptly, a small bomb erupting inside his head. Colors swirled before his eyes and shapes started to form but were never completed. Danny blinked, then felt his head, finding only smooth skin. None of the wounds had returned, but it felt as if someone in concrete boots were tap dancing on his brain.

In Danny's voice, Kalyde was screaming, "NO! Don't hit me anymore!"

As the men recovered from their surprise and tried to catch the shapeshifter, it sounded like a herd of buffalo were stampeding through the upstairs. Danny wished he could see what was going on.

Suddenly, as if he were there, he could see upstairs! Were they still mindlinked? Is that why he was seeing through Kalyde's eyes? Hands reached for him, and the board was roughly yanked from Kalyde's grasp by a tall, thin man with dark eyes. Danny didn't like the looks of the man; he was coldly stiff, just like his father had become.

A light was shined into Kalyde's eyes, blinding both he and Danny. "Well, well, what do we have here?" asked the man. His voice was deep and rumbling.

To Danny and Kalyde, the surrounding men were shadowy and faceless hulks behind their glaring flashlights. Danny tried to be brave for his friend, hoping that his emotions would carry through their link.

"Not what we're looking for, Lieutenant," came a second voice from somewhere out of Danny's view. Behind and holding Kalyde, maybe. "He doesn't look like an ex-fugitive. The footprints and the bicycle probably belong to him."

The flashlight was no longer directed into Kalyde's eyes, and the men's grip shifted, allowing him to stand. Tears were rolling down his cheeks. "Don't hit me, please," Kalyde said in Danny's voice. "I thought you were Spike and his buddies. I'm sorry . . . I'm confused, and my head really hurts," Kalyde weakly stammered.

Could Kalyde really feel his headache? Danny wondered.

"Who are you?" the lieutenant demanded.

"I'm . . . I'm Danny Chase," Kalyde stammered. "I live at 115 Oak Ridge Road. It's a couple of miles from here. My dad, Captain Chase, works security at Carswell Air Force Base."

One of the men groaned, and they released him. "Henley," the lieutenant said over his shoulder, "go get Dotson. Son, why were you hiding here?"

"I was hiding from Spike – a mindless brute I go to school with. You see," he began to explain, "I just moved here – and Spike, the jerk – and his buddies pick on me. He steals my lunch, my money and even hits me." Kalyde's voice grew shakier as he explained about delivering newspapers, the chase, and his fall. Kalyde pointed to his bicycle. It had been shoved aside and was surrounded by splinters from the broken door and shattered frame.

Danny wanted to clap his hands together. Kalyde was doing wonderfully. Do I really sound like that? Danny wondered. Boy, am I a wimp! Somehow he had to grow tougher – develop a spine.

A large, stocky man wearing a cap entered and stood behind the others.

Kalyde glanced at him, then finished his story, "And I don't remember much after that. When I woke up, I heard voices and thought Spike had found me. Did you know this place is haunted?"

The man who had just entered laughed, then said, "It looks like this place is a dead end."

"Dotson, do you know this boy?"

"Yes, sir."

"Damn, man, I thought we were close to finding one of the fugitives," the lieutenant said. "At least the new satellites proved they work as designed."

"Maybe we'll find something we can use at the . . . crash."

"Dotson, load up the boy's bicycle and drive him home, unless," he addressed Kalyde, "you want to see a doctor? You have a nasty cut on your forehead. You might need stitches."

Danny's heart almost seized. How bad had his head wound been? How bad was it? A concussion? Brain damage? His head was still pounding, and his vision was blurry.

"No, I just want to go home," Kalyde told them. "I know how to take care of myself. It's not the first time. Besides, my dad, Captain Chase, always tells me to hang tough."

"Okay, then off you go," the lieutenant said. "Sorry to scare you, son."

Kalyde didn't have a key, Danny thought. How would he get inside the house? Then Danny laughed at himself; from his memories, Kalyde knew where the spare was hidden.

As Kalyde left with Dotson, Danny heard, "Sir, should we continue to search the estate?"

"Yes. I have a nagging feeling about this place."

Danny jumped to his feet. His head swam, and he teetered, barely grabbing the steps in time. What was going on? Kalyde had healed him! Oh, oh, Danny thought, maybe the meeting of the minds had damaged his brain! Was he on his way to becoming a vegetable? He shuddered at the thought, then pushed it away. His imagination was wild; even wilder than usual.

Danny rubbed his neck and his temples. His headache subsided, a little. He didn't have time to worry about it right now. Any minute they would investigate the basement. If they found him, Kalyde's story would be proven false, and his friend would be captured. And tested. Maybe dissected.

Danny searched for a place to hide. His eyes had adjusted to the darkness, and although his vision was still doubled, he could see a few feet in front of him. There didn't seem to be any place to hide. The basement was almost empty except for the mattress, a box spring and a few scattered boxes.

Then Danny spotted a boarded doorway. He looked around for Murg. The calico was waiting under the stairs. "We've got to hide," Danny whispered.

He tried to move quietly, but water gushed from his soggy shoes. He cursed quietly, then quickly removed his shoes and socks. He didn't want to leave wet prints, so he wiped his feet on the mattress, then continued toward the boarded doorway.

Murg followed quietly behind him.

Why was it always so hard to be secretive? Secrets always wanted to leap out of his mouth – to tell people something he shouldn't. And he was an awful liar. This time loose lips might cost a friend's life.

Danny ran his hands over the boards and two shifted. He allowed himself a tight smile. Maybe there was someplace to hide in there. Danny stuffed his shoes and socks in his pants, then moved a board aside and squeezed between a pair. From what he could see, several empty racks stood before him. Was he in a wine cellar? He found it strange that there was a basement at all. His father had told him they didn't build basements in Texas. But this was a strange house; there was a tower to the diving board.

After Danny rearranged the boards as he'd found them, he searched the cellar. He was still receiving images from Kalyde, and it was a bit disconcerting to be in two places at once. He coped by pretending to daydream; he'd been told he was an expert at that.

Kalyde limped outside. Dotson, a big blocky man with short dark hair and BBs for eyes, carried Danny's mangled bicycle. Kalyde and Danny were dumbfounded by the crowd gathered among the vehicles surrounding the mansion.

White, red and blue lights flashed and whirled about, creating a circus atmosphere. Waves of color washed across the landscape, briefly highlighting the unmarked vehicles, the numerous vans and all the people. Their grim faces reminded Danny of his mother's car accident, except these people were armed.

Was Kalyde some sort of criminal? Danny wondered. Surely not. Had he made a mistake in helping him? Doubt nagged him even as he tried to push it away.

Kalyde passed by a van with its back doors open. Several darkly dressed men were unloading a large piece of equipment. "What's that?" Kalyde asked, pointing to the shiny metal contraption. With octopus-like arms and shiny dials reminding him of eyes, Danny thought it could be a robot. Possibly an android. He could easily imagine it slithering out of the truck, then scuttling forward after him.

Dotson hesitated, then said, "This contraption will help us find who we're looking for. You'll probably read about it in the newspaper or see it on TV in a couple of years."

"Oh," was all Kalyde could muster.

Danny could feel his friend's fear slowly slide away.

The military man loaded Danny's damaged bicycle into the trunk of his dark blue car, then secured the lid with a bungee cord. Dotson helped Kalyde inside the car, then climbed behind the wheel. As they drove off, Kalyde began giving directions.

The contact was suddenly lost, and Danny felt very alone. Was Kalyde out of range? Danny suddenly smiled. It didn't matter. They'd done it! They'd fooled the hunters! He was two for two today! Danny wished Kalyde well, hoping he'd find his friends and family, and have a safe journey home.

The basement door opened and a pair of voices carried clearly down the steps, echoing throughout the cellar. Danny could see snatches of light through the gaps in the plywood. He held his breath as the two men descended the stairway, their footsteps hollowly dancing about the basement.

Danny began to sweat; he felt like a mouse in a cage with a cat waiting outside, licking its chops. He still couldn't see very well and was afraid to move for fear of knocking something over. But he couldn't stay put. He might be discovered.

On his hands and knees, Danny crept toward the back of the wine cellar. What if he ran into a rat? Or a spider? He cringed. Then he touched something. He jumped back before realizing it wasn't alive. He ran his hands over it, feeling the rough cloth. Burlap! It was large enough to hide under. Or would that be too obvious?

Suddenly, he had an idea. Danny rolled the burlap and put it on his shoulder. As footsteps approached the wine cellar, Danny quietly began to climb one of the ten foot tall wine racks. The finish had worn away long ago, and the wood was rough, digging into his hands. What if one of the cross boards was rotted? He tried not to think about it.

About halfway up, the wood creaked under his weight, and Danny held his breath. He thought his heart would explode.

"Hey, Larry, I thought I heard something." Twin beams of light splayed through the boarded entry way, illuminating the wine cellar.

Danny heard their footsteps cautiously approach. He couldn't wait any longer. Praying as he went, Danny continued to climb.

"Let's check in here." The wine cellar was flooded with crisscrossing rays of bright light. They danced through the racks, creating distorted shadows. Were they getting closer? Were they using infrared?

In his mind, he could see them clearly, strange goggles on their faces. Danny tried to curb his imagination, but it was like trying to hold onto a greased pig; it kept slipping free and running loose.

Another board creaked as Danny reached the top, and he winced, knowing they would really come looking for him now.

"I heard it this time! Whoever you are, come out of there!" one of the men shouted. When Danny didn't respond, he called again.

"Should I call for backup?" the other asked.

"Let's check it out first. I'd hate to call for backup if it's a field mouse," the first man replied.

As the men began pushing the boards aside, Danny stretched the burlap across the top of the racks, lay down, and then pulled the cloth over him. He could barely breathe, afraid they would see him move.

Could they hear his heart? It was thundering so loudly he feared it might draw attention. What if they had sound or movement sensors? Danny tried calming himself by breathing slowly and steadily – something his mother had taught him when he'd had anxiety attacks.

The last board squealed loudly as it was removed. One of the men entered the cellar. The second waited at the doorway. The room brightened as a beam passed over him.

Danny stopped breathing, even after the light continued to search the room.

"Maybe it was a mouse," he said. There was the shuffling of feet followed by some scraping. "Nothing."

"This place gives me the creeps."

Danny almost jumped. The voice had come from just below him. As if hoping to leap free, Danny's heart crammed into his throat.

"Nobody builds a house like this in Texas."

"You heard the boy say this place is haunted," the other responded.

His companion laughed.

Suddenly, the wine rack shook, swaying back and forth. Danny lost his balance. He swallowed a gasp and grabbed onto the edge with his hands and toes. He felt a shoe slip from his pants and start to fall away.

"Careful about leaning on one of those things."

Danny tried to catch the shoe but couldn't. It seemed to hit the floor with the loud pop of a gunshot.

"What was that!"

"Hey, something just brushed by me!" Their lights immediately targeted the wine cellar doorway. "Oh, just a cat."

"That's probably what we heard."

"Was it carrying something in its mouth?"

"Probably a field mouse."

"Damn! I thought we had the alien cornered."

"Let's go upstairs and see if the Analyzer is set up. It should find what we can't."

"At least we have its ship."

"What's left of it."

"Well, it's only a matter of time. I'll bet our satellites bring down another one soon."

Danny heard them ascend the steps and depart. When the basement door closed behind them, Danny let out a heavy sigh that seemed to release all his tension, and he deflated like a punctured balloon. He would wait until the lights were long gone before trying to leave. Kalyde needed the time to get home.

Wondering how long he'd been asleep, Danny awakened in a bit of a daze. He thought he remembered most of what had happened. When he threw off the burlap cloth, he realized he was stiff and sore. His headache wasn't any better, either. Danny didn't think he could see straight, but it was too dark to be sure. At least he wasn't brain dead. Murg meowed just below him.

Danny climbed down the wine rack to the floor. Every muscle ached. What was wrong with him? Hadn't Kalyde healed him? Could it have been temporary? Maybe Kalyde hadn't healed him; maybe he just thought he was healed. Danny's thoughts spun around and around. He was no longer sure if Kalyde had helped him, except his ankle didn't bother him at all. It handled weight just fine. Danny stretched and felt a little better.

Murg rubbed against his leg.

Danny reached down and stroked the feline's back. Murg was almost dry.

"Thanks, gal. Kalyde and I owe you. Your timing was perfect."

Murg meowed in response, and it sounded to Danny like she was saying, "Of course, it was." His shoe lay at her feet.

As he picked up his sneakers, Danny smiled. He didn't know how long he'd slept; but if Murg was almost dry, it should have been long enough for the authorities to leave.

All the lights outside were gone, and it was very dark. He could barely distinguish differing shades of darkness. Just in case they weren't gone, Danny listened quietly for a while. Over the throbbing in his head, all he heard was the creaking of the house as the wind blew through it.

Murg rubbed against him, as if telling him it was time to leave. Danny picked up his cat and held the calico close. "I guess it's just you and me again, Murg."

With one arm outstretched to guide him, Danny maneuvered toward the cellar entrance.

Murg leapt from his hands but circled around quickly to wait in front of him.

Danny discovered that if he walked slowly, Murg could guide him; and she did between the boards and to the steps.

Danny stopped and listened at the top of the steps. It was quiet, except for thunder in the distance. Trying to prevent the door from squeaking, Danny carefully pushed it open the rest of the way.

The house was pitch dark, until interrupted by an occasional flash of lightning, and seemed deserted. Although the creaking and shifting caused by the wind made his imagination conjure otherwise. Pushing skeletons, evil spirits without heads, and flesh-rotting zombies from his thoughts, Danny moved from window to window, peering out and discovering he'd been right. The surrounding yard and driveway were empty.

"It's going to be a long walk home," Danny sighed. "At least we won't have to roll the bicycle back to the house."

Danny sat on the floor, and put on his wet shoes and socks. He hated walking in squishy sneakers, but he didn't have a choice unless he wanted to go barefoot. Looking at the bright side of things, it had quit raining.

For the first time Danny thought about what an amazing day it had been. He had done something right after all. Kalyde was free!

Danny smiled broadly, and a sharp pain flared inside his head. He wondered if his brain was expanding or something, trying to escape his skull.

Wishing for a flashlight and some aspirin, Danny headed

out the back door and down the porch steps. Feeling a little turned around, he decided to try backtracking his trail.

Murg was right beside him, her tail swishing saucily back and forth.

When Danny stopped at the fence atop the weed-covered hill, he glanced back at the House of Blue Lights. He couldn't see the gray stone mansion clearly, but it still made him smile. No ghosts inhabited it, only visitors from the stars.

Danny walked into the woods. Water dripped from the trees, and once again he was being rained on. Murg meowed, and Danny gathered her in his arms, carrying the calico.

When he thought about how much trouble he would probably be in when he arrived home, his mood sank. Surely his dad would be home by now. How was he going to explain this? He could see his father's angry face, flushed and pinched. Deep set eyes glowered like burning coals.

Danny wondered if he should tell the truth. He always tried to tell the truth, although it wasn't always easy. Still, it was easier to tell the truth than remember a series of lies.

Danny pictured this: He told his father about giving his bicycle and memories to a shapechanging alien so Kalyde could escape the military. Danny laughed. Even if his father didn't believe him, with a story like that he'd be grounded for the rest of his life. Never to eat ice cream again. And comics? Say goodbye to the Silver Surfer, Thor and all the rest.

Danny wondered how he was going to explain his bicycle, if it were already home. It might be better if Kalyde hadn't returned it. Then he could tell his father that he had left it at the House of Blue Lights.

Why was life so difficult? Things always so confusing?

Danny didn't want to lie to his father, but he wouldn't believe the truth anyway. Adults were like that sometimes. They asked for honesty, then they didn't believe it or didn't like it when it didn't suit their views. He resolved not to be like that when he was older.

Suddenly, he wondered what if his father had already been home when Kalyde arrived. . . . That almost made him start running. Could Kalyde still be there, impersonating him?

Without noticing he'd left the woods behind, Danny stumbled onto the dirt road and walked along the muddy trail toward the unfinished homes. His legs were tired and didn't seem to obey him very well.

At the end of the long muddy road, a crescent moon was setting over the neighborhood. Along that half of the sky, the stars twinkled brightly. Suddenly a set of bright lights engulfed him. The glare stung his eyes, blinding Danny. He was momentarily confused; then he heard the oncoming car and stumbled off the road.

The car approached slowly, then stopped.

Danny started to run, but his legs wobbled, and he tripped over a rock. He landed in the mud, scraping his knee. Yes, Danny thought, his luck was holding true to form.

When he started to rise, Danny heard, "HOLD IT!" Danny froze, knowing he couldn't have gone far anyway. He was exhausted.

The door opened and a large figure carrying a flashlight emerged. He inspected Danny. For a moment, there was silence. "You look familiar, son. Who are you?"

Danny's heart sank, and he thought about making up a story, but he was too tired and his head hurt. "My name's Danny Chase. I live nearby. I had a bicycle accident. Who are you, and what do you want?"

The man seemed surprised. "Wait a minute. Did you just come from that strange house at the bottom of the hill?" Danny nodded.

"I thought you were taken home. Wait, weren't you injured?" The man sounded very confused.

Danny once again thought about running, but he noticed

the man wore a uniform of sorts. He would probably be caught quickly anyway. Danny wished he was older so he could run faster. By the time he was an adult, Danny thought, he would be an expert at running away. It seemed that all he did was run away and hide. At least this time he'd done so to help someone else. To help Kalyde.

"Something's wrong here. You better come with me." The man firmly gripped Danny's arm and led him to the car.

All Danny could think of was a procession he once saw in a movie – one which led to the executioner's block.

Chapter Four

The Magic Bicycle

*M*onday afternoon, a tired and downhearted Danny Chase stumbled in through the front door. He staggered to the couch and collapsed, burying his face in the cushions. He was so glad to be home.

As usual, school had been terrible. The kids didn't like him, and Danny swore the teachers didn't either. He didn't even want to think about his grades!

To say the weekend had been awful was an understatement. No matter how hard he tried, things went wrong. Danny was so caught up in events going awry that he hadn't even noticed that his headache had disappeared yesterday. All Danny thought of was how extremely unfair the world was to him.

Maybe he was trying too hard. He felt as tightly strung as a piano wire. His mom used to say that some things might come to him more easily if he would let things happen naturally, instead of pushing so much. In his dreams. Maybe.

Danny pushed his face deeper into the pillows and agonizingly reviewed the last three days. He recalled meeting Kalyde, which always made him smile. Then he remembered what had happened afterward, some too vividly, hurling him back into black despair once more.

At the airbase in Lieutenant Chambers' office, the tall man relentlessly questioned Danny. Each answer only further confused the officer. Next the lieutenant called on Sergeant Dotson, who was flabbergasted.

Dotson hemmed and hawed, then stammered that indeed he'd taken Danny Chase and his bicycle home.

The lieutenant immediately sent several men to the Chase house.

"Could this one be the alien?" Dotson asked.

"I wouldn't think so, but we were fooled before," Lieutenant Chambers said.

Danny felt like a criminal, despite the fact he believed he hadn't done anything wrong. He didn't always understand why adults did the things they did; they seemed to think differently.

"We'll test him," the lieutenant concluded. "Is the Analyzer still in the van?" Dotson nodded. "Come with us, Danny."

Danny didn't want to go, but they threatened to carry him. When he faced the shiny contraption, Danny remembered Kalyde's fear – as if it were his own.

Dotson turned on the power, and with a click and a whir, the gleaming machine came to life. Lights blinked as though eyes, then stared at Danny. Dotson repositioned its arms to surround Danny, and Danny wondered if this would hurt.

Now Dotson punched a button, and Danny's hair stood on end as though the air were electrified. Kalyde's fear was so strong,

Danny started to run. They grabbed him, holding him still. When nothing happened, they were disappointed.

"We should have done this to the other Danny, instead of just checking the house," Lieutenant Chambers said, his voice heavy with disgust. "But who would have guessed the alien was a shapechanger."

Danny was embarrassed. The ol' Chase bravery had once again reared its ugly head.

He was taken to a detention room – a small room with a bed, a desk, and a chair. The walls were white and bare. After an hour, a lean man with dark eyes entered to announce that his father would be arriving shortly.

Danny preferred electrocution over facing his father. What his father would do to him would almost certainly be worse, and certainly longer lasting than death.

Rolling over on the couch, Danny stared at the ceiling.

Murg jumped on his stomach and started to pad back and forth.

Not being in the mood, Danny set the calico on the floor.

Murg protested and returned.

Danny held his cat so tightly that Murg couldn't paw him anymore.

The calico finally squirmed free and leaped onto the floor. A blur, she ran part way up the stairs, then came halfway back. She did this several times, trying to get Danny's attention but failed.

Danny was reliving unpleasant memories – again. Poking at them. Digging at them.

With a grim scowl, his father entered his "cell". His dark eyes glowered, and his salt and peppered hair was wild as if he'd been running his hands through it. Or trying to tear it out. His face was slightly flushed, and he moved stiffly as if worried he might lash out.

He didn't ask Danny how he was doing or how he felt – no pleasantries at all, no sir. His dad started right in with cold, hard-edged questions as if Danny were a criminal.

"What were you doing around the old Johnson estate?" And, "Why did you help a stranger? And an alien at that, for God's sake! What did you think you were doing? Didn't you think at all!"

Most of the questions weren't supposed to be answered, so Danny just nodded. Ever so slowly, his father's anger changed into disappointment.

"I know you wish I'd done otherwise. I'm sorry I embarrassed you. I did what I thought was right at the time." Danny could tell that statement had further disappointed his father.

"Now you know otherwise," his father said. "Let's go home. Helluva way to start a weekend."

His father didn't look at Danny or say a word to him during the drive. At home, Danny was marched into the house and forced to sit on the couch.

His father looked him in the eye and said, "Danny, you know I am extremely disappointed. You've done something very wrong, and you've embarrassed me. You know how I feel about being a good citizen and cooperating with the authorities. We can't all just do as we please any time we want, or there'd be chaos." His father sighed. "I'm glad your mother and sister aren't around to see this."

Danny was so sad and angry that he couldn't stop the tears.

"You made the decision to do this, Son, so don't cry about the consequences! Before you decide to do something next time, think about all the things that might happen, then make your decision. Don't just look at the way you want things to be. Stand up and take your medicine like a man."

Danny sniffled.

"Well, there's nothing I can do about it now, except make

sure you learn from this," his father said. "As for punishment, there are several things I expect from you. Are you listening?"

Danny nodded.

"You're only allowed to leave the yard to deliver papers or go to school. That means no free riding. If you hadn't wandered off this never would have happened." Danny knew better than to emphasize that he was being chased.

"There will be no television, no video playing, and no reading comic books. All of this will remain in effect until I say otherwise. Do you understand?"

"Yes." How much worse could it get? Danny wondered.

"I can't truly express how deeply disappointed I am in you, Son. What would your mother have thought?"

Danny was positive his mother would have approved. She had loved life and all creatures, but to have said so would have led to more trouble.

"Your bicycle is out front. At least the alien returned it. Put it in the garage and go to bed."

Danny trudged outside and found his bicycle. To his surprise, it was undamaged! The tire wasn't flat, the frame wasn't warped, and the front wasn't crooked. Even the handlebars were straight, and they'd been a bit off even before the crash. This . . . miracle buoyed his spirits, and Danny sent off heartfelt thanks to Kalyde wherever he was hiding. Danny hoped he was safe.

The repaired bicycle hadn't sustained Danny's spirits for long. Riding was freedom. Riding was adventure. And recently, riding had become his life. He obeyed his father. Sort of. All weekend he took the long way for delivering papers. His father hadn't said anything about direct routes; Murg had agreed. She was a witness.

Come Monday, Danny was sent to the principal's office. Somehow, Mr. Cripes had come across a brown paper bag with Danny's name on it and kitty droppings inside.

Danny tried to explain, but it was like talking with his father. Danny didn't even try to understand grown-ups anymore. As punishment, he was given detention.

Spike was furious about not catching Danny last Friday and cuffed him several times. He yelled at Danny to tell him what happened.

Danny silently rose to his feet and trudged away. Spike hated to be ignored; and so, Danny just suffered in mute silence. He hoped that Spike would get bored and go away.

Starting tomorrow, Danny decided to quit eating lunch and to leave all money at home. Instead, he would eat a huge breakfast to sustain him for the whole day.

As far as riding home, he also took a long, out-of-the-way route. The detention had one benefit; Spike wasn't waiting for him when he rode home.

Danny sighed as he climbed off the couch. He started to walk to the kitchen, then he changed his mind; he didn't really feel like eating. His mother would have said he must be sick if he wasn't hungry. He missed her. Maybe he'd quit eating and waste away. His father probably wouldn't even notice.

Danny went upstairs to his room. He didn't notice that his bedroom door was open or that Murg, with her dancing tail, waited for him. He looked around his sanctum; here, he could be himself – or even better yet, be a super self. The walls were covered with posters of superheroes, and two bookshelves were crammed double-rowed with books. Another bookshelf was full of boxed comics.

As Danny entered, he stared at a poster of the Silver Surfer, wishing he could fly away. He didn't notice the red bicycle and stumbled into it. "Hey!" Danny barely managed to grab it and stay on his feet. "What's this?"

His face lit up as he examined the bike. At first, it appeared to be his bicycle, but upon closer investigation, this one was brand new with gleaming metallic paint. It also had some minor additions, which included reflectors and a gel-padded seat. Danny's smile broadened as he ran his hands along the frame. They tingled with the contact. There was a certain feel to the new bicycle, a freshness similar to the beginning of Spring – after a long, hard winter.

Danny hefted the bicycle with one hand. It was incredibly light. He lifted it with one finger and was truly amazed. Something about the gears looked different, so he played with them. It had eighteen gears! Wow! Not that he needed them in Texas, but with the way his family kept moving, he might some day!

Danny turned to the calico. "Murg, where did this come from?"

Murg meowed as she rubbed against Danny's closet door. When Danny just looked at her, she scratched at the door.

"What's in there, girl?" Danny asked as he approached the door.

Murg simply meowed again.

Danny opened the closet door. Two glowing blue eyes stared out at him. As the sunlight filled the closet, Danny saw a wide grin and electric blue hair cut in a thin row and standing straight atop a large head. "Kalyde!" Danny jumped forward and hugged his friend. They tumbled backward into the closet and landed in a heap. Clothes fell down atop them, and they laughed and laughed. "You escaped!" Danny kept repeating.

Murg sat back and watched with a satisfied expression. She was too dignified to join the romp.

Eventually, Danny climbed out of the closet and helped Kalyde stand. "What are you doing here, buddy?"

"I brought you a gift," Kalyde projected, his thoughts sounding inside Danny's head. "My thanks for your help. I know it landed you in . . ." Kalyde paused, searching, " . . . boiling water?"

"You didn't need to do this! I mean, you fixed my other bicycle! That's thanks enough. Heck, if you hadn't healed me, I'd still be hobbling around. Jeez, Kalyde, the new bicycle, it's . . . it's fantastic! No! It's AWESOME!"

Kalyde beamed, and a happy golden glow radiated from him. "It is very special."

"It looks, even feels, special."

"I mean there isn't another bicycle like it anywhere."

"Really?" Danny said, his curiosity running wild. "What makes it different?"

"The metal comes from the heart of an exploding binary star. It reacts to thoughts, and more importantly, your imagination."

"Will it fly?"

"Not exactly, but it is very, very fast. And it will take you anywhere you want to go."

"Anywhere I want to go?"

"It is powered by your imagination. You have a very powerful one, as I know," Kalyde said. "I see you are still confused. You have lived many places, yes?" Kalyde asked.

Danny nodded.

"You have friends scattered all about the world. Friends you miss and would like to visit?"

"Yeah, but they're all so far away. Some are overseas. I can't ride there."

"Not true. Now you can ride there, and it will only take you minutes. If you so choose, you can ride around the world," Kalyde told him.

Danny's mouth dropped open.

"Hmm, friend Danny," Kalyde projected with a cocked eyebrow, "I see you don't believe me."

Danny started to deny it, then said, "I'm sorry. It sounds too fantastic to be true."

"Then we will go for a test ride, and I will show you."

"All right! Uh, it only has one seat," Danny pointed out.

"Right now that is true, but you," Kalyde pointed to him, "can change that. In fact, you can make this bicycle take on any appearance you can imagine."

Danny's look was skeptical.

"Your expression reminds me of your father."

Danny's eyes widened in alarm, and Kalyde laughed heartily. Danny joined him in laughter.

Then, Kalyde spoke, instead of projecting his thoughts. "Now you're in the right frame of mind. You can never create anything special when you are angry. Now, close your eyes and picture a two seater, a . . . ah, hmmm . . . a tandem bicycle. Now – touch your bicycle. Concentrate very hard. See and feel the bicycle stretch, growing another seat. Pretend you're using magic, that you're molding it like a sculptor shapes clay."

Danny pictured the two-seated bicycle in his mind, then pretended that his hands ran over a second seat. His fingertips tingled, and the bicycle seemed to vibrate ever so slightly. Suddenly he felt two seats, not one! Danny opened his eyes, and to his astonishment, there really were two seats on the longer bicycle!

"See, now we are ready to go."

Danny's expression suddenly grew serious. "Uh, Kalyde, you took a big risk coming here. What if you'd been seen?"

"When I came to your door, I looked like this," Kalyde said as his features and coloring changed.

His skin grew pale, losing its metallic quality, and his hair turned blonde, although it still stood up straight. Kalyde raised his hands; he'd grown a thumb to go with his four fingers.

Danny clapped his hands and watched in wonder as the jumpsuit changed to jeans and a green sweatshirt.

Kalyde wriggled his toes in emerald high top sneakers, then pronounced, "I am ready."

"That should do it," Danny agreed. "Let's go cruisin'!"

Murg let out a loud caterwaul.

"Murg's ready to ride, too!"

Danny steered the bicycle out the door and carried it down the stairs, still amazed by its feather light weight. He wheeled the bright red bicycle through the living room and out the front door. Danny hadn't really noticed it before, but it was a beautiful October day. Indian summer had arrived.

"Uh, what if my dad finds out?" Danny said, suddenly worried.

"Has he ever come home before five?"

"Not since Mom and Sarah . . . not since the accident," Danny replied.

"Then we are safe. What time must you deliver papers – the afternoon edition?"

"Around four-thirty."

"Good. It is three o'clock. We have plenty of time. Are you ready?"

"Yeah!" Danny hadn't created a place for Murg, but he had a better idea. He ran inside and grabbed his backpack. He quickly emptied it, and Murg climbed inside. The calico purred with approval as Danny slipped it on over his shoulders.

Kalyde sat behind him, and they were off. They immediately found a rhythm, working in tandem and riding along smoothly. Kalyde began to hum, and Danny joined him.

Danny smiled as the wind ruffled his hair and sang past his ears. Murg stood up in the pack and leaned over his shoulder. Eyes closed to half mast, the cat enjoyed the wind as it ruffled fur and played with her whiskers.

Danny was amazed at how easily the bicycle moved along. It glided – no, it sailed like a cutter on the high seas, and he was the captain – yes, Captain of the Wind, Danny Chase! He pedaled effortlessly, and their speed increased.

They raced along the street, going faster than Danny had ever gone before. And he wasn't even breathing hard!

Danny knew exactly where he wanted to take it – out in

the open where there weren't any stop signs, cars or people. He thought about some back roads, but they were dirty and potholed. Danny wanted something smooth so he could fly. Along the highway were frontage roads that cars rarely traveled. From there, he could find a deserted farm road and head out into the country. He and Kalyde pedaled even faster, and soon they were out of the neighborhood.

They briefly halted at a stop sign, then took off, burning rubber before streaking forward. "Wow!" was all Danny could manage as he looked over his shoulder to watch the smoke drift away.

They raced past the entrance to the highway and shot down the frontage road. As expected, it was deserted. Danny let go of the handlebars. The bike was perfectly balanced! They soared along, enjoying the sun, the wind, and the freedom found in speeding along the road.

"Shall we 'shake it down'?" Kalyde asked.

Laughing, Danny said, "Let 'er rip!"

Together, they pedaled furiously.

"Don't worry about pedaling hard or fast. Don't punish yourself to go fast," Kalyde's thought popped into Danny's head. "Just think about going fast. Being fast. Don't close your eyes. Just see yourself sailing along free and easy. It's a smooth, fast ride. Use your imagination."

Danny nodded and followed Kalyde's advice. Soon they raced along so fast the wind whistled through the wheels. Trees blurred, vanished, and then the dotted white line nearly became a solid stripe.

Danny was singing. He didn't notice that they were easily passing cars on the highway. The telephone poles became a picket fence. "We must be doing over sixty!" Danny yelled, significantly underestimating their speed. "Yee-haw!" The doldrums of the past few days were whisked away.

Then a cautious thought somehow crept into Danny's mind.

"How quickly and how easily does this thing brake?"

"Not to worry, my friend," Kalyde sent calm thoughts. Then, "Look out! Stop!"

As it jumped, Danny's heart nearly ran over his tongue. He squeezed the hand brakes as tight as he could.

"Think of a smooth, quick stop!" Kalyde said. Danny did.

The bike immediately came to a smooth, easy stop.

"It stops on a dime," Danny breathed heavily. He was a bit pale. "Kalyde, please don't scare me like that!"

"I'm sorry. I just wanted to show you how effectively and easily you could stop. You are in no danger while riding unless you don't pay attention – see, I know you are a daydreamer. This bicycle can stop on a dime, but you are not invulnerable." Kalyde's tone had taken on a teaching tone. "You can be hurt if you don't stop. Don't crash through things. As you can tell, it handles extremely well, is perfectly balanced, and has excellent brakes.

"If you believe you're safe, you will be, unless you ride off a cliff or into a wall. Remember to always pay attention to what you're doing, and where you are, but more importantly where you want to go. You don't want to hurt anybody getting there. Be responsible."

There was that word again. It seemed to get thrown around a lot. "I'll do my best," Danny said.

"That's all I can ask, my good friend."

They began riding again, their speed rapidly increasing. Telephone poles whizzed by. Soon they were out of town, racing along a farm road.

"Kalyde, did you get back to your family?"

"Just after I arrived at your home, my father contacted me. All Cor-ror-o'lans are telepathically linked. We arranged a rendezvous. After I had repaired your bicycle, and it was safe to leave, I . . . hitchhiked out to a place north of town. It was a joyous reunion. When I'd told them what you'd done, they thought that you deserved a special gift. And we are riding it!"

"I am so glad. I was afraid for you."

"Once I could look like a human, it was easy to move about unnoticed. Danny, is there someplace far away you'd like to visit?"

"You mean in Texas?"

"No, much farther away than that."

"Well, I really miss the beaches in South Carolina. There was a little bay where Sarah and I used to collect sea shells," Danny recalled. "Sometimes we'd even follow the inlet and do some shrimping."

"Shall we go there?"

"How?"

"The same way you changed this bicycle into a tandem. Picture this place, the beach in Carolina – in your mind. Don't worry about how you're going to get there. Just assume that you will. In fact, be absolutely positive you will arrive safely. If you like, pretend you are already there. Don't close your eyes. See the color of the water and of the sky. Hear the sea gulls cry and the thrashing of the waves. Can you hear them?"

Danny nodded.

"Feel the sand underneath the bicycle tires and smell the salt in the air. Is it not a beautiful place?" Again Danny nodded.

"You know it well."

The world around them suddenly blurred into a whirlwind of colors. Danny felt lighter and was sure they'd lost contact with the road. But he still felt safe.

There was a roaring sound like a thousand charging lions, followed by a tremendous clap of thunder. Bright sparks exploded all around them, then the world went white for a moment, followed by a hazy grayness as if they were riding through clouds. Danny suddenly noticed it was quiet. Where was the sound of the wind?

The clouds parted, and they rode atop a gleaming rainbow. Below them were brilliant streaks of red, orange, yellow, green and blue. Forming walls along each side of them was an electric purple. It was so bright that when he looked at himself, everything he wore, even his skin, glowed brilliant violet.

Murg meowed loud and long, and Danny looked over his shoulder. The calico was standing on his shoulder and staring upward. Stars sparkled in the darkness above. They were riding across the sky to South Carolina!

The world suddenly went white, then flashed brightly as if they rode directly into a star. The lions roared once more, and the thunder cracked as if a giant hole were being ripped in the sky.

Danny was disoriented for a moment, then he realized they had done it! They had ridden to the east coast near Myrtle Beach.

The sun danced along the bay and glistened off the sand of the beach. The three of them, Danny, Kalyde and Murg cruised along the shore. The waves came gliding in, then crashed, spreading across the sands. Danny breathed deeply, both smelling and tasting the salt in the air. Gulls circled overhead – just as he'd pictured in his mind; and they cried out to him.

"As amazing a journey as I've ever experienced," came a strange and somewhat superior-sounding voice in Danny's head.

"Kalyde, did you say . . . I mean, think something to me?"

"No."

"My guess would be speeds approaching light," the voice returned. "Actually, I believe we split the seams of our plane of reality and hopped through space from the flat lands to the beach. Sort of like in PROTONMAN. We reach optimum speed, which is being there."

"Murg?" Danny asked incredulously.

"Danny, if I live eight more lives, I don't believe I'll experience anything quite so exhilarating," the calico responded.

Danny gasped, astonished. "Kalyde, I can understand

Murg!"

"My companion has always had a scalpel-sharp mind," Murg observed dryly.

Kalyde laughed. "It might have something to do with the bicycle. I told you it had . . . magical properties, limited only by your imagination."

Danny was amazed. "Kalyde, what else can it do? Can it fly?"

"Not exactly. It needs something to ride on. The only way it seems to fly is if you're traveling a long distance, as we just did from Ft. Worth. Whatever you do, don't try to ride across a canyon or off a cliff, okay?"

"I don't fully understand all of this, but I'll follow your directions. So I can cross the ocean, visit Gretchen in Germany or Peter in Scotland?"

"Of course you can!" Kalyde told him.

"What a wonderful way to travel the world," Murg thought. "There are so many places I have memories of that I'd like to see."

"I don't understand," Danny said.

"Cats have the memories of famous felines so that nothing important will be lost."

"A racial memory?"

"Something like that, yes. So there are places I know that I've never visited, that I would like to visit. You see, cats are indeed very special."

"You need to know where you are going. At least be familiar with it," Kalyde told the calico. "With Danny's imagination, if he studies some place enough, scrutinizing pictures of it, you should be able to travel there."

"Shoot!" exclaimed Danny.

"Danny, what's wrong?" Kaldye demanded.

"Oh, it's a little after four. We need to be getting home," Danny said with disappointment.

"Well, one thing we can't do is alter time. No matter how fast you ride, the time will always move at the same pace in the place you leave and the place you arrive. Time may seem to move quickly due to all the excitement, but it doesn't change. Your actual travel time only takes a few minutes. Do you see?"

"Yes, so if I'm already late for something, there's no way I can ride fast enough to arrive early or on time. Is that it?"

"I told you he was passably smart for a human," Murg thought dryly. "That's why I keep him around."

"Well, we better return home. We wouldn't want to disappoint all those people who are waiting for their evening paper. You know, I can't wait for Spike and his buddies to try and catch me now!" Danny laughed, feeling suddenly confident and smug.

"Remember what I told you," Kalyde said. "You can make it look like any bicycle you wish. Change its shape and color, disguise it, just like me. Okay?"

"It's just too cool!" Danny cried, then sighed. "I'd like to ride all night, but I guess it's time to get home."

He began picturing the long stretches of flat plain, the scattered trees covered with olive-colored leaves, the bare sun, and the amazing sunsets he had come to know in Texas, where the earth and sky seemed endlessly expansive. With a rush of sound and light, the beach disappeared.

Danny, Kalyde and Murg appeared on the rainbow, riding homeward bound.

Chapter Five

The Challenge

*A*s Danny carried his dishes to the sink, he was thankful for the day's first small favor. His father had been called into work early, leaving before Danny awakened. Mornings had typically started with cold silence between the two which always ruined Danny's mood.

The canary yellow kitchen was brilliant from the bright sunshine and matched Danny's sunny mood. He hadn't slept so well in a long time; and, yet, he couldn't wait to go for a ride on his new bicycle. It almost made up for Kalyde having to leave. He could have used a best friend. But if he couldn't have a best friend – or even a friend – a bicycle was a good second choice!

Danny tossed his banana peel and apple core in the trash, then started to rinse his cereal bowl. Murg yeowed, halting

Danny. "Sorry," said Danny. He set down the bowl of milk for the calico. "I guess my mind is somewhere else this morning."

In his thoughts, Danny was already on his magical bicycle – his ticket to speed and anywhere he wanted to go. To freedom from care or worries. When he was cruising, nothing else mattered. Standing before the open kitchen window, he smiled, daydreaming of riding the wind on Kalyde II. He could go anywhere! Anywhere! Where was he? The beaches of South Carolina? The rolling hills of southern Indiana? Or the mountains of Germany? Thank you, Kah-laye-dee!

Pressure against his leg brought Danny back to the present. With an arched back, Murg was rubbing against him. "Want some more?" The calico shook her head. "Then what?" Danny knelt, but the cat danced away, then leapt gracefully onto the kitchen counter. With her tail waving to and fro, as if she were walking in a parade, the feline moved back and forth in front of the clock. It read 7:30.

"Oh, yeah! It's almost time for school." Danny stroked the cat. "Thanks, Murg, I would've forgotten. I was thinking about riding."

The calico responded in catspeak.

"I know, I'm a space case." Danny replied, grabbing his backpack. "I'm off. I don't want to be late." He'd even remembered to do his homework. Danny scratched Murg once more, then swung his pack over his shoulders.

Murg caterwauled, the sound echoing through the kitchen and carrying into the dining area.

As Danny passed the table, he called back, "Of course, I'll take you riding with me this afternoon! It wouldn't be as much fun without you!" A satisfied purr reached Danny's ears as he shut the front door.

He all but skipped down the front sidewalk to the garage where his bicycle awaited him. What a day! He breathed in the sweet morning air. It was invigorating, even if a bit humid. The light drizzle last night made everything smell so fresh.

His smile widened as he opened the garage door and rolled his magical bicycle outside. Danny marveled at Kalyde II. Right now, it looked identical to his old bicycle – an assembly of old and spare parts polished and cleaned with loving care but still looking like a third generation hand me down. But it felt different. Magical! He could sense it!

Danny ran his hand over the ramhorn-shaped handle bars and the gleaming red frame toward the padded seat. The bike appeared to undulate under his hand . . . just like Murg! The bicycle quivered, then wavered, briefly changing shape and color. It became longer and sleeker as it turned blue with gold wrapped handle bars and a matching seat.

"No," Danny shook his head and watched his bike revert back to look like his old bicycle. No one could know that he had a new bicycle. Besides, who would take him seriously when he told them it was made from star metal that responded to thoughts? To imagination!

Danny glanced at his watch. "Oh, oh. I better hurry." He hopped onto his bicycle and took off, coasting down the driveway and into the street. The bicycle rode smoothly without a shake, shiver or shimmy. Each movement was effortless as though the bicycle transformed every ounce of energy – mental and physical – into forward motion. With this bicycle, he would be at school in minutes. Usually, it took him about twenty minutes, but today he would be there in five. He was careful not to picture himself already arriving.

Even with the breeze streaming through his wild, curly red locks, Danny somehow shifted moods, the joy departing as he thought about his dad. Danny forgot about the energizing feel of the magic bicycle and focused on last night. Would his dad ever speak to him again? Or smile? Last night had even overshadowed yesterday's excitement, his first ride on the magic bicycle.

Danny had asked his father if he could begin riding again. With a grunt, his father had shook his head no. Usually they attended an air show whenever there was one nearby. The Blue Angels were flying over Ft. Worth this weekend. Danny asked if they would be going. His father responded with stony silence. Finally, Danny had asked what he needed to do to be forgiven. Without a word, his dad had snapped the paper open to full length, shutting Danny out. Not another word was spoken.

What could he do to change things? What would he do if he could time travel and do things all over again? In retrospect, he wouldn't have done anything . . . except not get caught.

"There he is! Get 'em! Get the wimp!" came a nearby yell.

Danny quickly looked around and took stock of the situation. Spike, Rocky and Hank were after him again.

Spike had been hiding behind a tree. Rocky bolted from behind a truck. Danny had no idea where Hank had been concealed; he seemed to simply appear out of thin air.

"I still owe you for that lunch bag trick, Chase!" Spike bellowed. The bully's full, fleshy face was flushed. His black eyes were blazing below bushy brows. Curly hair waved in the breeze as Spike's shoulders heaved, urging his bicycle ever faster.

Danny vividly remembered being sat on, the feeling of being crushed. That fear suddenly overwhelmed him. The trio of bullies were going to catch him and pound him again. His legs tried to freeze on him. He just knew they would catch him sooner or later. Wouldn't later be worse?

"I got 'em in my sights!" Hank yelled. With a Super-Soaker in hand, the burr-headed boy came from Danny's left. Hank's glasses bounced up and down on his nose as he took aim, then pulled the trigger. A jet of water spat from the gun.

A few drops rained over Danny, and he smelled something funny. What was it? PERFUME! They were squirting him with perfume!

Hank closed in from behind, while Spike grew ever nearer

along Danny's right. Both were carrying Super Soakers!

If they got him, he would arrive at school smelling like a beauty shop. Everyone would think he was a sissy. That thought galvanized Danny. He began peddling furiously. Even if they had fancy bikes, they couldn't catch him! The magic bicycle bucked onto its back wheel, performing a wheelie, then shot ahead, leaving the bullies far behind.

Danny suddenly remembered what he was riding. With a beaming smile on his face, he glanced over his shoulder to see the astonished looks on the trio's faces. Unable to help himself, he coasted to take it all in. Even without peddling, the magic bicycle was outdistancing the threesome.

"Hey, come back here!" Hank yelled.

Rocky's mouth hung open, his eyes wide in disbelief.

"Chicken!" Spike yelled. His face was twisted in anger as he shook his fist.

Danny knew better than to gloat. That kind of stuff just came back to haunt you. Danny began pedaling again, leaving them far behind.

"You little . . . " Spike began to yell, again shaking his fist.

Spike wasn't watching where he was going and bumped into Hank's bike. Hank lost his balance as his two-wheeler wobbled. A flailing arm caught Spike across the face, and he reeled backwards. His bicycle collided with Hank's entangling a mass of cloth, flesh, and metal. In a heap, they bounced once on the pavement, then slid into a yard.

Not hearing their screams, Danny peddled onward. In less than two minutes, he was at school. Early. Safe, once more. Thank you, Kah-laye-dee!

The morning went by quickly and smoothly. Danny had his homework ready for all his classes and even did well on a pop quiz in Algebra, which he despised. Probably because numbers were not his strongest subject. In his opinion, numbers lacked creativity. Let somebody else be an engineer, architect, or accountant. He would rather write. Or even draw.

As Danny walked alone behind his science class toward the cafeteria, he wondered why Spike hadn't been in his English class, then was thankful for small favors. Whatever had kept Spike out of his life was okay with him.

Instead of eating lunch, Danny planned on reading a book during the break. He was engrossed by one of the Mad Scientist Club books about a group of boys who were always getting in trouble with their wild experiments.

Danny wandered past the lunch line and headed toward the empty table in the farthest corner of the room. As he passed a pair of tables inhabited by the "in" crowd and cool kids, their chattering grew quiet. Danny expected some teasing or snide comments, but nothing came his way. Even Rocky didn't say anything, probably because Spike wasn't around to start it. Danny ignored the glances and stares of the other kids. Their expressions showed disinterest, scorn, or outright contempt for the "new kid".

Except for Jason.

For some reason, Jason eyed Danny speculatively. Jason had also been new at the beginning of the year, but he played basketball and had quickly been accepted. The dark-skinned giant with the angled flat-top had been chummy with Spike. Recently, though, Danny had heard that the two had fought; something about Spike calling Jason 'boy'.

Danny wished he meshed with kids that easily. But, as he well knew, it was sort of a ritual – a test – for kids to give new kids a hard time. If one was different . . . watch out! It might be catching. The first week he had tried to make friends, but he'd received enough cold shoulders to make an iceberg.

With his back to the corner in gunslinger style – so no one could sneak up on him – Danny sat, opened his book and began reading. The boys in the novel were entering a haunted house, ready to test a contraption they'd invented to locate ghosts. Danny had only been reading for a few minutes when he noticed that somebody – no several somebodies – were standing on the opposite side of the table waiting for him to look up. Well, Danny thought, two could play this game.

One cleared his throat. Danny ignored him. His mother once told him that if someone really wanted your attention, they would use your name.

"Chase." It was Rocky. "Chase, I want to talk to you!"

Trying not to show any fear, Danny casually looked up. Three people were standing there, waiting on him. Besides Spike's square-jawed brother, a cute girl named Cynthia was next to Jason, holding onto his arm. She looked as if she'd rather be somewhere else.

Rocky glanced over his shoulder at Jason, frowned, then turned back to Danny. "I guess you're damn proud of yourself. Think you're so cool, don't you?" Rocky accused.

Danny didn't have a clue as to what Rocky was talking about.

For some reason Jason smiled while his dark eyes bore into Danny's.

Everyone waited. Cynthia looked away and spun several strands of dark hair around her finger. She popped a bubble of gum, then continued chewing.

Rocky grew tired of the silence first. With balled fists, he leaned forward.

"Easy, man," Jason stepped in his way, putting out a restraining arm.

"You know my brother and Hank spent most of the morning in the emergency room because of you!" Rocky shouted, pointing an accusing finger at Danny. "And Spike won't be able to play football for weeks! You've crippled our team!"

His eyebrows shooting up, Danny's expression was a mixture of confusion and surprise. "Oh, really?" He fought back a small smile. It wasn't right to be amused by somebody else's pain, even if they deserved it.

"They took a real bad spill, and you caused it, Chase," Rocky continued. "You're gonna pay."

"I've no idea what you're talking about," Danny finally told them. "They never got close enough for me to touch them or them to touch me. Do I smell like perfume? And are you saying my . . . my mere presence caused them to crash?"

Suddenly, Jason laughed harshly. "Man, Chase, you are one cool dude." His dark gaze grew piercing. "Hmmm, maybe you aren't spineless after all." Jason stood back, his face taking on a thoughtful expression. "I think maybe you deserve a chance to prove yourself against even odds."

Cynthia hugged Jason's arm and smiled winningly.

I can't wait to hear this, Danny thought sarcastically.

"Rocky, are you afraid of Chase?" Jason asked.

"No way, dude!"

"Is Spike?"

"Of course, not. Danny's nothing. Even Hank," Rocky chuckled, "isn't scared of him."

"Then you could beat him at anything – any competition, right?"

"Hands down, man. Chase is a total wimp."

"I hear you were cruisin' pretty good this morning on your bicycle," Jason said to Danny. "Not bad for a small dude. I wonder how you are over a long distance. Think you could beat these guys in a bicycle race?"

Danny hid his smile. "Easily."

"What?" Rocky exploded. "He's a weenie! A wimp! A nerd who reads all the time! Y- y-y-you . . ." Rocky sputtered, "you can't take us, Chase! Not even in your dreams!"

"I'm ready to prove you wrong," Danny replied evenly.

"Well, well," Jason said. "There's a race this Saturday. It's the Oktoberfest 20k. It's held on the blacktop south of Ft. Worth.

It's not too late for you to enter. I did. And so has Hank, Spike, Rocky and a couple of other guys. I already have a bet with Spike boy, so he's been practicing. Not that it'll help. If there's one thing I can do, it's ride."

"Whose side you on, Jason?" Rocky asked.

"Not Spike's, that's for sure."

"Listen, Rocky, I'll make you a bet," Danny told Spike's brother. "If I beat all of you, you don't bother me anymore. No more chasing, hounding, beating or fleecing. If I lose to any of you, you get my bicycle."

"And you bring us lunch every day!"

Danny thought for a moment. "I'll let you know tomorrow."

"What's wrong Chase, chicken?!" Rocky jeered, then began to make squawking noises as he flapped his arms.

"I'm grounded. I have to get permission to ride."

"Turkey," Rocky spoke again.

"Can it man," Jason told Rocky. "I can relate. I get grounded all the time. It's a Mom thing. It means he might not be a total wet blanket like we thought."

" 'Til tomorrow Chase," Rocky said, making it sound threatening.

Danny nodded.

Rocky left, but Jason hung around, his smile growing broader. "You got your chance, man. Make the most of it."

"Why'd you help me?"

"Let's just say I don't like people who pick on people cause they're different.?"

"Right," Danny said.

Jason nodded, then left with Cynthia.

All eyes in the cafeteria were still on Danny. He ignored them.

He would ask his dad tonight. Danny hoped he said yes, then he would show these guys what riding was all about. With the magic bicycle, four days should be enough practice.

Danny allowed himself a small smile. Spike might have gotten what he deserved, if he was hurt badly enough.

Maybe things were looking up. In four days, he'd race past Spike and the others, and end the harassment. He hoped it would be all right with his dad.

The afternoon went as smoothly as the morning until school was out. Nobody was waiting for him, probably because Rocky had already done the dirty work.

Stunned, Danny stared at his bicycle. It sat crookedly in the bicycle rack; they had trashed it! Much of the damage looked irreparable. TOTALED! The frame was bent, just as it had been after his wreck outside the House of Blue Lights. The tires had been slashed, and the spokes kicked in. The wheels were no longer round, appearing more egg-shaped. Even the seat was missing.

Holding back his tears, Danny knelt for an even closer inspection. Someone had taken a key to the paint, scarring it with crisscrossing marks. He looked on the ground where the chain lay. Someone had taken a rock to it, smashing the links.

Danny shook his head, then put his face in his hands. What was he going to do now? He had lost his chance to get back at the bullies, to win something from them. He should have known better. And Kalyde's precious gift – Danny's magical bicycle – was destroyed.

For a long time, Danny just knelt there and quietly raged in frustration. No one stopped to ask him if he needed help.

Finally, after all the buses had departed, Danny began walking home. He didn't wonder how he was going to deliver newspapers; he only thought about the destruction of a special gift – Kalyde's gift of friendship.

It was a long, lonely, depressing walk home.

Chapter Six

Magical Transformations

The walk home seemed agonizingly endless.

Devastated and heartbroken, Danny trudged along, never looking up, encouraging his feet to keep going. If he didn't, they would stop; they felt weighed down by concrete.

All he really wanted to do was sit down and cry, but that wouldn't solve anything. Danny sighed heavily. The string of disasters continued to mount with the destruction of Kalyde's gift. The magic was gone.

Finally, after what seemed like days, Danny guided the mangled bicycle up the driveway, then leaned it against the garage door. Barely able to walk and his head hung so low that if he stumbled his chin would scrape the ground, he dragged himself to the front door and inside the house.

Danny didn't see Murg watching him as he entered. But the calico immediately knew something was wrong. She hopped off the back of the couch and ran to Danny, where she stretched and rubbed against him.

"Oh, hi, Murg," Danny muttered.

Murg meowed, asking what was wrong.

"No, we won't be going on a bike ride . . . " Danny sniffled, then wiped his red nose. "The slugs at school, they – they –" he choked on the words " – destroyed my bike. It's TOTALED!"

Murg immediately trotted to a window to peer outside. She looked at the bike, then back at Danny. With a defiant expression, the cat shook her head.

"What?" Danny mumbled.

Murg hissed, then darted to the front door where she meowed loudly.

"What?" Danny asked again.

Murg responded with a prolonged meow.

"You want to see it up close? Okay?" Danny opened the door.

Murg darted outside and raced around the corner. With a clatter, the bicycle fell.

Danny followed the calico, finding Murg trying to get comfortable atop the warped rear wheel. "Why did you knock down my bike? Not that it matters. What's another scratch?"

"I'm going to cheer you up," Murg responded.

"Whhhat?" Danny had almost forgotten that Murg could speak when on the bicycle. "You can still speak?"

"So the bicycle must still be magical," Murg finished.

"Hey! That's right!" His smile appeared, then faded just as quickly. "So?" he asked, looking puzzled.

Murg gave him a parental look of disappointment.

"I don't understand. So the bike still contains magic. What good does that do me? The bicycle is trashed. I won't be able to race. Let alone ever ride it again. Just look at it!"

"That's correct, just look at it." Covering her eyes with both paws in frustration, Murg said, "You're not thinking. You're just feeling! THINK! What powers the bicycle?"

Danny was taken aback. "My imagination? So?" So what if the bicycle was magical, what good did that do him? Danny scratched his head.

Murg peeked out from between her paws and frowned.

"Wait! If it's powered by imagination, then we can still change its shape and color. We can repair it."

"Yes!" Murg exclaimed.

"Uh, I don't know," Danny replied, bridling his enthusiasm. Murg was impatiently tapping the spoke with a paw.

"You really think we can transform it from trashed to as good as new?"

Murg was nodding her head. "Do you doubt your own imagination?"

"No."

"Good. All you have to do is remember what Kah-laye-dee told you."

"You mean – see the bicycle as I want it to be?"

Murg nodded. "And believe in the magic of your imagination. That this magical gift of friendship can be anything." The calico climbed off the bicycle to give Danny room to work.

Danny moved quickly to Kalyde II, putting his hands on it and closing his eyes to concentrate. In his mind, Danny saw the bicycle as it should be – as he wanted it to be. He put all his desire, all his hopes and dreams into his thoughts – into his imagination. He believed that the magic was strong enough to restore his bicycle. It would be as it was . . . as good as new!

Danny ran his hands over the spot where the seat should be and thought he suddenly felt it. With his eyes still closed, his fingers wandered over the frame. He felt the scratches in the paint, then wished they were gone – and he no longer felt the grooves or chips!

Smiling, he placed his hands on the chain, focused, and soon it changed, appearing brand new. Magic! Danny could barely contain his excitement. His fingers traced the warped wheel rims, and they smoothed, becoming round once more. Magic! Nearly giddy, Danny felt the flat tires expand. The spokes were back in place, too!

Danny opened his eyes. "IT WORKED!" He beamed, his smile stretched wider than ever. Bright red and gleaming as if newly polished, Kalyde II was whole under his hands.

"You're so smart," Danny said as he hugged Murg.

"I'm a cat," the calico replied.

Later that evening at dinner, the moment Danny dreaded, finally arrived. To race – to beat Spike, Rocky, Hank, and even Jason – to be free of harassment, Danny had to have his father's permission. They had to talk. Really talk. Danny hoped his father would listen. Would understand.

Eating pizza at the kitchen table, Danny and his father sat in cold silence. His father was reading the paper. Only a few single words had been spoken since his father had arrived home with a pepperoni pizza. The two hadn't carried on a true conversation in three days now.

Pizza was undoubtedly one of Danny's favorite foods. As he savored a piece of pepperoni, Danny thought back and remembered Kalyde's words about how the magic bicycle worked when traveling long distances. "In your mind, picture the beach in South Carolina. Don't worry about how you're going to get there, just assume that you will. Be absolutely positive that you will arrive safely."

"Assume you are already there," Danny mumbled. His father scowled at him as if Danny had just broken a cardinal rule. His eyes were still dark, almost black, as though full of storm clouds.

Assume you are already there, Danny thought to himself

this time. He scooped up another piece of pizza, looped the hanging strands of mozzarella around the wedge, then stuffed a good portion in his mouth. Danny wondered if imagining things working out the way that he wanted would work in this situation – imagine that his father would say yes. Had to say yes. Why not? Well, for one, he wasn't on the magic bicycle right now.

Oh, well, Danny decided. He would pretend that he was . . . wishing he was magical! Danny imagined that his father had already given him permission – that he knew the right words to say to make him understand. Now all he had to do was get confirmation. "Dad?" Danny began.

His father grunted but didn't stop reading the newspaper.

Danny stared at the top of his father's graying head. Examining his father's face, Danny saw that his dad's attention was forced. He was working hard to ignore Danny. This time, Danny wasn't going to be deterred. "I'd like to ride this Saturday in the Oktoberfest 20k bicycle race."

His father just shook his head no. He flipped the page of the paper, and when it didn't settle naturally, he snapped it.

Murg suddenly rubbed against Danny's leg.

Danny forged ahead. "I have the money."

"No," his father spoke but still didn't look at Danny.

"I can get a ride there, you won't have to drive me," Danny continued. He reminded himself that he was just asking for confirmation, not permission.

"I said no."

"It's important!" Danny blurted out.

Danny's father raised an eyebrow, obviously surprised. Then annoyed, glowering as his jaw tightened, he leveled a stare at his son. "What did you say?"

Danny stammered at first, "It . . . it's . . . it's really important."

His father continued to stare.

At first Danny squirmed, then he discovered that he had his father's full attention for the first time in a long while. Encouraged, Danny grew bolder. "It's sort of a bet."

His father stiffened. "You know I don't approve of betting."

"Okay, it's not exactly a bet, it's more of a fight. It's self defense," Danny corrected.

Danny's father did a doubletake, then looked confused. "What? A fight? Self-defense? What nonsense are you talking about?"

"You remember the bullies I told you about?" Danny asked.

His father nodded.

Danny was thrilled. They were actually having a conversation! "Well, the past several days they've been hassling me on my bicycle, but I've been outracing them. They can't catch me! Not even three of them!"

His father waited patiently, and his gaze had softened. "You've been running away from them?"

"Tactically avoiding them," Danny corrected. "I may not be as strong as them, but I'm faster. This morning two of them crashed into each other trying to catch me. So they're really mad," Danny spoke quickly as if a dam had burst. "At lunch, they challenged me to a race. If I can beat them in the Oktoberfest 20K this Saturday, they've promised to leave me alone."

"I don't know, Danny. I can't see ending your punishments already. What you did . . ."

Danny's mind scrambled to find the right words. "I might even gain some – respect by showing them I'm good at something. Maybe even make some friends."

"Hmmm," Danny's father stroked his chin.

"It's not exactly fighting, but I'm still fighting back. Proving myself," Danny claimed. "I'm defending myself – and my family name. I'm fighting back with what I can do best. Instead of using my fists, I'm using my bicycle. It's just — just," Danny's mind whirled " — another type of weapon." Danny smiled.

"Yes," his dad agreed. With that, the second magical transformation of the day was complete. "You can race on Saturday, IF you pay your own way and can get there on your own."

Danny clapped his hands. "YES!" He bounded to his feet and raced out of the room.

From somewhere, Murg jumped into his arms. She nudged him and meowed. "I can't wait to practice, either!"

Chapter Seven

Practice, Day One

*A*fter school Wednesday, Danny rushed homeward. He hoped Murg was ready. It was time to practice for the race. Danny had never been in one, and he had only three days to prepare. He wasn't going to let the fact that he rode a magical bicycle go to his head.

As the wind blew through his hair and his eyes watered, Danny wondered where the best place to practice would be. The bicycle seemed to know how to get home by itself, so Danny contemplated locations – the beach, the desert, the central plains or the rolling hills. Maybe even the mountains. With Kalyde II, he could go anywhere!

Since all he thought about all day was getting home and riding, Danny hadn't noticed the day had gone smoothly. Glowering, Spike had reluctantly accepted the deal, thanks to Jason shaming him into it. Spike's wrists and hands were wrapped, and the left side of his face scraped and bandaged. He didn't look healthy enough to bother Danny. For now.

Jason had called for a truce until the race was over.

Danny had pointed out that also meant leaving each other's bicycles alone.

Despite his obvious shock, Rocky had never asked about Danny's bicycle – how it had been repaired so quickly.

Guilty as charged, Danny thought.

Danny suddenly found himself at home, coasting into the driveway. He hopped off his bicycle before it fully stopped and walked it to the front door. He leaned Kalyde II against the wall, then raced into the house. "MURG! Come on!"

The calico was asleep on the couch with her feet in the air.

Danny couldn't believe that she wasn't excited, too. "MURG! We don't have much time before I have to deliver papers."

Murg cracked open an eye as if to ask where they would be going and whether it would be worth getting up.

"Let's go to the desert," Danny suddenly decided. "There we can find out how fast we can really go!"

The calico appeared vaguely interested at best.

"No one will bother us there," Danny continued. "The highway north of Las Vegas is usually deserted. We can add a speedometer and see about breaking the land-speed record!" Danny laughed.

Murg stood slowly and stretched languidly as if there weren't any reason in the world for a cat to hurry. Then she jumped off the couch and walked outside, her tail twitching more excitedly than usual.

Danny smiled; he knew Murg loved speed. Sometimes down a good hill, when they were really flying, she'd let out a long caterwaul of pure pleasure.

Within moments, the duo was on the bicycle heading out of the neighborhood. They passed the entrance ramp onto the highway and cruised along a frontage road.

"Are you ready?" Danny asked.

"Most definitely," Murg said, although she sounded a bit bored. "Are we going to Nevada?"

Danny nodded.

"I've never been there," Murg allowed.

"It's dry, mostly flat and barren with sandy looking mountains. There's sagebrush, bitterbrush and tumbleweeds. Not many trees. Just thinking about it makes me thirsty."

"Sounds like west Texas but with mountains," Murg replied.

"I remember deserted concrete bunkers along the road, too. They used to do nuclear testing in that part of the country."

"Wonderful. Radioactive Racer. Your own comic book, maybe?"

Danny laughed. "We won't be there long. In fact . . . " Danny began. He pictured the two lane road leaving Las Vegas far behind. The valley was flat with a stripe of black heading toward the horizon. Sometimes close, sometimes far off in the distance, barren brown rocks jutted forth from the sandy ground to form mountains. The sky was high, cloudless and light blue. "We . . . " The bicycle raced forward even faster.

The air was hot and dry. Danny imagined gusty winds and dust devils dancing like brown tornados in the distance. In his mind they seemed to come alive; he could feel the air, and he was thirsty already.

" . . . are . . . " Danny continued speaking to Murg while he visualized where they would soon be. A sign read, "Just Leaving Beatty." Kalyde II raced faster.

Another sign flashed by as Danny raced along Highway 90. It read, "Death Valley 80 Miles." Below, it read "Tonopah

128 Miles."

Danny was getting even more thirsty; the desert had moved into his throat. The sun was merciless and blistering. The wind gusted and swirled, blowing dust and tumbleweeds across the road.

". . . already . . ."

A kaleidoscope of color exploded around the bicycle, then a legion of trumpets blared. A sharp crack of thunder ended the blaring and shook the bicycle. As though suddenly swallowed, the duo was surrounded in a brilliant white light.

Danny opened his eyes just as they broke through some clouds to cruise along the glittering rainbow. Danny tried not to let his mind wander, keeping focused on the Nevada highway. Arid lands cut by a black ribbon that rolled along valleys and over mountain passes.

At the end of a rainbow was a blazing ball of light, reminding Danny of the "on ramp" onto the sky bridge. They flew into it, momentarily engulfed by a sensationless void, then they were riding atop pavement.

" . . . there!" Danny finished with a cough.

The wind was hot and dry, almost immediately wicking away moisture from their skin and breath.

Murg blinked as a speck of dust caught her in the eye. "A giant litterbox. Wonderful."

Danny's gaze wandered over the desolate landscape. Just as he'd pictured it, the foundation of a paradise left unfinished . . . or one that had been worn away. The highway was totally deserted, matched only by the barren mountains surrounding it.

"Did you bring water?" Murg asked.

"I forgot."

"That's being prepared," Murg said coolly, then began licking herself clean.

"We won't be here that long." Danny closed his eyes and concentrated. He ran his hands along the handlebars, then cupped them as if forming something. The metal flowed into his palms, then took shape as a speedometer grew from the ramhorn handlebars.

"I'm thirsty now," Murg complained. "Fur is, by nature, intended to keep animals warm."

"All right. Hang on," Danny breathed. He reached down to a support rod leading to the pedals. Moments later, a black water bottle appeared set in a small rack.

"Is it full?" Murg asked.

Danny pulled the bottle free. When he shook it, water sloshed noisily. "Mind over matter. I just love magic, don't you?" He poured some water into a cupped hand and let Murg drink.

"Ah, much better. Water is a nectar only exceeded by milk."

"Are you ready?" Danny asked as he put on his sunglasses. Murg nodded.

"Then let's go! We don't have much time." He put one foot into the toe clip and pushed off. "Remember what Kalyde said. We can't change time, so I have to return in an hour. Mrs. Wilson will be mad if I'm late with her evening paper and her new planter."

"We can see plenty in an hour," Murg said.

That wasn't exactly true, though. The duo had been riding for ten minutes, cruising effortlessly, and all they had seen was a snake and a buzzard. Danny wasn't tired; but he was thirsty, so they stopped next to a sign that read, "Alien Highway," for a water break.

"Alien Highway?" Murg mused. "We must be near Site 51. A perfect place to test pilot Kalyde II."

Danny laughed in agreement. He noticed the calico's eyes were tearing. "Would you like some sunglasses?" Danny asked.

"No, thank you. Cats don't need sunglasses to look cool, suave or debonair."

"I thought it might help with the brightness or your eyes watering," Danny said a bit testily.

"That would make a fashion statement that we aren't happy with the way we are, and we know we are already perfect."

Danny wanted to throw up his hands in exasperation. "At least the bicycle doesn't mind changing. Speaking of which, since we're on the Alien Highway, I think we should be riding the Spacelander bicycle."

"What's that?"

"A futuristic bicycle built in the 1950's. It was designed in 1945 by Ben Bowden. I read about it in an article on antique bikes in *CYCLING* magazine. There were only 522 Spacelanders made, and only 38 still exist, so one in good condition is worth about 15 grand."

"Wow! What does it look like?"

"This," Danny said, then closed his eyes and concentrated. Kalyde II transformed to match the image in his mindseye, a red two wheeler with white-walled tires, a molded frame that was thick but curved aerodynamically to encase the entire bicycle. At the front, protruding ahead of old-fashioned handlebars, were twin headlights looking like rocket tubes. Similar ones stuck out from the rear where tail lights were mounted. Danny made some modifications of his own, creating handbrakes and multiple gears.

Sort of ugly and garish, Murg thought. "It looks rather unwieldy."

"It reminds me of the cars back then with their big fins," Danny laughed.

"I guess it doesn't matter. It will ride just the same. I am still amazed by all of this," Murg said. "Without trying, you reached 80 miles an hour. The race is yours, hands down, but if you win the race by too much, everybody will think something is amiss."

"I think I'll just concentrate on beating Spike and the crew, and see what happens. I really don't need to win the whole thing. It wouldn't be exactly fair. Not everyone has a magical bicycle."

Danny really didn't care about winning at all, except to beat Spike and the others, so that they'd leave him alone. What he really enjoyed was the freedom the bicycle had given him. Freedom and speed. Think of all the surprised friends he could visit. There was Dano in Hawaii, Gretchen in Germany, Kelly in Indianapolis, Tony in Connecticut . . . .

A red blur roared past them. Then a whoosh assaulted their ears. The after draft tore at them, sucking the air with it, but leaving road dirt and exhaust fumes.

Gasping, Murg said, "The nerve of that Ferrari." She coughed, then wheezed, "If you're warmed up, I think we should show that hundred-grand-toy a thing or two." Danny looked confused.

"Let's catch it, then pass it as if it were standing still!"

"Yeah!" Danny cried. He took one more swig of water, then they raced off in hot pursuit. "We'll rocket past them!"

As Danny pedaled rhythmically, he concentrated on catching the Ferrari. He didn't worry about speed, focusing solely on catching the Ferrari. They would travel as fast as they needed. Danny pictured the rear end of the red sports car growing larger and larger. The wind seemed to bend around them, protecting them, then blowing from behind, propelling them ever faster. Murg let out a tremendous caterwaul.

In less than five minutes, he could see the back bumper and tail lights of the Ferrari. Glancing at the speedometer, Danny couldn't believe his eyes. They were doing over 160 miles per hour! Everything close by was a blur, and the far away mountains appeared to rapidly shrink and grow. The lines along each side of the road and the blinking white streak seemed to lead to the red car ahead. How was that possible?

Suddenly, they began to slow down, and the Ferrari pulled away. The dotted white line became more distinctively separated. The telephone poles no longer looked like a fence.

"What's wrong?" Murg asked.

"I don't know," Danny replied. He was confused. One moment they were cruising along, the next they were slowing to a crawl, down to 50 miles per hour.

"What were you thinking?" Murg asked.

"That this was unbelievable."

"Stop that!" Murg admonished. "Of course, it's possible to go as fast as a Ferrari, and even faster. We were doing it! Plus, we've already traveled to Nevada and South Carolina from Texas in less than a minute, right?"

Danny nodded.

"So there isn't anything not to believe – right?"

"Right!"

"Good, don't let reality interfere with your imagination."

"Yeah!"

"So just concentrate on catching and passing that snooty red car!"

"RIGHT!"

Again, they raced forward, but even faster this time as though they'd left some weight behind. Danny ignored the speedometer. It disappeared, melding into the handlebars once more. Speed didn't matter. The time it took didn't matter because . . . Danny was . . . already . . . there!

Suddenly, they were right behind the red Ferrari. A tall, dark-haired man and a pretty blond woman were riding in it.

"Pass 'em!" Murg cried. "They're parked!"

With a huge smile on his face, Danny whipped into the oncoming lane to pass. The road was flat, empty and appeared endless.

Danny examined the car as he slowly passed. He could see his reflection in the glossy paint! Cool! It was a beautiful automobile. It looked fast... BUT HE WAS FASTER!

The dark-haired man glanced to his left as if he sensed something, then did a doubletake. His mouth opened and his cigarette fell into his lap.

Murg waved.

With wide eyes, the driver peered over the top of his shades. He said something, and the woman leaned over to look at them, wonder on her pretty face.

Danny suddenly wondered if he were on TV. He could see the *Makers of Kalyde II* selling their magical bicycle with this kind of ad. Danny laughed. He doubted he'd be their poster boy!

The driver's expression grew determined. The Ferrari leapt forward, racing ever faster, but Danny kept up with it.

The driver constantly glanced over at them, wondering if they were real. The woman tentatively waved at them.

Danny smiled. Feeling wonderful, he doffed his cap.

Murg bowed. "Kick it in, Danny, get serious and have some fun passing this guy."

Danny thought of leaving the Ferrari behind. As if a launching rocket, the magical bicycle blasted forward. Danny glanced over his shoulder and smiled at the receding Ferrari. Without a second glance, Danny focused on being farther down the road. In his mind, the Ferrari was nowhere in sight.

Danny, Murg and the bicycle blurred, becoming a streak of light racing along the road, leaving the Ferrari far behind. They continued to speed along for a while, going up one mountain at an elevation of over 8,000 feet, then screaming downhill into the valley. As they descended, they could see far ahead where a strong wind was driving tumbleweeds across the road.

"I notice that when you don't have a goal in mind," Murg began, "that it's harder to maintain your speed."

"I think so, too!" Danny yelled. "Let's go dodge tumbleweeds! I could use the practice."

They flashed by a Mack truck pulling two trailers, then raced across the valley floor. The side wind pushed against them, then seemed to whip around behind them, driving Kalyde II ever faster. Ahead, tumbleweeds danced across the road.

With the speed of thought, Danny easily steered around two tumbleweeds, then he was in the midst of them, dodging, weaving, and sometimes swerving. The bicycle tilted sharply, putting Danny's knee near the pavement, but he felt supremely safe. The bicycle was incredibly stable. It has tiger paws for tires, Danny laughed.

"What?" Murg asked. She was hunkered down across the padded bicycle carrier. Tiny paw railings surrounded it, allowing her to hang on. Her claws were out, and she looked a little nervous as they dipped low, then skirted around another cavorting bush. "These things are everywhere!"

"Yeah!" Danny exulted. He swept right, then left, then two rights and almost off the road to miss four tumbleweeds. "That was close! I'm Han Solo steering through the asteroid fields!"

"See your way clear! Don't worry about each bush!" Murg warned just as one scrapped across the back tire. Splinters flew.

"We're almost clear."

A strong breeze blew, carrying a tight cluster of bounding bushes across the road. "Gonna be tight," Murg hissed.

The bicycle danced wildly, swerving from the path of several rolling bushes, slipping around behind them, then in front of the next wave. A tumbleweed appeared destined for the front tire until the bicycle reared upwards. The bushes rolled on. Kalyde II scooted forward on one wheel, then dropped as they cut behind a huge tumbleweed. The bottom seemed to fall out, and the bicycle shook as they hit a huge chuckhole. Danny grunted as his face narrowly missed slamming into the handlebars. The bicycle recovered, handling steadily. "That wasn't . . . "

A tumbleweed struck Danny in the face. "HEY!" Danny let go of the handlebars, and then they hit a second crater. Kalyde II jumped high, flying off the road.

"Watch out!" Murg cried as they sailed into the desert, racing down the brush-covered easement. They crushed a bush and kept rolling. "See yourself back on the road!" She snagged his shirt tail with her front paws and hung on for dear life.

"I wish this was a mountain bike!" Danny shouted. The old fashioned handlebars of the Spacelander changed, then the rest of the bicycle quickly followed, looking as though pulled from an Erector Set compared to the 1950's model. Fat tires appeared and the ride smoothed as shocks settled atop the wheels. "Cool!"

They careened downhill toward a gully. Danny aimed for a rock sticking out of the ground, looking like a ramp.

"Hey!" Murg cried as they hit it, then shot airborne. Still holding onto Danny's shirt, Murg bounced up from the carrier but not as far as she expected. Due to the bicycle's magic, she wasn't in any danger except being jostled to death. They sailed ten feet, then landed softly, rolling across the bottom of the gully.

"That was incredible! Let's do it again!" Danny laughed.

"Oh, can we? Please?" Murg asked sarcastically.

"You sound like you didn't enjoy that." Danny was breathless.

"I won't be hungry for a while. Maybe a week."

"Kalyde II is amazing. It's a mountain bike. Do you think it could become a motorcycle?"

"Why? It couldn't run any faster, could it?" Murg asked.

"I don't believe so."

"That answers that question. What time is it?" Murg asked.

Danny checked his watch. "Ah, man. It's time to deliver."

"We can come back tomorrow after school."

Danny looked at the mountains surrounding him. "Good. I know I can go fast. Now I want to see how it handles off road."

"What a wonderful idea. After that, we can go play on some crowded highways, give you some real practice dodging obstacles," Murg finished dryly.

Danny laughed. Tomorrow, he thought, they might try something new! Maybe they could get Kalyde II to fly yet!

Chapter Eight

Changing Terrain

Murg was breathing easily, but Danny was almost out of breath when they reached the top of the barren, Nevada peak called Battle Mountain. "Over 9,000 feet high. A 3,000 foot climb. You should be proud of yourself, Danny."

"I only," Danny wheezed, "did the first thousand. Mountain . . . biking is . . . really work." He took a deep, sighing breath.

"As long as you don't hurt or kill yourself," Murg yawned, "it will definitely get you in shape for Saturday's race."

Since his father had agreed to let him race, he'd also agreed to let Danny practice. Now he could fully defend himself. No excuses.

Danny had delivered the Thursday evening edition, then

they were off, returning to the site of yesterday's off road experience. Clusters of tumbleweeds were everywhere.

They had raced along the road for a while, then Danny changed Kalyde II to dirt bike mode. After a little off-roading, Danny had turned uphill and began climbing. After the first thousand feet, he was exhausted, his legs leaden. Because of the altitude, he could barely breathe! He stared at the peak, willing himself to be there. He didn't care how they arrived, as long as they made it to the top. He was doing this not only to get in shape, but he wanted to ride downhill!

Along a clear stretch, he closed his eyes. With all the sweat in them, he couldn't see very well anyway. Moments later, when he peeked through the perspiration, he discovered they'd arrived atop the summit.

"Very interesting," Murg said. "We 'jumped' here . . . ."

"I like to think of it as teleporting . . . "

" . . . without riding the rainbow bridge," Murg pointed out. "Possibly because it was a short jump. We should experiment further. Get a good grasp of the bicycle's capabilities."

"First, we're going downhill," Danny said as he pushed off.

"Wait!" Murg commanded. "First, we pad this carrier so I can hang on and ride in comfort befitting a feline of my stature!"

Danny visualized the change, padding the seat and railing around it.

Murg tested it, able to grip with her claws. "If we must, I'm ready."

"Hang on!" They raced downhill, careening over rocky mounds and sailing airborne with each jump. "We can fly!" Danny said as they hit a slanted rock that worked as a launching ramp, giving them big air.

"If cats were meant to fly, we'd have wings," Murg murmured morosely. Her back arched and her eyes closed, she was hanging on with all four paws.

The bicycle hit hard, but Kalyde II seemed to absorb the blow. Danny barely felt the impact. Without braking, they continued plummeting down the steep slope. Bushes grabbed at them, but they ripped on by.

Murg peeked through hooded lids. "That wasn't too bad. Good thing this bike is magical or – even with handles, I'd have been thrown off long ago."

Danny steered sharply, guiding them toward another rocky ramp. As they left the stone behind, Danny pulled a midair wheelie.

"Danny, please!" Murg didn't sound as if she were pleading. Much.

"I've seen them do this on television!"

"I prefer speed to flight. Remember, I eat avians!"

For dropping 20 feet, they landed fairly softly. "Yee-haw!" Danny cried. It was a long way downhill, full of bumps, jumps, snatching bushes and radical air.

When they reached the road, Murg was exhausted, lying collapsed across the carrier, although she tried to hide it within typical feline repose. "I'd rather be sleeping," she told him, her eyes appearing a bit unsteady.

"What do you think about participating in the bicycle jumping contests? I bet we could learn some cool tricks!"

"Felines do not need to perform tricks to be cool. There's no sophistication in it. Besides, tricks are just learned responses. And, no, I don't like the idea. You should be concentrating on Saturday's race. Not 'catching air'."

"You're right."

"Of course. I am a cat."

"And you think we should keep experimenting?"

"Most definitely."

Danny stopped the bicycle. "It snowed in the Sierras last night. I'd like to see how Kalyde II does in snow. Would it sink?

Or would we stay atop the snow?"

"You wouldn't have any traction."

"We could outfit Kalyde II with tiger paws."

Murg groaned. "Have you ever been there?"

"On vacation. We learned to ski, sort of, on a vacation up from San Diego. And we snowmobiled an area above Zephyr Cove. That was a blast! I remember the area well. Dad shot some video. This morning I taped the broadcast from the Weather Channel, and studied it and the video. I think I can take us there."

"At least you've thought this out. This should make an interesting entry into my memoirs," Murg said.

"You have memoirs?"

"As I told you before, great cats and great achievements are passed on from cat to cat."

"How?"

"Often times we just know."

"From birth?"

"Yes. Other times, the deeds are passed along."

"How?"

"Through the cat language. It is much more subtle than your speech. Much more efficient, I might add. Less is more, in cat tongue."

"Then you're ready?"

"Reluctantly."

"You really didn't enjoy plummeting downhill?" Danny asked.

"It was fine when we weren't airborne. The speed was exhilarating."

"See, I thought you enjoyed that. Maybe with practice."

"Practice? Experimenting?"

"Let's go," Danny agreed and pushed away.

After gaining a little rhythm, he thought back to snowmobiling. He recalled racing through the woods. Genoa

Peak was off to their right, a communications tower and a building atop it. Below them, a ring of trees cut by a dirt road surrounded the summit. Evergreens and pines were abundant. Danny breathed deeply of the mountainous scent, a clean perfume full of pine and brittleness.

The bright flash swallowed them, then they burst from the clouds to race along the rainbow. Seconds later, they rode into the light and appeared in the snowy woods.

"I do believe the length of our ride has something to do with how long we cruise along the rainbow," Murg surmised.

"Look at all this snow! There must be nearly a foot, and it's not even winter yet."

"The mountains have longer winters," Murg informed him. "Brrr." Murg shivered. "Aren't you cold?"

Danny shook his head. "Think about tiger paws for tires," he told her.

"You want me to help you reshape the bicycle?"

"Sure? Why not? You know what tiger paws look like, don't you?"

"Of course."

"See them as the tires."

Soon, they were riding along, Kalyde II still working as a mountain bike. At first, they'd sunk into the heavy snow, slushing along. Then Danny said, "Think light." He thought of himself as lighter than air.

Kalyde II slowly rose to the surface and skimmed across the top of the snow. They barely left a track, unless they turned, braked, or dug in to go uphill. The tiger paws gave them incredible traction.

"It's a lot like mountain biking," Danny said, "except we're riding on frozen water. Sort of."

"I do not suggest ice riding. Tiger paws might not be enough."

"Not a big deal. We've already hit some slick spots. What I

was thinking about was water. Let's try riding Kalyde II on H_2O!"

"Water? Water!" Murg didn't like getting wet.

"It would be warmer," Danny said as they rode out of one snowy valley to pause on a ridge.

"Where?"

"Hawaii! I remember it well. Here we go!"

"But . . . "

Danny thought about a beach on an island; he didn't remember which, but it was composed of black sand – volcanic stuff. In what seemed an eternity ago, Danny had walked hand in hand with his mom and dad along that stretch. He also remembered chasing Sarah down the beach. Riding a raft! Riding the waves!

Danny pictured it, recreating the sights, colors, sounds, smells and even the feel of the air. Humidity and warmth. Tropical breezes. The smell of salt. White caps washed shoreward, then crashed among the dark, sandy shallows to ride upon the beach. Rustling palm trees along the edge of the sands were the only shade around.

The wind arrived, followed by the loud roaring. Bright light engulfed them. The clouds vanished quickly, then they dashed across the rainbow into the blazing exit. "We're here," Danny said as the bicycle slowly rolled along the beach. The back tire spewed a fountain of sand behind them, barely missing Murg.

"So I see." The calico turned around. "Another litter box, but with running water this time."

Danny laughed.

Instead of looking prissy like Danny might have expected, Murg appeared very pleased. "You need to laugh more often. It's good for the soul."

"You never laugh," Danny replied.

"Not true," Murg replied. "We are just so dignified about it that you cannot tell."

"And you don't want me to be embarrassed because you're

laughing at my expense, right?" Danny asked.

Murg seemed to smile, then began preening.

Danny stopped the bicycle and surveyed their surroundings. Palm trees, bushes and wildly colored flowers stolen from every ray of the rainbow lined the deserted beach. They were alone, and it was peaceful with the calming sound of the slowly rolling surf and the soft sighing of the breeze through palms. Danny looked to the sun and smiled. It was time to explore paradise.

"I don't know about this," Murg suddenly moaned. She was staring at the ocean. "Puddles are quite annoying. Maybe I should just wait on the beach."

Ignoring Murg's comments, Danny pushed off and began pedaling rapidly. He headed along the beach for a while, then swerved right, kicking up sand as he raced for the water's edge. Danny pictured himself skimming across the water, leaping from wave to wave. "Here we go!"

"Oh, no!" Murg covered her eyes with her paws. "I think I'm gonna be ill," she said as the tire struck the water.

Spray drenched the duo as the front tire seemed to sink. Murg hissed. Kalyde II popped to the surface as if it had struck a chuck hole. The rear tire had no such problem, rolling smoothly along the ocean's liquid surface. A groove trailed them, quickly collapsing upon itself.

At an amazing speed, they seemed to skate across the surface. The wheels spun, propelling them along a rolling highway of clear green. Up the side of one swell, breaking its crest, then rolling into the valley toward the next wave. "Wow!" Danny exclaimed.

As they rode farther from shore, the waters changed to blue and the waves grew larger. They continued to race from peak to valley to peak, from swell to swell. If he closed his eyes, Danny thought it wasn't much different than riding off road in the hills, except these hills moved!

And he could see another world below him in the crystal-line blue waters. There were ridges of coral and numerous schools of brightly-colored fish. "Hey, Murg, there's a giant turtle!" He pointed at the slowly moving sea turtle. When it saw them, it dived away, disappearing rapidly.

Having shaken off the water and composed herself, Murg was staring down at the ocean. Her eyes were large as she watched angelfish swim and swirl below them as if set under glass. "So many colors, shapes and sizes to choose from," Murg murmured. "I do so love fish for dinner or breakfast and lunch. Even a snack." The calico flattened low across the bicycle's carrier rack. While she hung onto the rail with one paw, Murg reached down with the other. It was farther to the surface than she'd thought.

Murg wasn't sure it was a good idea, but she was very hungry. And she hadn't had fresh fish in a long time. And never fish this fresh. This would make an interesting entry into her memoirs. Unable to resist, the calico leaned more and more, stretching toward the water. Some of the spray from the front wheel splashed over her, and Murg shivered, but she was determined. Her paw nearly touched the water. A long slender silvery fish neared the surface. Murg extended her claws: "LUNCH!"

Suddenly, the fish burst free from the water, the splash slapping Murg in the face. Surprised, the calico scrambled back as the flying fish skipped across the water as if it were a thrown stone. Danny's mouth dropped open, and his eyes widened. Then an even bigger smile appeared on his face, stretching from ear to ear. "We're gonna catch a flying fish!"

"Yeah!" Murg encouraged, waving a paw. "CATCH MY LUNCH!" She grabbed hold more tightly as the bicycle burst forward. The blue below blurred, losing its transparency.

Soon they were airborne, skipping from crest to crest as if they were a flying fish. Danny laughed uncontrollably, wiping the spray from his face when he nearly choked on it. "I'm gaining!" Danny yelled.

A drenched but determined feline, Murg leaned forward, her tongue peeking out in anticipation. They were closing in on the flashing knife-shaped fish. It sailed across the surface, sometimes careening as if it were a boat on rough waters. Suddenly, there were more. At least a dozen. No. Two dozen.

"Hey, it's a school! Or is it a squadron?" Danny laughed.

The fish dipped into the water every so often, barely skimming the surface before they shot forward. Danny followed them as they turned this way, then that, trying to lose him.

"So many fish," Murg murmured, her tongue flicking out and about. "Lunch for a month."

Danny gained on the fish, then put on a burst of speed, bouncing quickly across three swells. They were suddenly inside the school, surrounded by the airborne seafood. Murg leaned out. She was going to catch her dinner yet. The calico wailed a hunting cry and took a swipe, her claws catching a fish.

The change in weight threw Murg off balance, and she was pulled from her perch. "Help!" Her back claws scraped across the rails as she slid off the carrier.

Danny looked back and started to reach out, but it was too late. He closed his eyes and concentrated. Two baskets immediately appeared, one on each side of the rear wheel. Murg fell half in and half out of the one on the left.

"How undignified," the calico said. "Sometimes I'm just a slave to my appetite." Never losing a grip on her fish, she twisted and fell the rest of the way inside the basket.

"You're welcome," Danny replied. "I'm getting good at this!"

"Yes, you are! Let's celebrate with dinner!"

While Murg was eating, Danny spotted a huge catamaran. It was a tri-hull with a gigantic and brilliantly multicolored sail. A dozen or so people were sitting about drinking, soaking up the sun and taking photographs. With a smile, Danny raced past it. All they saw was a blur.

Danny had definitely gotten the hang of handling the bicycle, from off-road and dirt, to watery surfaces – snow and the ocean. It was easy; it was magic, powered only by his imagination. Kalyde had been wrong. A little bit anyway. He could fly for short distances on the mountain bike, and it seemed like flying when they went from wave to wave. But what about clouds? he thought suddenly. They were made of evaporated water that had condensed.

"Think we could ride on fog?" Danny asked.

"I don't see why not," Murg replied, "but fog is usually found in the morning."

Danny checked his watch. He'd been riding for three hours! No wonder he was hungry. "Let's go home. I wanted to visit Dano, but we'll have to do that another day. Tonight I'll watch the Weather Channel and figure out where the fog will be."

"Home, Daniel." Murg settled comfortably on the padded carrier.

At five o'clock Friday morning, Danny snuck down to the garage, where Murg was waiting for him. He'd watched the Weather Channel late last night, taking note of temperatures, humidity, and especially dew points. He figured the Smokies of North Carolina would be packed with fog. Maybe he should just visualize the perfect spot, Danny suddenly thought. A hilly road where the valleys were socked in thick but the peaks were clear, poking through the mists. Why not? If that didn't work he could always head for Boone, North Carolina.

Danny quietly rolled Kalyde II out the side door into the early morning darkness. A hint of predawn glow silhouetted the houses to the east. With the moon already set, the stars were sharp and radiant. Were they trying to tell him this was a good morning to fly? He set Murg on the feline carrier above the back wheel.

Yes, a good morning to fly, Danny thought. Kalyde said they couldn't fly, but perhaps that wasn't so. He'd blown past a Ferrari. He was lighter than mud, snow or water. . . .

"Maybe you should add wings or foils," Murg said dryly.

"We seemed to fly down Battle Mountain," Danny said as he climbed onto the bike and pushed away from the driveway.

"Please! Don't remind me."

"We were catching air!" Danny whispered.

"We were plummeting. The bicycle just lands well."

"After all, it is magical."

"I know you have a powerful imagination, so I think this is as good a time as any to say that I'm not interested in racing off cliffs, going higher and higher, just to see how far we can fall before landing too hard."

"Really," Danny said, sounding a bit crestfallen. "Then we'll stick to riding fog."

"We should know immediately whether we can or can't. With your imagination, I believe we can. You, and your imagination, might even allow us to ride smoke."

"Now that's a thought." Danny turned out of the neighborhood then onto a main street, heading for a frontage road. There was a hint of a fog that was thicker in the trees. Danny looked for an opportunity to get on top, but it was very patchy. He wanted low fog or patches atop hills. He needed an opportunity to ramp atop it.

Danny mentioned trying to visualize the perfect spot. Murg agreed to help. Danny pulled onto the frontage road where he looked around for cars. There were a few on the highway, but nobody was on the side road.

Danny found a riding rhythm, then said, "Let's do it." Danny squinted and imagined the perfect place, where the fog was so thick, the beginning and ending were clear. Almost like a wall. Or a ramp. Even a bumpy access road. He pictured fog laying heavy in a valley and thought they'd been surrounded by a thick forest of vibrant trees. He could hear rivers in the distance. One even seemed close by. The weather was cool but heavily laden with moisture.

Even with his eyes closed, he could tell when it abruptly became bright. The air grew crisp and lights danced through his lids. They were on the bridge! Danny concentrated on the fog, the way it lay along the land. All through the misty blanket, peaks jutted upward, standing out like giant fingers poking skyward through the clouds. There was the brightness again, then it was chilly.

He should have worn a jacket, Danny thought as he opened his eyes. "We're here."

"You've found fog, all right."

They were riding uphill on a steep grade. Danny could barely see ahead of them. The gray fog was so thick it walled off the rest of the world and clung to him like a wet cloth. Even if he couldn't see, Danny keep thinking he was safe. "Let me know if you hear anything," Danny told Murg.

"Only thing I'm worried about is hitting an animal," Murg replied.

"I'll put it on obstacle avoidance," Danny joked.

"A good idea."

They abruptly burst from the fog as they neared the peak of the road. The trees were more barren than he expected, and it was colder, too. The road was still wet and glistened with the light of dawn. As they crested the hill, Danny was awestruck. Ahead in the dim light to the east, a second hilltop was across the fog. It was very close to what he'd imagined. Behind it, a bright glow grew even brighter beyond the mountains.

"Look at this, Murg. Perfect," Danny said as he pointed to the clear delineation of road and fog ahead. The thick mist was spread out like a comforter, blanketing the valleys.

"A bit bumpy."

"Think light," Danny said. "And since we're going to fly . . ."

He changed Kalyde II into Spacelander form, then pedaled faster and faster, hoping speed would help. When they were close to the mists, he stopped, letting them coast while he concentrated. They'd know immediately, either passing through the fog and down the road or cruising atop it, riding the clouds. He imagined invisible wings spreading, flaps adjusting.

As they reached the fog, Kalyde II ramped atop the mists, bumping about a little. Danny tightened his grip on the handlebars. "We can fly!"

"In a very real sense, we can," Murg agreed. She tightened her grip, too. "It feels a bit like riding a dirt road but spongier. Softer."

Danny began pedaling again. "We can fly!" He headed for the distant peak. The sun suddenly rose from behind the mountains, nearly blinding them as they rode into the sun. "We can fly, Murg! We can do anything! Anything!" Danny cried as they seemed to fly atop the world.

Chapter Nine

Race Day

*D*anny had never experienced anything quite like race day. Bright-eyed, he looked around trying to absorb everything.

The day was sunny and warm with a carnival atmosphere. Hundreds of bicyclers of all sizes, ages, and sexes surrounded him in a sea of bright colors. Men wore numbered jerseys of red, while women wore blue. Underneath the numerals, the division was printed. Danny thought he remembered there being a dozen classes. He was amazed at the wide variety of entrants and their outfits. Most wore skintight spandex biking pants, serious looking helmets and radical shades. He'd never seen so many people in such good shape.

Danny stared at himself, taking in his physique and clothing. No one else was dressed in cutoffs, a tank top, and a baseball cap; he felt a bit underdressed. Or at least out of fashion. What else was new?

Well, he was also the only one with a riding companion. Murg was apparently asleep on the back of Kalyde II. She had already drawn plenty of attention and had done her best to ignore it with typical feline disdain. Eventually, people no longer stared at them, but they still snuck amused glances now and then. Eventually, the calico had responded quietly, "Did they expect a dog . . . or maybe a hamster?"

Beyond the racers, a large crowd of bystanders and race volunteers lined the road. Camcorders and cameras seemed to be required equipment. Ahead, the break and first aid stations were staffed and waiting.

Danny and Murg were positioned in the middle of the pack. The start time was nearing, so all the riders had crammed together. It reminded Danny of sardines. He felt hemmed in and tried to relax. Murg didn't seem to notice, somehow still sleeping, even as Danny rolled into position.

Danny noticed his hands were shaking and shook them to relax. What a morning this would be! Excitement made him jittery and restless. This day could change his life! If he won, no more beatings by the bullies!

Danny took another, deeper breath and thought back over the morning.

Wolfing down breakfast, Danny had grabbed Murg and hopped onto his magical bicycle. He'd followed the Ft. Worth and entry instruction maps, and arrived at the starting line early. At first, the place was deserted. Danny checked in without any trouble and received his jersey. It was red. Below the number 521, it read: 16 UNDER. Looking around, Danny couldn't imagine 500 racers showing up. Then people seemed to appear from everywhere and chaos reigned.

Some arrived on bicycles, but most came in sport utility

vehicles, pickups, vans and station wagons. As if metallic antennae atop beasts of prey, all types of bikes – sports, touring, leisure and even tandems – were attached by racks to the automobiles. On the smaller cars, the two-wheelers appeared to be erector-set insects. Only the vans and pickups actually gave the impression that they carried the bicycles instead of the other way around.

Danny had never seen so many brands of bicycles, both American and foreign: Schwinn, Specialized, Bianchi, Cannondale, Lotus, Cruise, Mongoose, Guru and many, many more. Most of the bikes seemed to outshine their more expensive porters, and unlike the automobiles, few of the two wheelers were colored a solid hue. Most had racing stripes or splatters of bright neon. Turquoise, hot pink, lime green and electric purple were the colors of the day, along with traditional reds, blacks and metallic blues. Often, the seats and handlebar wrapping were brighter than the frames. Red and white reflectors were set in the spokes and glinted in the sunlight. Bicycle flags waved above it all as if some celebration were underway.

Danny looked down at his old Schwinn and felt a crazy pang of jealousy. All the other bicycles looked newer, more state-of-the-art. All their parts and colors matched, designed to work together with a smoothness of style and mechanics. Danny's bike appeared to be worn – a relic not really suited for racing.

To anyone else, it appeared that Danny had entered a jalopy in a sports car race. Danny knew he could change Kalyde II's appearance, but that would set Hank, Rocky and Spike wondering.

"What are you nervous about?" Murg whispered in his head, bringing Danny back to the present.

"Ever raced before?" the elderly man next to him asked. He was trim and dressed in all the right equipment, even gloves.

Underneath his jersey, his shirt read, "Denton Turkey Trot".

"No. Can you tell?" Danny asked as he thought: This guy does this all the time and probably has for years. His bicycle was an Aegis and looked very expensive, probably thousands of dollars.

"Yes," he said with a knowing smile. "It's written all over your face. Now, don't be nervous. Just have fun. That's why you're here, isn't it?"

"Uh, yes, that's right. Thanks. I'll remember that."

"Don't let competition carry you away," the man cautioned. "You know – that desperate need to win. You'll enjoy it more if you just focus on having fun."

Danny knew those words could never have come from his father. If you were going to do something, do it to your best, and prove that by winning, not losing. In this case, victory was important to Danny's physical well being.

"Fancy bicycle, hah!" came the voice inside of Danny's head. "Your bicycle is magic!" Murg told him. "You don't need to worry about winning or losing. With magic, you can turn a dud firecracker into a rocket. You, my friend, can outrace any-thing!"

"You're right! My bicycle can do whatever I want. What-ever I imagine. Someday we'll even fly!"

Murg purred loudly. That unusual noise drew some atten-tion. The calico yawned in response to all the stares. "Kalyde says you're safe as long as you don't ride off a cliff or crash into a wall or a car. And we've already ridden off a cliff. A short one, but still a considerable drop. You know, if you'd paid more at-tention when things got rolling, you'd be closer to the front."

Danny nodded.

After the people had started arriving in mass, the race co-ordinators had put things into motion. Seeded riders and the competitive entrants were placed near the front. The rest of the bicyclers had to jockey for position. Before Danny knew what was going on, he'd found himself in the middle of the pack.

Danny wondered about racing. He preferred riding the open road, up and down the mountains, or along the ocean front or lake shore to this jungle of dazzlingly clothed bicycle riders. Would this be boring compared to riding atop fog? Racing a flying fish? Or rocketing past a Ferrari?

"One minute to go," the nearby man said.

Danny nodded and concentrated on remembering why he was racing. Danny was going to prove he wasn't a wimp, chicken, turkey or nerd.

"Don't worry about starting in the middle," the man said.

"I'm not. Are you, Danny?" Murg telepathically asked.

Danny nodded. He kept telling himself that with magic and imagination, all things were possible. He could outrace any-thing.

"You sure you're not?" Murg asked.

"Yes. Why do you keep asking?"

"It's written all over your face. I'm sure Jason and Spike have already spotted it. Try smiling broadly. That will unnerve them a bit. Besides, this is going to be fun!"

"You've seen them?" Danny asked, surprised.

"Yes. But that shouldn't be a concern."

"Where are they?"

"Remember, we crossed the state of Nevada in no time, and that wasn't counting the Ferrari!"

This made Danny smile broadly. Outrace anything, he kept thinking. Even his past he suddenly wondered? If so, could he catch up with his present? "So where are they?" he asked Murg.

"In front of you," the feline told him.

"Already?" Danny scanned the riders ahead of him. Spike and Rocky were easy to spot, taking up more space than most of the other riders. Jason looked like a typical racer in a black helmet, dark pants and a red shirt. He smiled broadly, then waved at Danny. Hank frowned at them both.

Spike turned around and yelled, "Chase, I'm gonna kick your — "

BANG! The starting gun erupted. The race was on!

"Go!" Murg projected, then caterwauled, startling Danny.

Everyone stepped onto a pedal and pushed off. Bicycles wobbled as feet slid into toe clips, then everyone was settled and riding. Smiles became more determined. As if they were one giant centipede, the mass moved forward in stages.

For the first few kilometers, Danny was hemmed in. There was no place to go unless he forced his way through, and that might cause an accident. As Danny bided his time, he recalled the conversation he and Murg had yesterday about racing intelligently. "Be sane. Your cycle can fly . . . in a manner of speaking. Remember, if you think about the finish line, you'll suddenly be there. Concentrate on passing people one at a time and beating Spike. As we discussed, you won't have to sandbag the whole way, but mainly at the beginning."

Danny asked what sandbagging was.

"Holding something back while appearing as though you're trying your best. Make it look like work."

"That makes sense," Danny agreed, but he didn't like it. It went against one of Mom's constant reminders to always do his best. Were there good reasons for not doing your best? If so, this would surely be an acceptable case. "I guess I can't go whizzing through the crowd at a hundred miles an hour."

"Obviously," Murg agreed. "Just lie low until we have room to move and then casually cruise. We can get serious at the halfway mark." Murg rubbed her paws together. "Keep suspicions at the minimum. Remember, you don't have to win. Just beat the Spike and the others."

As they passed the five kilometer distance marker, Danny finally had room to breathe, the riders no longer tire-to-tire and wheel-to-wheel. Danny searched ahead but couldn't see the bullies. They were probably way ahead. Danny let that thought slip away. With magic, he could outrace anything and anybody.

"Start working your way forward to the front of the pack," Murg suggested, speaking this time. "These people are slowing you down. I think you'd win without magic. Now, forward ho." She leaned forward and stretched out a paw, pointing the way. People stared unabashedly as the duo passed them.

Over the next two kilometers, Danny casually weaved in and out of traffic. With each minute, he sped up a little, making more room for himself. He watched for signs of his tormentors but didn't see the bully crew. Or Jason, either.

As Danny swerved, weaved and dodged in and out of traffic, he was reminded of the tumbleweeds, except this was easier. He was once again impressed by how well the bicycle maneuvered. It was incredibly graceful! As if his wheels were magnetized to the road, tight swerves and turns were accomplished easily, especially when compared to riding atop snow. He shifted easily from left to right without losing a beat. Born to ride!

They moved as one, the bicycle gliding ahead in concert with his thoughts. Mind, body, bicycle . . . and cat were in time and tune! Danny found himself humming a song he didn't recognize.

"What's that tune?" the calico asked.

Danny thought for a moment. "Strange, I don't know."

"And you're humming it?" Murg said.

Danny nodded and shrugged.

They passed the ten kilometer mark, and their speed continued to increase. Danny put his heart into humming, but still the words wouldn't come to mind. They had a foreign sound to them as if they were alien. "I think it's a song Kalyde knows."

"Oh," Murg looked around.

As the riders watched them pass, many were amazed; others wore defiant, even angry expressions as if they were being passed by an inferior. Danny barely noticed; he was concentrating on the task at hand. He wasn't breathing hard, and he was barely sweating, his legs churning in clockwork fashion.

"Well, whatever that tune is makes you ride fast," the calico concluded. She motioned to a rider on their left.

The young man was clad in skintight black that appeared to have been splashed with a rainbow and a helmet with a bird-like beak turned backwards. He did a doubletake, then shook his head. Even though he worked the pedals harder, Danny easily passed him.

Danny weaved between a brightly dressed woman and an Asian rider wearing a white t-shirt and trunks. His number was 125. The magic bicycle angled left, right, then left again. Zip, and Danny sped by several riders. The air whistled about the duo.

"Yeah!" Danny had spotted Rocky riding a Grant bicycle. The heavyset boy never saw Danny coming and barely glimpsed him passing, leaving Rocky far behind. The twelve kilometer marker came into view. The tune rang in Danny's head, and the magical bicycle seemed to throb with life. "Slow down! Be smart!" Murg urged. She looked at Danny, who appeared lost in thought. "The leaders aren't all that much farther ahead, maybe a kilometer. SLOW DOWN!"

Danny spotted a bright red flag. There was a black fist symbol painted on it. Spike's bicycle was just ahead!

The brute was wearing a torn red t-shirt that was darkened with sweat. Just behind him was Hank. His pale skin was flushed, matching the stripes on his bright yellow shirt and baggy shorts atop riding pants. He appeared to be laboring even as he reached down for his water bottle. Hank drank, then gasped before spitting water.

Danny slowed a bit. He planned to pass them in the same fashion he'd passed the Ferrari but at a considerably slower speed. Instead of traveling at 180 miles per hour, they might have been going twenty-five.

Hank spotted him first. With wide eyes staring through crooked glasses, he watched Danny calmly close. The magic bicycle's front wheel was parallel with Hank's rear one. "No way, Jose," Hank cried. He jumped out of his seat and stood, pedaling as if he were running. His GT bicycle shot forward. "Eat road dirt, turkey!"

Danny slowly inched forward, gaining with inevitable slowness, but knowing he would pass. Hank would know – must feel – there was nothing he could do. Kalyde II's front tire was even with Hank's pedals, then his handlebars. Within moments, they were even.

Danny kept his eyes on Spike's sweaty back.

Murg didn't. She was enjoying this. The calico thumbed her nose at Hank.

"This can't be happening!" Hank howled. "Spike, look out! Chase is gaining!"

Spike glanced over his shoulder, then turned around. He snarled, then spat at Danny before whipping back around. Spike attacked the road with his bicycle. Tiny pebbles shot out from under the back tire. Smiling and grunting, Spike thought he was pulling away, giving it everything he could muster.

"RRROWRrrr- OWRORRrr!"

Spike looked to his right. Danny continued staring straight ahead. "Damn you, Chase! I'll get you for this! You can't beat me!"

Danny paid no attention to Spike's string of taunts. He was frustrated, not only was Chase winning, but he was hardly sweating, barely straining. As Danny agonizingly inched past the desperate bully, Murg turned her tail to him and flicked it. "I'll . . . " Spike sputtered.

Danny looked him directly in the eye, smiled broadly, then put on a burst of speed, leaving Spike some fifty feet back. The distance between them stretched farther and farther.

Danny began humming again. There weren't many riders

ahead of him, the road fairly clear. He passed an aid station. He didn't stop. He wasn't tired or thirsty. His speed increased. Danny passed several more riders. A bicyclist paused along the side of the road, grabbing the back of his leg.

The fifteen kilometer marker blurred. Danny barely noticed it, reveling in the feel of the bicycle and the speed, the wind whipping past him. Danny wondered if this was how a cheetah felt. It was incredible! He could outrace anything, maybe, just maybe even his past and his troubles with his father. Danny never noticed passing Jason, who was slack-jawed with amazement.

Murg pawed at his back. "Danny, slow down. Down. SLOW DOWN! SLOOOOOW DOWN!!" Murg projected, then yelled. More than one rider rubbed their eyes. "You're passing everyone like they're standing still. You're going to win!"

Not hearing a word, Danny continued on, humming and pedaling, driving the bicycle ever faster. He wished Sarah was here to see him ride.

After delivering the Friday evening paper, they'd taken a final practice run along the Nevada highways and somehow ended up at Hoover Dam. Since then, Sarah had been on his mind more than usual.

Just ahead of them, a dark haired man on a silver bicycle attempted to pass a trim Hispanic guy on a red Schwinn, number 66 trying to get by 101. The challenge was being hotly contested when the metallic colored bicycle hit a rock. The back tire jerked sideways, hitting the red bike.

Danny heard the sound of sliding rubber, alerted in time to see a two-wheeler tumbling directly into his path. Panicking for a moment, Danny forgot what type of bicycle he was riding. He braked, wished he was elsewhere and partially backpedaled as if hoping to go into reverse.

The bicycle vibrated wildly, then jerked. There was a tearing blackness and earth-shattering explosion of sound. Stars rushed by Danny, turning them into comets, and he thought he was racing backwards. Everything was cloudy, then the pavement turned into a ragged rainbow. They bumped along, thrashing about, then there was another ripping flash of darkness followed by light.

They were suddenly cruising along the road atop Hoover Dam!

What was he doing here? They coasted toward a car which looked very familiar. A young, blond haired girl got out of the back of the Lincoln Continental. "Sarah? Sarah!" Danny yelled.

"That can't be Sarah!" Murg told him.

"You're right! Sarah's dead!" Danny choked. And . . . hadn't he just been racing? "What's going on?" He looked again. It looked like her, but that couldn't be Sarah! She was dead! And he was racing in the Oktoberfest 20k in south Ft. Worth! Wasn't he? Was he brain damaged?! If so, why was Murg seeing her too?

"Let's go find out!" Danny pedaled forward and felt the bicycle shudder. Then it shook mightily. Everything around them – the valley walls, the dam and its buildings – appeared to contort, then caved into a circle that materialized in front of them. Danny was sucked forward into the darkness just like everything else.

Now back in the race so suddenly it all seemed to have happened in several blinks of the eye, Danny had an overpowering sense of *deja vu*. He recognized the rider in front of him. Wasn't he going to fall. Or had he fallen already?

"What was that?" Murg asked. "It seemed like some sort of temporal shift."

"What do you know about those?"

"As many have surmised, cats have a different view of time."

Before Danny could respond, the accident happened – or happened again – just as he'd known it would. The red bike shot to the right, then skidded. The silver two-wheeler tumbled over and over. Danny blinked, braked slightly, then steered around it.

"Odd. Didn't that already happen?" asked Murg.

"The accident?" Danny asked. "I thought so, too. It's why people wear helmets. They don't always land on their feet."

"And that – place," Murg continued. "And that girl. She reminded me of Sarah." The calico sounded very sad. "But it couldn't have been Sarah."

"I guess we better slow down."

"I think that would be prudent," the calico agreed.

They finished twenty-second, but first in Under 16. He'd beaten the bullies, but all he thought about was Sarah and Hoover Dam. Had they really traveled there? To the past? Time traveled as he'd dreamed of doing? Or was his imagination running wild – again?

Chapter Ten

Rewards

The moment Danny crossed the finish line, the rest of the day became a blur. He didn't recall the time they gave him, but he did hang onto the number 22.

A nice lady in red and white came to Danny and told him, "Congratulations, you've placed first in your division. We'll be handing out the trophies shortly."

"Trophies?"

"Yes, you won your division!"

"I won, Murg! I really won! That's a first. I can't remember ever winning anything!"

"History is made. What an incredible story about a boy, his magical bicycle and his companion, an amazing calico! We'll switch to our roadside reporter for an up close and personal conversation with the trio."

Danny laughed. He had given up participating in such events.

Danny overheard someone tell a rider that the competitive divisions were recognized first, then they progressed backwards from the oldest to the youngest. That was fine with Danny. He wasn't in a hurry. He was revelling in the thrill of the adventure and winning for the first time ever.

Yes, he had won. Yet, the images he'd seen of Hoover Dam unnerved him, preoccupying his thoughts. What had he seen? Sarah? Really Sarah? Alive? Were his parents also there? Hadn't they visited Hoover Dam just a few years ago? But why hadn't he seen himself?

Was it just his imagination? Was he mentally wandering into the past? Danny rubbed his head. It had seemed so real. Oh, oh. Maybe he had been injured in the exchange of memories with Kalyde. The meeting of the minds certainly seemed to have changed him; he imagined so much more vividly now. Maybe the headache had been an early warning sign that his mind had been altered.

Or . . . maybe, the bike was even more magical than they first thought! Maybe, just maybe, he actually did travel back in time! Could the magical bicycle actually travel time?

What had he been thinking? He'd been telling himself that with his magical bicycle he could outrace anything, hoping to put distance between him and his unpleasant past. Could the bicycle ride so fast that it broke the time barrier? Was there even such a thing?

He had been thinking about Sarah and Nevada just before the . . . images had appeared. She'd been on his mind even more since yesterday and his visit to Hoover Dam. What had he been doing besides thinking? Had he been picturing her and that place in the same way that he imagined the bicycle carrying him to far away destinations?

There had been an accident in front of him, but all he could remember doing was braking, then swerving. Wait! The second time he'd known the accident was coming! What was going to happen! And he had reacted accordingly.

"Are you thinking about what you saw?" Murg asked. The calico was reclining on the back of the bike, which was propped against a bench.

"Yes."

"We were somewhere else, that's for certain."

"How do you know?"

"As I said before, cats are familiar with changes in time. We live across time sometimes. When we do, we appear to be sleeping."

"Is that why you sleep so much?"

Murg appeared a bit miffed. Then her ears twitched. "Hey, we'll talk about it later. Right now, they're calling your name."

"Danny Chase, first in the boys' 16 and under division," came the call a second time. "Danny finished twenty-second overall, beating many older riders even in the competitive category. That is the best ever by someone in 16 and under. Come on up, Danny!"

Atop a small platform, a man with a microphone held up a modest-sized trophy of a boy crouched on a bicycle and riding low. The sun glinted off of it as though it were cast from gold.

"It's time to collect your award. Don't blush! You won!"

Danny blinked. He must have been out of it. How much time had passed? Murg dug a claw lightly into his arm. "Ow!" Danny jumped, then looked all around. People were looking about, searching for him. Danny moved toward the platform. There was no need to call his name a third time.

"Here he comes! Make room, ladies and gentlemen."

Danny wished his mom and Sarah could have been there to witness his first victory! That depressing thought overshadowed his receiving the award. He said nothing when it was handed to him but forced a weak smile. Danny wished, knowing it was futile, that he could reach back and change the past so they could be a happy family once again.

"Hey, Chase!" came a voice, "I want to talk with you!" Jason was sweaty with curly helmet hair and road grit stuck to his shirt. Jason carried his backward bird helmet in one hand while Cynthia held the other.

A second pretty girl caught Danny's attention. For a moment, his sadness was forgotten. She was tall, with long, golden blond hair and eyes the color of the water in Hawaii. Her smile was broad and charming.

"Congrats!" Jason said. "You beat almost everybody! I'm very impressed." He looked at Danny strangely. "Hey, I thought you'd be excited, man, you know, about winning."

Danny glanced away. "Oh, I am. But I was thinking about my mom and my sister, wishing they were here."

The golden haired girl leaned forward and asked boldly, "Didn't anyone come to watch you race?"

"No, they couldn't make it," Danny replied quietly. Murg meowed loudly. "I take some of that back, Sarah's cat, Murg, came along for the ride." Danny managed a smile.

"I like cats," the girl said. Murg beamed as she moved within petting distance. Danny was suddenly embarrassed by the situation, both by the attention that winning brought and the interest of the golden-haired girl.

"Where is your family? Your fans?" the girl persisted. Her blue eyes were locked on Danny, pinning him.

He felt exposed. "Murg is here. My dad had to work . . . and my sister and mom, well, they died in a car accident a while ago."

"Oh," the girl said and covered her mouth.

"Yeow!" Jason said. He gestured to the blushing girl. "This insensitive clod is Christina Mornay. Chris, meet Danny Chase."

"Uh, hi . . . hi," she stammered, her face flushed.

"Yes, Chris is a clod. It takes one to know one . . . and I should know," Jason said, pointing to himself. "Because I can be a brute, too. My sister, Angelina, tells me I'm insensitive all the time."

"Christina Mornay! I've seen your artwork hung in the halls! You're very talented."

"Not just an artist," Jason said. "She's also a cheerleader, like my sister Angelina and Cynthia here."

"Jason, unlike some people I know, I don't define myself by one thing," she said, then smiled sweetly.

Jason laughed.

So did Danny. Then he asked Jason, "Do you think Hank, Rocky and Spike will honor the bet?"

Jason looked a bit uncomfortable. "That's a good question. Spike comes from a screwed up family. Bullies and bigots. His father hits Spike all the time, so he smacks Rocky. And they smack others. Smaller guys like you. Different guys like me. You get the picture, I'm sure."

"Yeah," Danny said. "I do."

"That doesn't make it right," Christina said.

"I didn't say it did."

"I didn't really win if Spike is still going to harass me," Danny said.

"Hey, I'll do what I can," Jason said. "I'll embarrass him about not keeping his word."

"That sounds like fun," Christina said, her eyes aglow. "Me, too."

"And if that doesn't work, there's the old-fashioned way," Jason said. "Though I prefer not to settle things street style."

"Thanks. I appreciate you backing me up," Danny said.

"My word is important to me," Jason said.

"Honor," Christina began, "now if we could only find chivalry."

Cynthia laughed with her.

"Hey, Chase!" Spike yelled as he approached.

"Speaking of honor," Christina murmured.

Spike was still sweating heavily and appeared to be simmering mad. Both hands were clenched. Rocky and Hank were behind him. Hank appeared reluctant. "If you think I'm going to leave you alone because you won, you're wrong," Spike snarled.

"But . . . " Danny began.

As Spike approached, Murg popped her claws and hissed.

"I agree," Christina muttered and stepped between Danny and Spike. "Spike, you're not going to break your promise, are you?"

"I didn't promise nothin'!"

"Your word means nothing to you, does it?" Jason said.

"He beat you fair and square," Christina said.

Danny didn't say anything; that wasn't exactly the truth.

"Big deal! I don't care!" Spike said. He started to move around Christina.

Jason moved to intercept him.

"Just because your father is an s.o.b. doesn't mean you have to be mean to Danny," Christina said.

Rocky's intake of breath was loud. Spike stiffened, his face a mask of surprise, then his eyes narrowed, and his expression tightened. "Little Miss Cheerleader, you don't want to start with me!"

"Don't start with me, Spike! If you break your word or screw with me, I'll make sure not a single girl speaks to you anymore. We will make your life a living hell! Rumors can have wings." She smiled sweetly.

"You wouldn't!"

"Try me," she said coldly.

They stared at each other for a time, then Spike hissed like a snake, whirled about and said, "Come on, guys. Every dog has its day. Even a poodle. Later, Chase. Count on it."

Jason started laughing. "Christina. You're one tough babe!

I knew there was a reason I liked you," he cackled.

Danny was so surprised he could barely speak. "Thank you, Christina. Thank you very much."

"My pleasure. I can't stand Spike."

"Well, it was nice to meet you guys, but I've got to leave now."

"No time to celebrate?" Christina asked.

"I deliver papers. Morning and evening editions."

"A working man," Jason laughed.

"I'll be seeing you at school," Danny said.

"Uh, Danny, wait a minute." Jason stopped him.

Danny turned, wondering what now.

"Do you ride a lot?"

Danny nodded.

"So do I. I hope to be the first black, I mean, Afro-American, cycling champion. Not many of us race. First here, then the Tour de France. Then the Olympics. Hey, what I'm trying to say is, would you like to go riding sometime? Have a riding buddy?"

Danny was dumbfounded. He'd been amazed that Jason had come looking for him in the first place. Now he was asking him to be a cycling buddy.

"I like riding out to lakes like Squaw, Eagle, and Crowley. I've even been up to Grapevine. It would be a trip! You, me and the wind!"

"I'm impressed," came Murg's thought. "I've ridden to the beaches of South Carolina, the Nevada desert, the Appalachians and Rockies and the ocean around Hawaii. Next week, Germany, here we come."

"Sure," Danny replied. "Riding clears my head, so I enjoy bicycling alone sometimes. You probably know what I mean. It's just me, the wind – and Murg," Danny said. He scratched the calico behind an ear.

"No problem. I'm training for the 'Hot as Hell 100' next

July in Waco." Jason's smile was broad.

Cynthia's matched Jason's smile.

"I'm heading out to Squaw on Wednesday. Want to join me?"

"I'll see if I can." Danny wouldn't be able to use the bicycle's magic when he was riding with someone, but it might be fun to have a second riding partner and a friend besides Murg.

The calico agreed. "You could use a friend."

Before Danny could leave, Christina said, "Danny, I'm so sorry for . . . asking dumb questions."

Danny didn't know what to say.

Christina continued, "Due to all the parties this month, we're having my Halloween party next Saturday night, and I'd like you to join us."

"Sounds great! But I'll have to check with my dad. I'm still grounded," Danny told her. "This race was an exception. I'll let you know at school."

Christina appeared disappointed.

"Thanks again for the invite. And the help with Spike. See you Monday," Danny said as he climbed on his bicycle, then rode off.

"Boy, moving up in the world, aren't you?" Murg purred.

Danny didn't respond. There was a lot to think about. He'd won, sort of. Spike would still be looking for him, but the others might leave him alone, unless Spike harassed them. Jason apparently wanted to be his friend. He found it surprising that Christina Mornay had invited him to a party! If she had still been alive, Sarah would have teased him until he'd wanted to die.

Sarah.

Danny swore he'd seen her at Hoover Dam just an hour ago.

Was he going crazy?

Chapter Eleven

Backpedaling In Time

The warm wind blew through Danny's red locks as he tossed another newspaper. He was smiling and daydreaming, paying very little attention to his work. On the book carrier, Murg sat with her eyes closed and a satisfied expression on her face.

All was going well. The week had been marvelous, and tonight's Halloween party was a perfect way to end Danny's first week of being a winner. Christina's party was at six o'clock. He couldn't wait to see her; this sunny day reminded him of her. The Texas forecast projected a high of 70 degrees, and currently, there were only a few puffy clouds in the light blue sky.

As Danny rode along effortlessly, he basked in the sun, reveling in the wind as it blew across his face. His skin felt electrified, and his heart pounded in time with his pedaling. Nothing was as thrilling or made Danny feel more alive than cruising on the magic bicycle. He looked into the sky and again sent thanks to Kalyde wherever he might be. Danny wondered if Kalyde would have believed the last week. Danny wasn't sure which made him happier – the transformation at home or the changes at school.

His dad was speaking to him, once again, and Danny hadn't been harassed all week.

When Danny arrived home with a first place trophy, his father was obviously surprised. He didn't say anything for a few moments, mixed emotions playing across his face. At first, Danny thought he was in trouble again.

Finally, his dad's face broke into a huge smile – the one Danny hadn't seen in months. "Amazing! Congratulations!" He shook Danny's hand, then lifted him off his feet when he hugged him.

Danny felt ready to burst.

"Tell me all about it!" Danny's father requested.

Danny told him about everything except for the "magic bicycle" and his short "visit" to Hoover Dam.

His father beamed for a while, especially when he recounted his conversation with Jason. His father encouraged him to go cycling with Jason but didn't look too concerned when Danny mentioned that Spike was still after him. "I guess so," his father responded when Danny mentioned Christina's party. "But I expect to see an improvement in your grades."

"Sure," Danny agreed.

"I'm glad you're finally blending in. You could use someone to talk with, besides Murg. People worry about you if you talk to animals," his father said.

Murg protested loudly but was ignored.

"Still, some of last week's punishments are still in effect.

Remember, I will never condone what happened last week. No
Nintendo or comics, right?"

Danny nodded.

All week, things were close to being normal. Or as normal
as they could be without Mom and Sarah. Danny admitted to
himself that things might never be the same, but at least this
week was acceptable. His father talked to him over dinner and
helped him with his Algebra homework. He hadn't done that in
a long time. All of it inspired Danny, and he spent some time
writing on the computer.

As Danny mentally returned to the present, he casually
flipped a paper toward the front porch of a brick house on his
right. The mailbox read, 'The Earvins'. On each side of the
porch sat a small stone lion. The paper bounced off the right
statue and landed on the sleeping dog, a pit bull.

Surprised awake, the dog yelped. With an angry snarl, the
pit bull jumped to its feet and raced toward Danny.

Murg opened her eyes at the sound of the enraged dog.
"Get it in gear!" the calico cried.

"Huh?" Danny said, not yet fully in tune with the real world
of Now.

"Haul tail! Pit bulls are born killers!" Murg cried.

Danny glanced over his shoulder, finally seeing the dog as
it raced nearer. Its claws scrabbled across the asphalt, bringing
it closer to the duo. The ugly, squat beast slobbered in anticipation. Viciousness glinted in its dark eyes.

Danny finally kicked it in gear, pedaling much faster. Instead of picturing his escape, Danny romped down on the pedals. Before Kalyde II could shoot forward, the front tire hit a
rock and skidded. It slipped into a pothole in the road, then
jerked sideways before magically righting itself. Danny's head
snapped back, his vision briefly blurring.

The pit bull struck, snapping jaws scraped skin as it caught

Danny's pant leg. "Ouch!" Danny yelled.

Teeth gnashing, the pit bull hung on tenaciously.

Danny kept pedaling, but the dog's weight was a drag. Its back legs scrabbled across the pavement. The bicycle wobbled, then righted. "I can't pedal!" If he didn't do something immediately, they'd crash. Then they'd be at the beast's mercy. Danny grabbed a newspaper from his satchel.

"I'll take care of it," Murg said as she flexed her claws. "Stupid dog, disturbing my ride." The calico swiped at the pit bull; her claws caught the dog's ear.

The pit bull yelped, letting go of Danny's leg.

Finally free, Danny stood on the pedals. The magic bicycle raced off. "Whew, that was a close one," Danny said, then wiped his brow. "I guess the bike's magic doesn't protect us against attack dogs."

"Just a speed bump in the highway of life," Murg murmured.

"Hey," Danny said, "how did you get so philosophical?"

"Your mother. She would have said something about letting sleeping dogs lie."

"That's right, Mom did study that stuff in college. I'd forgotten." Danny hurled another paper. This time he was alert for dogs, even sleeping ones.

"And she always wanted you to do well in school."

"Yes, but she didn't always talk to me about 'fitting in' at school like Dad does," Danny responded.

"He is the establishment," Murg replied.

"Mom always encouraged me to be just who I am and not pretend to be somebody else. I think she said something like 'be you before you try to be someone else.'"

"Hmmm," Murg pondered. "I believe she said 'be who you are before you try to be what you want to be, and let both shape you.'"

"That's it!"

"Well, she would be happy about the way things went this week at school." He thought back to the beginning of the week. Apprehension had dogged him all the way to school. None of the bullies, not even Spike had bothered Danny during his ride to school.

Monday had been strange, especially when he first walked into school. He strolled past the kids lounging in the front hall, those waiting until the last minute to run to class before the school bell rang. Some stared at him as if he were an alien with four eyes and antennae. Neither Hank, Rocky nor Spike were in sight, and they were almost always waiting in the front hall. When he could, Danny snuck into school through the gym door. Monday he didn't, wanting to see if Spike was still after him. That sounded brave, but he hated not knowing, wondering if they might jump him at any time.

A long-haired boy in a Red Hot Chili Peppers t-shirt looked amused and gave Danny a thumbs up. "Excellent, dude."

A cute, dark-haired girl with large eyes – one who never paid him any attention – surveyed him with covert glances at first, then bold stares.

Danny didn't know how to react. He wasn't sure if he was a hero, a celebrity, or a headliner in a freak show. Word about the race must have traveled fast. Would Jason be talking it up?

I'm not any different than I was on Friday, Danny told himself. But the kids at school saw him differently. Might he have appeared – have been – more confident? After all, he had won. Danny decided to be himself, not act any different than usual.

As Danny opened his locker, he thought back to something Murg had said on Sunday night. "Friendships aren't built in a day and friends shouldn't be created by word of mouth."

The rest of the morning contained more of the same. Classmates appeared not to know what to make of Danny Chase.

How had he changed?

Lunch altered the flow of the day and changed the entire week. Trailing the class as usual, Danny entered the lunch room. With a book in hand, he headed for his corner table. Danny had grown accustomed to not eating lunch and being alone. Today was no different, since he figured Spike was probably still after him.

"Hi!" As if materializing from thin air, Christina popped in front of Danny. Her golden hair was pulled back, and she already wore eye liner and lipstick that highlighted her beauty. Just the sight of her threatened to tie his tongue in knots. "Remember me?" Her crooked smile was dazzling.

"Of course! How could I forget the girl who stood up to Spike?" Something he should have done long ago, Danny thought. "I spoke with my dad. I can ride and come to your party – if the invitation is still good, that is."

"Of course, you're still invited, silly." Her eyes brightened as if she had a brilliant idea. "How about having lunch with us?"

Danny wanted to, but Rocky was sitting at the table. The larger of the "Bash Brothers" was scowling in their direction. "Uh, I didn't bring any lunch. I usually read." He didn't want to start trouble.

Giggling came from somewhere behind Danny. Christina tensed but wasn't intimidated. "That's all right," she said.

Danny realized she wasn't going to accept his lame excuse. He glanced in Rocky's direction, then said, "I don't think everyone would appreciate my company."

Christina noted his glance, and her eyes narrowed. "I think I understand." She pursed her lips, then said, "Some people can be so dense. Do you mind if I sit with you? I have a feeling much of what I've heard about you isn't true at all."

"Uh," Danny didn't know what to say. He felt a sharp pain, then said, "Sure." Danny swore that Murg had swiped him across the ankle! But the calico was at home! How strange; it was certainly something Murg would have done to jar him into action.

Picking up her tray and saying goodbye to all, Christina joined Danny. "Where's Jason?" Danny asked.

"In the bathroom. He'll probably join us." Danny was startled when she mentioned, "Jason was really impressed by you. He's been talking about you all morning. Said that he's never seen anyone ride like you. A natural, he said. If he's not playing basketball, Jason's riding. It's the NBA this or the Tour de France that."

"Odd combo," Danny said.

"I said the same thing!" Christina laughed.

They sat down across from each other at an empty table. "You read a lot, don't you?" Her blue eyes sparkled, and her lips twitched as if she were slightly amused.

He nodded.

"Why?" she asked.

"Two reasons, I guess. Moving from place to place a lot – I'm a military brat – I spend plenty of time trying to make new friends, which means being a stranger in a new place, and being alone a lot," he rambled, "especially now that Sarah is gone." Danny blushed just a bit. "She was my sister. We were best friends."

Christina's expression was sorrowful.

"The second reason – I want to write science fiction one day, like Asimov and Heinlein."

"Really? A writer?"

"Yeah, I have a whole bookshelf full of their stuff, and lots of ideas."

"All right! I want to be an artist. When you publish one, maybe I can paint the cover!"

"Cool!" Danny smiled. He'd rarely felt so comfortable around anyone, let alone a girl, except for Sarah and Gretchen, and they didn't count. Christina had a different effect on him. Just sitting with her made Danny feel as if he were coasting downhill on his bicycle, both hands tucked behind his head.

"What have you written?" she asked.

"Not much recently. I used to play on my dad's computer a lot, but I haven't touched it for a while. I've been . . . uninspired."

"Anything I can read?"

"Maybe," Danny hedged. "I have a time-traveling story."

"Like HG Wells?"

"Sort of. Are you a good artist?"

Christina looked surprised, then gave him a mock frown. "Yes, but not as good as I'm going to be one day!"

Danny liked her attitude.

"I'll bet you thought that cheerleaders couldn't do anything besides smile and bounce around yelling and clapping."

"They can?" came a familiar voice. "Hello Champ!" Jason announced as he set his tray on the table, then sat down. "I see you have a racing fan seeking your autograph." Both Danny and Christina blushed, then she hit Jason in the arm.

He grabbed it and groaned.

From that moment on, Danny had plenty of company for lunch, which he finally started bringing again. He ate with Christina, Jason and Cynthia every day. More kids joined them, but they just seemed to hang around, wanting to be seen with them. During his free time at school, Danny talked with Christina.

He wasn't bullied all week, and Spike seemed to avoid him. Danny wondered if Spike was a time bomb ready to explode when he least expected it.

Jason canceled their ride on Wednesday, which was all right with Danny. He was a bit overwhelmed by all his 'new friends.' Murg told him not to get a big head. Danny needed space and spent most of his time after school riding about. Danny didn't travel any place far, far away. He cruised northward to Lake Texoma on the Oklahoma border, then south to Lake Travis near Austin, and finally east to Broken Bow Lake in Arkansas.

As Danny hurled the last newspaper, he concentrated on one of the two questions that had dominated his thoughts all week. How was Christina similar to Gretchen and Sarah? Was it her blond hair or blue eyes? Or was it her crooked smile, which reminded him of Gretchen? She was about the same height. And Christina's laugh was abrupt, much like Sarah's had been. No. It was something more. Christina seemed to accept him for himself, not who she expected him to be. Christina was persistent too, just like Gretchen. She wanted to read some of his writing. Despite being a cheerleader, he laughed to himself, Christina seemed to be a creative soul.

"LOOK OUT!" Murg yelled.

"WHAT?" Danny snapped to attention. Straight ahead, not ten feet in front of him, a taut rope quivered, suspended across the road between two cars. Danny wished he was elsewhere, braked and backpedaled.

The bicycle appeared to sail through the stretched rope. Danny saw Spike open-mouthed with surprise. Before the bully could yell, a loud crack of thunder shattered the air. The cold breeze ripped at Danny, then he was suddenly gone. Just as quickly, they reappeared on the rainbow highway.

"What's going on?!" Murg cried. "We're going backwards!"

As they raced backwards along the rainbow, the bicycle jerked and vibrated. The force of the wind tore at Danny's back. He glanced over his shoulder. Murg was standing, amazement shaping her expression.

The rainbow was no longer just below him, it surrounded him, now a long tunnel instead of a bridge. Colors streaked by and blurred, mixing with white and black splotches, tattered tears in the rainbow tunnel. The holes shot by so quickly that Danny couldn't tell if there were stars or a sun outside the shaft.

The twisting sensation heightened. Danny felt as though they were going every which way at once. Wait! Did he see a reflection of himself in the surface of the rainbow? Or were there many Dannys riding their own Kalyde IIs with Murg on the back?

In one of the light holes, Danny swore he saw a moving van in front of their house in Texas. The crumpled remains of a car appeared, then was gone. The scenes continued, stringing along one after another: the mountains of Germany; an Oktoberfest celebration; his dog, Prince; Sarah, looking much younger.

WHOOOSH!

With a great gust of wind, the rainbow suddenly shattered into shards of bright light. Then the wind faded to nothing. Danny rolled to a stop atop a lush, green hill. As he looked around, Danny immediately recognized the area. They were in Germany! He rubbed his chin. Yes, these were the mountains outside of Garmisch-Partenkirchen. He, Sarah, and Gretchen would often ride the train to GP to hike.

Danny smiled at the memories as they played through his thoughts, then he looked up at the sky. A huge, dark thundercloud crawled over the mountains to the east. The oncoming storm was unusually shaped and shifted as though alive.

The clouds reminded Danny of a band of marauding, medieval warriors astride horses bearing down upon a helpless city. He felt lightheaded and placed a hand on his forehead. Danny's eyes suddenly widened. "Murg, I recognize that storm! Those clouds!

"Sarah, Gretchen and I got drenched in a storm one day when we were hiking, and the clouds looked just like those over there." Danny couldn't believe what he was saying. "Not just like that. But those exactly!" He pointed. "See the knights with their swords and horses? Look at the frontrunner's helm. It has wings. Behind them, there are dragons."

Murg was no longer looking at the clouds, she was staring down into the valley. Three laughing kids hiked along a trail in the meadow far below. They appeared to be heading toward the city a couple of miles away. "Look there!"

"What?" Danny asked as he tore his gaze away from the clouds to follow Murg's shaking paw. A boy and two girls were hiking. One of the girls had a bright pink and turquoise backpack. She was skipping ahead. The boy's pack was red, white and blue with stars and stripes.

Gasping, Danny recognized both packs. "I don't believe it! That's Sarah, Gretchen – and me!" Danny looked back to the sky. "It's the same day we were drenched in that awful storm! But that was over a year ago! How can this be!"

Danny rubbed his eyes, then opened them again. Yes indeed, it was Sarah. No one else had curly hair the color of a fireball. He, himself, had worn – was wearing? – a Chicago Cubs baseball cap.

"Murg. We've traveled back in time! Sarah's alive!" Danny started to roll forward. "I've got to talk to her!"

Chapter Twelve

Back To The Future

"**W**ait!" Murg cried.

Danny leaned over the handlebars. The magical bicycle rolled forward – faster and faster. "I have to see Sarah!"

"NO, Danny! STOP!"

Danny kept going.

"You don't understand."

Danny began pedaling.

"Stop or I'll puncture a tire!" Murg bared her claws, then hissed.

Danny ignored her.

Murg slashed at the back tire once, twice, then a third time.

With a pop followed by a hiss, Danny heard the tire going

flat. The bicycle began to ride roughly. "Murg!" Danny accused. The calico had been serious. Danny squeezed the hand brakes. They slid for a moment in the long grass, then stopped on the side of the hill. "I can fix it with a thought!" Danny was furious, his face crimson, and his lips curled back in a feral snarl.

"And I'll pop it again!" Murg replied.

"And I'll make them puncture proof! Don't you want Sarah to live?"

Murg sighed. "Danny, we have to talk. Please."

Danny gazed longingly at the three kids, then turned to Murg. "Okay. What now?" he snapped.

The storm moved ever closer, the black clouds roiling toward them. Murg appeared to be unconcerned, licking the paw she'd used to puncture the tire. Finally, the calico tucked the paw underneath her and looked piercingly at Danny. "Let's think about this for a moment."

"Think about this! What's to think about? This is all I've been thinking about! I'm in the past! It's magic, and Sarah is alive! If she is, then so is Mom! I have to talk to Sarah! I have to see my mom and apologize! We can save them! They can live!"

"What about the storm?"

"I don't mind getting wet. It's certainly not the first time." As they spoke, Danny watched the trio climb a short hill, then head for the last ridge before town.

"Exactly my point," Murg said. Her gaze was almost hypnotic, as though she were enforcing her will on Danny. "You say you were caught in this same storm about a year ago, right?"

"Yeah. I think it was in June. Oh, Lord, what if we're stuck in the past?" Danny asked suddenly, worried now as well as excited.

"I don't think we're stuck."

"Or could this be some kind of alternate universe?" His imagination was running wild again.

"Danny, we don't know what this bicycle can truly do.

Kalyde said only your imagination would limit it. It might be capable of carrying us to the past, especially a past we know. With magic, anything is possible. Or so it would appear. This might even be a reflection or a resonance of the past, like looking in a mirror or a pool. You might not be able to interact with anybody or anything. And more importantly, we don't know what might happen if you meet your past self — or alternate self."

"I don't care!"

"Danny, I know a little about time. It's not linear, and a single change will be like dropping a rock in a pond, the effect rippling outward."

"I said I don't care!"

"We should go back to the future. Make sure we can return to our time before we start messing around. See if just our arrival back here has caused a change. That would tell us something. If we're going to mess with the past — alter time — let's gradually experiment, not jump in with both feet!"

"What if we can't make it back here again? I'll have lost my only chance to save Mom and Sarah — "

"Danny. You know I'm right, you just don't like it. And actually, I don't either. I'd like Sarah to still be alive, too."

"I know. I'm sorry for what I said. But — "

"You are frustrated, I know. Danny, let's go. Just see us outside our house in Ft. Worth."

"But you said we're not sure if we're really here or just viewing past events."

"That's true."

"To be sure, we should ask somebody," Danny pleaded. His anxiety had passed. He wasn't worried about the future. It was the past that concerned him — consumed him. With all his heart, he wanted to change it. Murg shook her head as Danny finished. "And the best person to ask would be Sarah!"

"NO. It could be a shock for the past you — if that is the

past you – to meet the present you." The calico wasn't sure about that case or the tenses she was using, but it sounded good. She didn't like the feel of this situation, and her instincts were always true.

"I'll chance it," Danny volunteered. His eyes shot to the trio. "Because if we really have traveled to the past, then I still have time to save Mom and Sarah! Don't you see? The present – the future – doesn't have to be so bad. I can make sure that the car accident never happens. I can make amends! I can change things! Be the hero for once! Save our family! Oh, Murg," Danny whispered. "I've prayed for a second chance. This is it!"

"If you do something, it might make the present even worse."

"Worse! How?" Danny looked up into the sky. "How could things get any worse? My life is a mess. We're half a family. Dad and I are barely speaking to each other. If I make a friend, we move. You tell me. How could things get any worse?" A large raindrop struck Danny, startling him.

"Do you remember the science fiction short story you read in English class last month?"

"The one about the guy who time traveled into earth's history to hunt dinosaurs? Sure, he killed one. Killing it wouldn't affect the future because the creatures were extinct."

"Wasn't time changed when he returned? Hadn't things gotten worse?"

"Yes."

"Why?" Murg asked.

"He left the platform and stepped on a butterfly," Danny recalled. He had been fascinated by the story; in some ways it reminded him of the story he'd written.

"That's right. If stepping on a butterfly might change the future, what might saving your mom and sister possibly do?" Murg asked.

Danny drooped. He was so close to solving many of his

problems, now suddenly they seemed far away again. "But that was just a story."

"Yes, someone's imagination at work. Someone like you. Danny, let's go home. We don't belong here. It's an accident waiting to happen."

"Or fate," Danny replied. "I have wished, dreamed, and prayed for something like this to happen. Shouldn't we take advantage of this miracle of magic?"

"What if this time you die along with them in that accident. Or another person?" Murg supposed. "Listen to me. Time and fate have a way of making sure certain things happen in the long run."

"I'll take that chance," Danny said firmly, eyes wild.

"And your dad? Gretchen? Maybe someone else dies?"

Danny choked as tears welled in his eyes. "This isn't fair!"

"You can still do it," Murg told him. "Instead of letting you blindly rush forward, I wanted to be sure that you were aware of the consequences. And . . . I feel rain."

Several raindrops struck about them heavily. Danny looked down the hill at himself, his sister and his friend. He squinted as the trio reached the ridge. Gretchen's blond hair streamed behind her like a cape in the strong winds, then they disappeared out of sight.

"Let's go home," Murg said.

Danny gazed upward. A raindrop splattered on his nose. Danny shook his head. "We can come back if we want," Murg told him. "The past won't change. Just think where you want to go in the past, imagine it, feel it as Kalyde mentioned, then pedal backwards."

"Think that will do it?"

"I do," Murg confirmed.

Danny looked at the ridge where Sarah, Gretchen and he had disappeared. Thunder rumbled ominously, sounding right above them. Lightning flashed brightly; a jagged trident lanced toward the top of a far knoll.

"Well?"

"All right," Danny agreed. "We'll go back to the future. I can always come back. Maybe Kalyde knows about time travel."

"Maybe."

Thunder cracked again, sounding as if a cannon had erupted. The echo danced among the hills, then lightning flickered about the two as the darkness encroached.

"First, I have to fix the tire," Danny said, sounding weary. He put his hand on the wheel. With his eyes closed, he pictured it whole, fixed and full of air. It expanded under his touch, filled with magic from his imagination.

A sharp crack of thunder sounded very near, and the sky seemed to open wide, releasing the deluge. Torrential rain didn't simply fall, it was driven. "Let's roll!" Murg commanded. "Just see yourself riding along our street in front of our house."

Danny pushed off and let the bicycle roll down the hill. They picked up speed. The rain was transformed into watery bullets. The bicycle hit a bump, and they sailed airborne.

Holding his breath, Danny closed his eyes, wishing they could fly. The moment was drawn out, but eventually, they landed softly, bouncing twice, then gained speed. Danny pedaled faster and faster. The grass ripped at his jeans.

"See home, Danny, with all your heart," Murg encouraged.

Danny wasn't sure he wanted to return to the future. Why return? Despite being on speaking terms, his dad was still aloof, and probably would remain so with Mom dead. The family was in shambles. School wasn't much fun. Danny only had his bicycle, Murg, and maybe – just maybe – new friends in Jason and Christina. But they only liked him because he'd won a race. Or did they? Danny wanted to stay. Yet, he felt he must go. Was it wrong for him to be here? Why was what you wished for wrong when you received it?

Danny imagined the street stretching before his front door. He saw the neighboring houses. He felt the Texas warmth and humidity. The sky was a high blue dome. The grass was browning. The trees were covered with olive-colored leaves. A few were beginning to change, their coloring now brown. Danny breathed deeply; the air was dusty. He felt the safeness of the neighborhood. It was Halloween and the Jack-o' lanterns were out among the other spooky decorations.

There was sound, light, and then the rainbow tunnel. This time the arching highway of brilliant colors appeared perfectly smooth. Unlike before, when they were riding backwards, the bicycle rolled along effortlessly, as if this were the path to be taken. They traveled for a time, neither speaking to the other – the sadness of their decision too heavy – then coasted into the sun burst that was the exit to the future.

Suddenly, Danny was home. His house was on his right. The sky was filled with several puffy white clouds. They started to take on color as the sun sank closer to the horizon. Danny guessed he had an hour or more before sunset.

"Ah, home sweet home," Murg breathed deeply.

"Yeah. Right," Danny said bitterly, tears streaming down his cheeks. Without another word, he rolled the bicycle into the garage.

Getting so near to what he'd wanted so much, then leaving, well, he felt as if he had been ripped wide open and his heart squeezed dry.

Chapter Thirteen

School Friends

*O*nce again, Danny rode backward through the rainbow-streaked tunnel, the wind tearing at his back. He watched the present recede as the past unfolded. Kalyde II was wobbling, but it seemed to be going faster than ever.

The rips in the rainbow stretched, now appearing to be long jagged tears. There weren't any scenes this time; all the gaps were as black as deserted coal mines. Usually the rainbow was brilliant, vibrant as if alive. Not now. It looked faded, its color flat.

The handlebars vibrated as the bicycle jumped and thrashed. Danny was scared. He wished Murg was here with him. Where was Murg? Oh, yeah, Danny remembered. The calico disagreed with him on what he was going to do and had stayed home.

With an explosive cough of air, Danny appeared in front
of his family's house . . . in Germany. It was early summer,
some four months past. Danny rolled to a stop next to their
blue station wagon. Sarah was already in the car. His mom was
just getting in.

"MOM! WAIT!"

His mother gave him a scalding look. Her face shining as if
polished stone; her usually soft green-blue gaze was hard and
seemed to cast sparks. Danny was frozen by it. Lost for words.
To speak now would be asking for a terrible tongue-lashing.
And possibly a spanking. His mom's hand could be rock hard.

"Daniel, I thought I told you to stay inside," his mother
said. Her words were abrupt as she brushed a red curl from her
face, "We'll discuss this further when I return home. Right now,"
she nodded inside the car, "Sarah is late for her piano lesson!
And I'm not in the mood to argue with you. Please listen to me
. . . and mind me!"

The engine turned over, coughed, and then started. Danny
finally found his voice. "Mom! Wait!" Danny rolled the bicycle
to the window. His mother put the car in gear. Danny tapped
on the window. "Mom?" he pleaded.

With an irritated expression, his mother rolled down the
window. Her eyes were blazing, the only true sign of her anger.
When her face grew unnaturally calm, as it was now, Danny
knew he was really in trouble. He would be grounded for years.
No more bicycling, no ice cream, no more comics . . . IT DIDN'T
MATTER. A torrent of words poured from Danny. "Look, Mom!
Look at me please! Don't I look older? Don't I?" Surely he had
grown some and had a few more hairs toward a mustache.

She frowned.

"Mom, I've . . . time traveled backwards. I'm the Danny
from this upcoming October. Dad and I live outside of Ft. Worth,
Texas, now. I helped an alien escape the police, and he gave
me this magical bicycle which time travels. Not long ago . . .

actually today . . . in a few minutes, you died . . . are . . . are gonna . . . will die in a car accident. A truck blows a tire . . ." Danny choked on his next words as he fought back the tears.

Frustrated, his mother interrupted Danny, "I've heard enough of your wild stories for one day. We'll talk when I get back." Casting her gaze heavenward and exhaling, she rolled up the window. The station wagon pulled away.

"Wait!" Danny cried. He couldn't let this happen!

Danny turned his bicycle around. He could catch them on his magical bicycle. It would be easy. It could outrun anything! Anything! He could catch them and prevent the accident.

Danny tried to pedal but couldn't. His legs were heavy as if made of lead. "WAIT! MOM!" Danny screamed. He tried to push the bicycle, coast, then hop on; but he fell off the bike, cracking his left elbow. Pain ran to his fingers and up his shoulder. Then his arm went numb.

Through squinted eyes, Danny watched the car drive out of sight. "Mom! Sarah!" Danny cried forlornly.

He put his head down. How could this happen? Danny wondered. The truck . . .

Now he heard sirens and bells. They rang in his ears, and rang and rang and rang. The police would be arriving. It was over. He'd tried to change the past and had failed.

"Well, that's it for now," Mrs. Carpenter announced. The stout, middle-aged woman with wide features and a bun hairdo put down the chalk and dusted her hands together. "We will finish discussing photosynthesis after lunch. Expect a quiz."

Groans could be heard from many of Danny's classmates. Most were already rushing for the door. A few others neatly stacked their papers and books on their desks before leaving. Danny didn't move. He wiped an invisible tear from his cheek.

"Danny, are you all right?" Mrs. Carpenter asked, sounding concerned.

Danny was sitting in the middle of an empty class room. His mind still faraway, Danny responded halfheartedly. "Uh, yes, ma'am." He stood stiffly as if his whole body had gone to sleep.

"How are you adjusting?" Her expression was friendly and concerned.

"What do you mean?" Danny didn't look directly at his teacher.

"Do you like Texas? And are you more comfortable with your new home and school now after a month?"

"Yes," Danny replied.

Mrs. Carpenter smiled and frowned at the same time. He'd answered all her questions with one word, different than last week when he'd been smiling and talkative. "I'm confused, too," Danny said and left before Mrs. Carpenter could reply.

Danny followed his fourth period classmates to lunch. What a wild daydream! So vivid! He really thought that he had time traveled. Danny shuddered at the thought – at the result. He wondered what it meant when daydreams felt more real than night dreams. Or even real life.

Was he supposed to know these things? He was only thirteen, but sometimes he thought he was too ignorant to be thirteen. Sometimes he felt like a total dork. Even Murg was smarter, and she was a cat.

Yesterday after church, he'd gone for a ride hoping that cruising would help him work things out in his head. The service hadn't helped any; it had been on forgiveness, but he'd been unable to forgive himself for arguing with his mother before the accident. He was sure her anger had contributed to the car wreck.

While riding he had suddenly realized that Kalyde could probably help. Just by visualizing the spike-haired Cor-ror-o'lan, Kalyde II could take them to him. Danny had tried and tried, but nothing had happened. The disappointment had been crushing.

Murg had told him he was being greedy. The bicycle could go incredibly fast, teleport to distant places, and even time travel. One day, Murg expected that they'd be able to fly; he believed in Danny's imagination. But wasn't asking for space travel a little much?

Danny shook his head. Despite not being able to visit Kalyde, he couldn't get his friend off his mind. "How did last night's dream go?" Danny mumbled to himself.

He was standing outside his house behind a group of bushes. It was dark and Lt. Dotson's police car had just driven away. Danny stood there, watching himself standing at the curb, damaged bicycle in hand.

Danny walked over to talk with himself. The Danny with the bicycle became Kalyde when he saw his young friend approaching.

"Greetings, Danny," Kalyde looked surprised but his tone was full of affection. "How did you get home so fast?"

"I rode the magical bicycle you gave me," Danny told him. "It travels space and time, too."

"I gave you a magical bicycle?" Kalyde asked. He looked thoroughly confused.

"Yes, because mine was damaged. I thought . . . thought," Danny became dejected. He'd hit a dead end – again. "It was a gift for helping you escape."

"What a marvelous idea! Xenozilit . . . star metal . . . can be changed into a bicycle. It changes shape with thought and amplifies imagination. Are you having fun? Do you like the bicycle?" Kalyde asked. The Cor-ror-o'lan no longer looked confused. As he walked the twisted bicycle toward the front of the house, Kalyde closely examined Danny's two wheeler.

"Do I like it? OH, YEAH!" Danny responded enthusiastically. "It's incredible! It can go really fast." His hands zoomed left, then right. "I've named it Kalyde II, after you. It can sort of jump from one place to the next."

Kalyde nodded knowingly and smiled. "You named it after me?"

"Yes, when I'm cruising on it, I think of you."

"Thank you."

"And it can travel time."

"Forwards and backwards?" Kalyde asked with surprise.

"I don't know for sure," Danny said and thought hard. "I can always get back to the present when I'm in the past. I haven't tried traveling farther forward than now. You know, not into the future." He grew quiet and thought about what he'd just said.

"That's a mouthful," Kalyde responded with a smile.

"Do you know about this time travel stuff?" Danny asked.

"Of course not, but Xenozilit is powered by imagination, and you have a strong imagination. I don't see why one couldn't use it to time travel."

"What is Zeynozit?" Danny asked.

"Xenozilit, for you, means 'magic bicycle,'" Kalyde said with a flourish as if he were introducing something new and different. "Suffice to say, it transforms imagination into reality."

"Oh." Danny didn't really understand and had a feeling he was better off that way. "Has anyone ever used it to time-travel?"

"I don't believe so. It is very dangerous to mess with time. It is not linear."

Danny's heart sank. "Murg said the same thing. Then you don't think it would be a good idea if I traveled into the past, and saved my mom and Sarah from dying?"

"No. Living in the past is dangerous. I am sorry, Danny. We know very little of time travel. We prefer to live in the now and look forward to the future."

"Then what am I doing here?" Danny asked.

Kalyde shrugged.

"Then what should I do?"

Kalyde shrugged again, then said, "If everyone told you what to do, you wouldn't grow, wouldn't learn to make your own decisions and live with them."

Danny's frustration reached a head and his anger burst. "What if I screw up something important?"

"Do not worry, Danny, my good friend. You are a good . . . being. Just do your best. I have the utmost confidence in you."

"You do?" Danny asked. "You have confidence in me?!"

Danny rubbed his eyes as he walked through the main lobby, past the front office and trophy case towards the lunchroom. Acting as a guide, a green stripe was painted along the wall of the corridor. Since his trip to Germany and into his past, Danny had been in a fog. He was daydreaming so much it was as if he had one foot in another world.

Maybe the dream was trying to tell him something. He should time travel to find Kalyde? Maybe that was it.

Time travel? What if Kalyde didn't know? Who would? What if he went back to visit great men and asked their advice? But who would he visit? He should probably spend some time in the library.

The noise in the hall grew louder. Kids were entering the main corridor from other halls. Danny barely noticed. He didn't hear a girl say, "See, I told you he was still alive."

Someone else said, "He doesn't look alive to me. A zombie, maybe, heh, heh." Several voices pealed with laughter.

"Well, he might not live for long after I'm done with him."

Lost in thought, Danny was staring at the floor and didn't see Christina before he heard her. "Danny Chase, my God, you do live! I figured for sure that you were run over by a car, got attacked by wild dogs, were kidnapped or – or were grounded . . . or something!" Christina was exasperated, her face flushed. Hurt was bright in her eyes, along with the desire to pass those feelings onto someone else.

"No," Danny said simply. He tried to concentrate on what was going on right now but had trouble doing so.

"Do you remember me? My name's Christina, my friends," she waved to several kids nearby, "help me stick my foot in my mouth."

"And you're an artist and cheerleader," Danny told her, "and the first person at school to be kind to me." He saw some of her anger slip away, replaced by concern. Christina brushed several golden-blond hairs away from her lovely face. Danny wished he could say something clever. He doubted the truth would work, but it was worth a try.

"I invited you to my party, do you remember?" Christina asked. She sounded catty and more than a bit put off.

"I . . . I couldn't make it," he whispered hoarsely.

Christina turned away and walked off.

"Smooth move, Danny my boy," came the comment.

Looking down, Danny continued toward his reading table. This week was starting off as poorly as last week had gone well. Why did such a wonderful present bring such a big burden to him? Too bad Christina wouldn't believe the truth. And what was the truth? He couldn't escape his past?

Christina was suddenly sitting at the empty table. "Are you following me?" she demanded.

Confused, Danny spread his hands. Given a second chance, he blurted, "I was really looking forward to your party. Really I was. I was so keyed up I had trouble sitting around the house, so I went out riding and lost track of things. I . . . I was daydreaming. See, usually nothing bothers me when I ride, except for Spike. I think it's the wind or the speed or something that clears my mind. Anyway," he sighed heavily. "I nearly had an . . . accident and . . . I sort of relived the past."

Christina seemed to instantly understand. They had talked about this before. "You mean the day of the accident? Sort of like a flashback?"

Danny nodded; that was close to the truth. After discovering he could travel into the past, he'd wanted to go back to the day of the accident. "I . . . dreamed . . . thought – I could time travel back on my bicycle. Sounds dumb, I know – "

"Go on. I know you wish you could go back and change things. Everyone does every now and then."

Danny sighed. "Everything was so real. I could touch things. See, hear and smell. But . . . but I couldn't change . . . things. You know? I was afraid I might make a mistake. Change things for the worse." Danny looked down. "I was so depressed that I rode around until it was dark. I didn't even notice the sun setting." He shrugged. "I'm sorry. My sister used to say I needed a podiatrist."

"Huh?" Christina was caught off guard by the word and the change in subject.

"A podiatrist, you know, a foot doctor. Someone to help me with my hoof-in-mouth disease," Danny managed weakly.

Christina laughed. "Is that an apology?"

"Someone I know used it once. It worked for them," he said shrugging. "Aw, why would it work for me? I swear, cheerleaders get away with murder."

Christina laughed again.

"Do they?" She looked innocent, as if to say, "who me?"

Danny felt enchanted, and for a moment, the past slipped away.

"Was it that bad? So bad I couldn't help?" Christina asked sympathetically, her eyes large and searching. "I've had people tell me I'm unforgettable."

Danny stared at her mutely.

"Okay, I had one person tell me I was unforgettable. I guess we can stay friends, but you only get one more chance. You hear me? One more chance! If you don't count on me being a friend, then we might as well not be friends. Deal?"

"Deal," Danny agreed. "And it's more than I deserve. Thank

you." He felt better. Now if he could only push the dreams to a corner of his mind where they could run crazy on their own without interrupting his life, things would be fine. Or would they fester? Why couldn't he just forget the past? Let it go?

"Hey, butthead!" came Spike's voice as he approached them. "Why don't you leave Ms. Pom Pom alone?"

Mr. Cripe looked in their direction.

"What happened to you the other day?" Spike asked. "You just disappeared."

"You mean how did I avoid your clothesline stretched across the road?" Danny asked.

Christina gasped.

"I ducked and took off so fast you'd never catch me."

Spike appeared to be thinking about that.

Christina was looking at him speculatively. "Spike, take a long walk on a short pier," Christina told him.

"Listen – "

"Don't go away mad, just go away," she continued.

Spike began to get worked up.

"Actually, go jump in a lake. Scram. Beat it. Take off. Go soak your head," she continued the onslaught.

Someone behind Spike added something rude. "Shove off. Shoo!"

Christina waved at him as if Spike were a pesky fly.

"I'm warning you, you blond cadet," Spike moved forward menacingly.

Instinctively, Danny stood. "Do you want some of this?" he asked, raising his fist. Christina gasped and touched Danny's arm.

He didn't want to fight, but he didn't think it was right for Spike to threaten Christina. There had to be another way to solve this, Danny thought. Nothing came to mind. He wished that he had claws to bare like Murg.

"Spike! Split! Now!" Jason barked as he moved swiftly toward the bully. A looming dark shadow, Jason seemed to have appeared from thin air. His eyes were glowering, and his face was twisted with malice.

"Vamoose!" Christina continued.

Danny looked at her and pleaded with his eyes.

"Okay, I'll stop. Spike brings out the worst in me," Christina said. "As Cynthia would say, he makes me want to barf!"

"You still standin' up for this puke, boy?" Spike asked Jason.

"Yeah! You got a problem with that?" Jason responded, his voice barely a whisper. "At least I keep my word."

Spike growled something unintelligible, then moved toward Jason.

"Jason! Spike! Stop that this instant!"

"Mr. Cripe!" They cried in unison.

The tall broad-shouldered and balding teacher approached. Somewhere the rumor had started that Mr. Cripe had taught karate.

"What's going on here?" he demanded.

Both boys started to explain at the same time.

The teacher raised his hands. "One at a time! Please!"

"I think we should move," Christina said. "We can thank Jason later."

Danny agreed.

As they left, he nodded to Jason, who gave a thumbs up and a smile.

Chapter Fourteen

Old Friends

"I'm sorry for getting you in trouble," Danny apologized to Jason. The two were on bicycles stopped at a traffic light not far from their houses. They had discovered they were nearly neighbors.

"That's okay. Spike-boy gets me in deep do-da a lot. He tries to make as many people miserable as possible. He's a mutation needing a lobotomy. Forget him."

"I thought you two were friends?"

"We weren't really friends. We just did things together. I met him late last summer, after we moved, playing some hoop and a little football. And the longer I know him, the more I dislike him. I don't like people with small minds, and I don't see any reason to hang around somebody I can't trust."

The light changed, and they continued riding. "Danny, forget about getting me in trouble, okay? Are you brain dead or what? Knock! Knock! Jeez, how could you miss Christina's party? She's a babe and a half, plus she's nice and fun to be with."

"Uh," Danny mumbled, "I thought she was your friend."

"She is. Oh, I understand. Listen, Danny. I'm goin' out with Cynthia. Chris and I are friends. We could never be boyfriend and girlfriend, you know, date. People would talk. So anyway, how did you manage to miss her party?"

"Uh, I . . . " Danny hesitated, then, " . . . the doctors call it some kind of depression. I've talked to counselors about it."

"Maniac? I hope not! Jeez. I had a cousin who was maniac depressed. He had really wild mood swings. I mean – from one extreme to the other. One minute he's on top of the world, the next he's so low he could kill himself. Scary."

"I'm not that bad," Danny said. "And I think you mean manic, not maniac."

"Yeah, right. Well, it's good you're not either of those. Did you and Christina talk?"

"Yes, we talked about what's been bothering me."

"Good! Hey, it's time for me to go. You want to ride tomorrow? We could cruise to Joe Lake."

"Sure."

"'Nuff said!" Jason stuck his left arm straight out to signal. "I gotta cruise. 'Bye." There was no oncoming traffic, so Jason swung left and disappeared down Ranchero Road.

In minutes Danny neared home. His dad's car was in the driveway and a red van was parked in the street before their house. The car's trunk was open. Danny's dad didn't usually arrive home until seven. Coasting by the Buick and onto the sidewalk, Danny stopped at the front steps. Murg was waiting for him, asleep in the sun.

The front door opened, and bags in hand, his father shouldered his way through. "Hello, Son. I'm glad you're home. I'm in a hurry. Here," he handed Danny a small bag, then turned around and called back into the house. "Big Jim! Danny's home!"

"Where ya goin'?" Danny asked.

"Los Angeles," his father replied and motioned Danny to carry his bag to the car. "I don't know when I'll be back, so Big Jim will be around."

Danny slung the leather travel bag over his shoulder. "Who's Big Jim?"

"Someone to share the house with while I'm gone."

"I'm old enough that I don't need a baby-sitter."

"Just someone to help in case you have problems. Not that you ever get yourself in any trouble, right, Son?" Danny was silent. "I hope things continue to go well at school."

"Howdy," came a gruff, booming voice. "This is Danny?"

Danny put the bags in the trunk, then turned to face Big Jim. He was tall and massive with a barrel chest, wide arms and thick legs that might have been truncated pillars. His face was broad and his jaw jutted out, shaped like a lantern.

"Pleasure meetin' ya, Son, my names James Roseberry. I'll be staying with you for a while. Put her there, pard." Big Jim stuck out his meaty hand. His big, toothy smile grew even larger when Danny shook his hand.

"Danny, Big Jim is a student minister at the chapel on base. He's a good guy. You two can have fun, but obey him, okay?"

"Yes, sir."

"Good. Big Jim has a key to the house. He has to leave this evening for a while, so you're on your own for dinner."

"Okay."

"You can fix your own dinner?" Big Jim asked.

Danny nodded. He didn't tell him it was either that or go hungry sometimes.

"Since we can't have dinner together tonight, I'll take you out for a ratburger tomorrow! Okay?"

Danny couldn't imagine a ratburger, but said, "Sure."

"I'll see you around eight tonight. Don't booby-trap the front door, heh?" Big Jim chuckled as he walked toward his red van.

"He's going to be a minister?" Danny asked. "He looks more like a football player."

"Something wrong, Son?"

"No. Fine, I guess."

"Good. Son, I notice you've added a lot of pictures of Mom and Sarah to your hero wall."

"Just thinking about them a lot recently. Dad, I miss Mom and Sarah."

His father paused as he looked skyward, then he continued walking to the car. "So do I Danny. That's why I work so much, and I guess why you ride so much. We try to escape."

Danny was suddenly uncomfortable.

"Danny, Son," his father kneeled, stared at him for a moment, then gripped his arms. "I wish I could bring them back. I wish I could, but I can't. And neither can you. We just have to grow up strong. Live with it. It's tough, and a terrible way to have to grow up, but it's part of life. It's part of being an adult. Being mature. You either adjust or you breakdown. Do you understand?"

Danny nodded but thought: I CAN CHANGE THINGS!

"Good. You know, I think I can see you maturing. I'm glad you're fitting in at school and making friends. Having friends is very important."

Danny nodded. Life wasn't any fun without friends. Or family.

"Well, be good. No more helping aliens or talking to your cat. Go to school. Do your homework. Keep riding and do as Big Jim tells you."

"Yes, sir."

"I'll call every day. 'Bye, Son." He briefly hugged Danny, then climbed into his car. Danny watched him drive off. He thought about what his father had said about needing friends. Danny needed to talk with some of them, but they were so far away.

"So what?" Murg asked. The calico had hopped onto the bicycle. Danny smiled. He would go visit them – today! Right now! He hopped onto the bike, then the duo took off down the road.

With images of San Diego in mind, its beaches, coastline, and his old house, Danny soared along the rainbow highway. It seemed brighter than usual today, but that might have been in comparison to his time travels when it appeared ragged and faded like an old rug. The stars above twinkled as if trying to pass on some mysterious message. There was a bright flash, and then the stretch of colors was gone.

The bicycle rolled to a stop before a one-story, brown house. Built in military style, it was geometrical and graceless, with no special trimming or personal touches. "4405 Beach Street, San Diego, California," Danny said.

"Do you think Bernie will remember you?"

"Of course," Danny laughed. "Bernie and I have been pen pals for years. We vowed to stay in touch forever. Cross our hearts and hope to die," Danny repeated.

"Not one of my favorite oaths," Murg replied dryly. "When did you last hear from him?"

"Uh, not sure," Danny rode out of the military housing area toward another neighborhood. The school they had attended wasn't far away. Neither of Bernie's parents had worked for the military. "Wow! What happened? This place sure has changed. Over there used to be a park. Where are the fountains?"

"The place has gone condo, a fate almost as bad as pollution," Murg murmured. "Real estate developers abhor a forest or a park."

"Well, my old school still stands," Danny said, pointing to the set of interconnected buildings to their left. It was made of pale orange brick with white trim and stout columns out front in the classic mold of institutions of learning – that's what his father had told him, anyway.

"Over there," Danny said, nodding to the playground behind one building but still visible, "is where we used to play all the time. This was one amazing playground. There were jungle gyms, sandboxes, baseball fields, swings, slides and all sorts of stuff. We used to whirl around on the spinner until we were almost sick. We probably would have thrown up if we hadn't been laughing so hard." Danny's smile was stretched wide.

"A wonderful thought," Murg replied wryly.

"He lives past the school a couple of blocks." They rode by a sign about a PTA meeting. "I loved San Diego. There's nothing like being near the ocean. I remember trying to sail. Bernie and I almost drowned."

"Tell me about it."

"Well, we had borrowed his dad's boat . . ."

"With or without permission?" Danny just gave Murg a look. "You expropriated it," Murg said dryly.

Danny huffed, then continued, "We'd been out for about an hour when a storm and strong winds came out of nowhere."

"Probably the west or southwest."

"Hey, this is my story. Anyway, the wind caught us and took us farther out to sea and –" Danny stopped short. He squinted at the two kids walking toward them on the left side of the street. The older boy carried a basketball. Danny swore that the youngest of the two was Bernie, but he was too young. "Bernie!"

Danny saw the taller boy respond. His hair was shaved in rows on each side, and he wore a long ponytail. His earring and nose-ring glinted in the sunlight.

"How long has it been since you've received a letter from Bernie?" Murg asked.

The older boy squinted behind his sunglasses, then asked, "Who are you?"

"You don't remember me? Danny. Danny Chase?" Danny couldn't believe it. Didn't want to believe it. "Man, Bernie, you've really grown. What's with the hair and the rings?"

"Who did you say you were?" Bernie asked.

The smaller boy was looking expectantly at the older boy, obviously his brother.

"Danny. Danny Chase," Danny said again.

Bernie's brow was furrowed as he thought, but he didn't respond.

"Chase. Your old friend and pen pal." Danny was stunned by the vacant look in Bernie's eyes. "We almost drowned sailing together! We played video all the time! You mean you don't remember me?"

"Oh, yeah!" Bernie said suddenly; he didn't sound convincing. "Have you moved back?"

"No, I'm just visiting," Danny replied.

With that, Bernie seemed to lose interest.

"Why did you quit writing?"

"I didn't. You did."

"I didn't. You did. I wrote you from Germany."

"Oh, yeah. Sorry about Sarah, man. So where are you living?"

"In Fort Worth."

"Where's that?"

"Texas!" Danny was so frustrated he was ready to explode. They had been such good friends. What had happened?! And why had he chosen to visit Bernie first? He should have gone to see Gretchen, but he was afraid to tell her about Christina. Girls could be odd about other girls sometimes.

"Well, I gotta go. We're gonna be late for our ball game. See you around, Danny," Bernie said, then walked off.

Danny was flabbergasted and speechless. For a long time, he just sat there, feeling empty. Murg said several things but Danny never heard them. Finally, Danny said, "Let's go."

"To Germany? To see Gretchen?"

"No, uh, it's too late with the time difference. Let's try Kelly Hoolihan in Indianapolis."

Danny began pedaling. He pictured the faded red brick of the old military housing on Ft. Benjamin Harrison. Nearby there was a football field, lots of other rectangular houses and a complex of large, squat buildings that appeared to have been designed with ugly in mind. The entire fort was sprawling and rolling, with some areas fenced off. Kelly's parents lived about a mile away.

They zipped across the rainbow highway and appeared next to the football field. They were still going fast, quickly cruising by the long stretch of grass, then the bicycle smoothly swallowed two speed bumps. Danny finally noticed their speed and slowed. He didn't want to draw any attention. And the MP's – the Military Police – were very strict about speeding, even with bicyclers.

It didn't take long to reach Red Stone, the neighborhood where Kelly's parents lived. It had only been a little over three years since he'd been here. Come to think of it, maybe it was closer to four. Time and years did funny things sometimes.

"I hope this goes better," Murg said.

"Me, too," Danny said as they pulled up in front of the two story house. Healthy bushes stood out starkly against the newly painted baby blue walls. The trees were tall and the leaves were changing colors. The neighborhood had an old, settled feeling to it, and the houses needed some slight repairs. Danny heard the moan of a lawnmower. "It was yellow."

"The mailbox says The Parkers."

"Huh? This might not be the right place."

"6522 Simon Court?"

"That's right. Everything looks right. Did we time travel? Great, now I don't know when now is."

"Ouch. I don't think it's that bad, Danny," Murg replied.

"Don't start confusing where you are with where you've been."

"Uh, right." This still looked like the right place. He checked the mailbox next door. Edwin T. Wall and Family. 6526 Simon. That was right. He remembered the Walls. Bunches of kids. The Barnetts were on the other side. As Danny watched, a golden retriever burst out the Parker's front door, pulling along a stumbling young boy. Danny didn't recognize him, either. "Kelly moved without telling me. I... I just received a letter a couple of months ago. I always wrote him when I was moving."

"Maybe he was waiting until he got settled," Murg said.

Danny couldn't believe that Kelly would do this to him. He'd been a good writer, at least every three months. Now that he thought about it, he hadn't heard from him since last spring – long before they'd left Germany in August. Danny didn't think he'd written him about Sarah, either. Maybe he was at fault, too. Maybe Kelly's letter was being forwarded from Germany.

"Let's try someone else. Happy, in Honolulu," Murg purred.

"Okay," Danny said and started down the street. "I should've gone there first, anyway."

"I think you should have gone to see Gretchen first. Should go there now."

Danny pictured the suburbs of Honolulu. Starkly barren volcanoes, lush green mountains, thunderous waterfalls and white beaches with palm trees seemed to surround the city, stretching in every direction over the island. The ocean was turquoise and so clear that it looked pure and delicious.

Happy lived up a steep hill, farther away from the beach. The trees were lushly tropical and the flowers verdant and abundant. Danny recalled the perfumed aroma of the garden-like woods.

The world around Danny split, then disappeared before becoming the rainbow bridge. He thought of Dano; his friend was short, dark-haired, smoothly tanned and had a smile as big and bright as the rainbow. Sarah had called him Happy, then so had Danny.

For a while, they just rode along the rainbow. "Shouldn't we be there?" Murg asked.

Danny nodded.

"Think about our old house on that hilly road."

"Okay," Danny nodded.

Clouds raced by, and the stars became comets, then the white ball of light appeared ahead on the rainbow highway. It flashed as Danny and Murg rode into it, then they were rolling up hill. The air was thick and warm, steam rising from the streets and into the cloud-shrouded mountains. Ahead, Danny spotted lots of cars parked along the street.

As he drew closer to Dano's, Murg commented on all the formally attired people. "Yeah, lots of black and white," Danny agreed. And there were so many sad faces among the people walking slowly, it was as if they ached with each step. "Did someone die?"

It was soft at first, then grew louder. Danny heard someone crying. He rode a little closer, then stopped. "Leila?"

Sitting on a large rock, a girl with long dark hair and dressed in a deep, wine colored outfit held her face in her hands as she cried.

"Leila?" Danny asked again as he climbed off his bicycle, leaving it standing on the incline.

Leila slowly raised her head. Her face was flushed and tear-stained. "Danny Chase?" She sniffed. "What're you doing here? Oh, you must have heard?" She briefly looked at his bicycle, then for a car.

"Heard?" Danny asked. A feeling of dread swept over him and his stomach turned, twisting into knots. "Heard what?" he asked. Murg had taken a deep breath.

"You don't know? Oh, no!" She stood and ran into his arms. Danny barely hugged her back.

"First Sarah, now Dano. Dano's dead!" Leila buried her face in his shoulder, her sobs rocking her and shaking Danny.

Danny was stunned and speechless. For a time, they simply held each other and cried. Finally, Danny managed a hoarse, "What happened?" He had to ask three times, his voice getting a little stronger with each try.

Leila's voice shook as she said quietly, "He drowned saving a friend. After the storms, the waves were huge, so he and Tania went surfing. We think that when Tania fell, she struck her head on her board. Dano helped her back onto her board, but for someone reason, he . . . didn't make it. And he'd always thought he'd be a surfing immortal."

So many questions raced through Danny's mind, but he couldn't grab onto them well enough to ask them. Somebody began calling Leila's name.

"It's my mother," she said, then sniffed back more tears. "I have to go. I'm so sorry about Sarah and your mother." She pulled away from Danny and started running uphill.

"When and where?" Danny yelled after her.

"Two days ago," she said. "At Breaker's Beach."

Danny watched her disappear into the woods behind Dano's house and along a trail he knew so well. He didn't feel like going in to see everyone. He could feel their sadness from here. Besides, they would ask questions he couldn't answer.

Happy was dead. He couldn't believe it. Oh, Dano! What was the world coming to?

"Murg. We're going to do something!" Danny remembered the beach, a hot spot for surfing, something he'd never done very well.

"Hey, now! Let's not be hasty!" Murg said. "Let's think about this a little."

Without a word, Danny jumped on his bicycle. He needed to talk with someone, and if his old friends weren't available, then he'd speak with a new one.

Chapter Fifteen

Way Back

"**H**ey, Danny, you ready to go?" Jason asked as he donned his bird-beaked helmet.

Danny just continued to stare across the surface of Joe Lake. The water was calm, not nearly as turbulent as his thoughts. To change or not to change? That was the question.

"That's bad Shakespeare," Murg projected her thoughts. "You really should try reading it before quoting it." The calico was in her customary spot, curled on the padded carrier atop an old navy-colored sweatshirt.

Jason looked at the sky. "Danny? It'll be getting dark soon. Hey, you okay?"

"Yeah, I think so. Thanks for going cruising on such short notice." He'd cruised by Christina's house, but nobody had been home. "I really needed it."

"Hey, what are friends for?" Jason leaned on his bike, then said, "You sure you're okay? You look sort of . . . I dunno . . . lost."

Danny told him about Bernie and Kelly, but he didn't mention anything about his travels or Happy's death. "Sorry to hear it. I lost a good friend to drugs. I mean, he's still alive, but he just changed. I guess some things aren't meant to last. Sometimes people just grow apart. You have something in common for a while, then you change, grow or move on." Jason shrugged.

"That may be what happened between you, Kelly and Bernie," Jason continued. "I can't imagine hanging out with the same guys I used to run with when I was in elementary school. And you move all the time. That must be tough. Hello today, *hasta la vista* tomorrow. I mean, you could move tomorrow, right?"

"Probably not for at least five more months," Danny replied. "Most likely, eleven months."

"Whoa – long time there! Hey, I have to confess, I'm a terrible writer, even with the Internet and e-mail now. Some people just don't communicate well. You know, out of sight, out of mind. My mom complains about her friends a lot, too. I get the feeling we won't be like that, Danny. We could just be friends forever. I have that feeling," Jason said with a smile. "It's you and me, American Flyers – Ebony and Ivory, some day Tour de Francers. Hey, maybe even a gold medal. I mean, we really scorched it on the way here. I've never ridden that fast. You can haul, man! How you do it on that old thing I'll never understand! It must weigh a ton!" he laughed. Jason rode a bright red Bianchi Rodesport Premio.

"Well, this old thing is tuned to vintage perfection and precision," Danny said, keeping a straight face.

Murg coughed.

"Wish I had a Beyond Fabrication Beryllium, man. Then I

could fly. Literally. It's made of aluminum bonded with beryllium, has Campagnola parts and Michelin tires. At seventeen pounds, it's so light it almost floats!"

"You know a lot about bicycles."

"You bet. I just don't have four grand to spend."

"Four thousand!"

"Yup. But if I had one, yeah howdy! I'd be flyin'! Doesn't matter. We can still haul. You know, we would've been friends a month ago if you hadn't been so standoffish."

"Huh? What do you mean?"

"You sort of stood off like you were better than everybody else. Or had better things to do."

"Really? That's what you thought?" Danny asked.

Jason nodded.

"I was just down about my mom and Sarah, and moving and all."

"I know that now. Hey, bud, let's go."

They climbed on their bicycles and headed home.

"Danny, what are you going to do about Christina?"

"I'm going to see if she wants to go riding. We have an old tandem in the garage."

"A Bielenki Airhog!"

"I don't remember."

"Doesn't matter. Doubleteaming! Too cool! Take Chris to a movie. She loves thrillers. Wanna sprint to that stop sign?" Jason asked with a smile Danny didn't return.

"Maybe the one after that," Danny replied, then told him about Happy. After a silence, Danny said, "I got a hypothetical question for you, Jason."

"Is that one of those questions that doesn't need answering?"

"No. That's rhetorical. Listen, if you'd died, and I could travel back in time and change things so you'd live, would you want me to?"

"You've been listening to Mr. Gordon too much," Jason suddenly laughed. "He's always throwing out questions like that. Trish asked if he were teaching history or philanthropy."

"I think you mean philosophy. Philanthropy is goodwill and charity."

"He teaches that too."

"Jason, just answer my question."

"Okay, I'll bite, but I have some questions first. How old am I?"

"What?"

"If I'm young, yes. Bring me back so I can ride and play hoop! But if I'm old, you know ancient, like forty or fifty, just let me stay dead. Life's almost over anyway. I'll probably be bald, half-blind, wear dentures and have arthritis and hemorrhoids. Sheesh! Just let me go, okay? And I don't want to be maimed. If I can't ride or play hoop, just let me stay dead. Man, what a weird question." Before Danny could respond, Jason asked, "How did I die?"

"How should I know?"

"It's your question. Did I keel over from a heart attack? Get run over by a car? Or was I heroic, you know, saving a damsel babe from a burning building or something."

"I don't know. How do you want to go?"

"Man, another weird question. I'm a kid, not Socrates. How about you?"

"That's somewhat Socratic," Murg projected to Danny. "Answer a question with a question."

Danny didn't say he'd wished he'd died in the car accident with Sarah and his mother. "Quickly. Painlessly. I don't know." Now after talking with Jason, he was more confused than ever.

"Me, I want to go while riding, maybe my heart exploding while racing – and winning – against a Lamborghini."

Murg mentally chuckled. "How about a Ferrari?"

"Really?" Danny asked.

"Nah. Just jerking your chain. RACE YA!" Jason yelled and bolted.

Danny raced after him.

"I'm glad you've thought this over," Murg said, "at least a little bit and planned ahead."

It was dark, and they were riding along the frontage road at a blurring sprint. Dressed in all white, Danny appeared to be a flying ghost chasing their headlight beam.

But not all the winds in the world could blow away Danny's cares.

"Well, you made some sense. I need to talk to someone wise about time traveling and changing the past. If I don't let too much time pass, I won't have to worry about changing the future when I save Happy. Change much anyway. See? He's only been . . . dead three days. You know, it seems much more. Wish I'd been there."

"Are you going to go see Albert Einstein?" asked Murg.

"Not at first. I'm not sure I understand how E= MC^2 is going to help me. I don't care how the bicycle works, besides that it's powered by imagination. Imagination is magic!"

"But time travel . . . Einstein had all sorts of theories on that kind of stuff. A theory of relativity for objects in motion and a special one for light," said Murg smugly, as if he had the answers to everything.

"How do you know that?"

"He had a cat!"

Danny rolled his eyes. "That stuff is quantum physics, I think. I need someone wise, you know, philosophical, not just smart. Like Socrates and Benjamin Franklin. Everyone's always quoting Socrates – "

"Actually," Murg interrupted, "they refer more to his Socratic method, the process of answering questions with questions so the original querist will divine the answer on his own."

"I always thought answering a question with a question was rude," Danny muttered.

"Not if you're Socrates, and not if you're trying to teach something. To make people think for themselves."

Danny sighed. "Yeah, well, I'll try him first, traveling farthest back in time to start, then travel forward through time, stopping to visit Franklin around 1742, HG Wells in 1894, and then Einstein in the early 1950's."

"Smart thinking. That way you only have to time-travel backwards once. Have I told you that I tell the other cats that you have potential? Have you thought about visiting King Solomon? He was wise."

"I think most of the information about him comes from the Bible, and it isn't enough for me to get a good mental image."

"I'm familiar with him. He was a great lover of cats," Murg told him.

"Do you know what he looks like?" Danny asked. "That would help?"

"No, in a way, all humans look alike to us cats."

"Then how can you tell us apart?"

"You feel and smell differently."

"I don't think I want to try time traveling backwards based on a smell and a feel," Danny replied.

"Suit yourself," Murg sniffed.

"I'm not sure if we'll even be able to find Socrates. I did some research, but there aren't any photographs or paintings of him. And all the drawings are based more on legend, so they're probably not very accurate."

"That could be a problem."

"So I studied him, trying to get an idea of what kind of person he was. I hope that will work."

"That's not a whole lot different than a feel."

Danny ignored the comment. "Ben Franklin should be

easier. He was a philosopher, a writer – like me, a frustrated one – a statesman and an inventor. He invented special four-sided streetlight lamps, whale oil candles, smokeless stoves, and our vocabulary for electricity, among other things. His experiments led to the Maxwell radio."

"Why HG Wells?"

"He wrote *The Time Machine*, and he was a visionary. Many say he predicted tanks and the atomic bomb, along with helicopters and the like."

"And you think he might have some inside ideas on time travel?" the calico asked.

Danny nodded.

"Good enough. Then you've researched all these gentleman?"

"This afternoon. I memorized pictures and photographs. I even dressed sort of generic to cover all the times." He was dressed in a long, white cotton shirt and baggy white shorts. "I'm hoping this will help us blend in."

"In Athens on a bicycle in 401 BC. Carts were big back then. I take back what I said a minute ago."

"I could wear spandex and a fancy helmet like the riders in the race."

"Please! Did you leave a note for Big Jim?" Murg asked.

Danny nodded.

"Then let's do it!"

Danny slowed to a stop. "Here we go! The quest for the answer to change time or not change time begins!" He began backpedaling, the descriptions of Socrates running through his mind.

Danny tried to imagine a mental picture of the man. He'd been described as a short, stubby and even ugly with protruding eyes that were too far apart. The writer Aristophanes had made fun of the way the Hellenic philosopher had rolled his eyes.

Socrates had believed in moral courage and had been the

first to espouse that the soul guided man. Goodness in a man was the quality of his soul. It was the source of his natural excellence, and along with his ability to think in an orderly manner, set him apart from the animals.

Socrates lived a simple life – a life of poverty – and rarely bathed. He would be dressed in the attire of the time – a chiton, sort of a woolen shift. Socrates refused to wear sandals, preferring to be barefoot. He walked in a dignified fashion and was always alert to his surroundings, unless he was receiving a sign, which some likened to premonitions.

Still on his bicycle with Murg on the back, Danny pictured being parked in front of the Parthenon in Athens. He was talking with the Greek philosopher around 401 BC, two years before Socrates' trial and death. The white marble Parthenon, a magnificently pillared temple to Athena, was set upon the Acropolis, and overlooked Athens and the city-state of Attica.

There was a loud tearing like fabric being savagely ripped apart, then darkness engulfed them. It was heavy and oppressive, but only for a moment, then they burst from the inky blackness, racing backwards and careening through the faded rainbow tunnel. As before, it was tattered with ugly, tainted hues. The violet tunnel was darker, now indigo and menacing-looking with jagged black holes. This time there weren't any images within the dark tears. Danny had the odd feeling that they were being watched. But by who or what? Was he just being paranoid?

The bicycle was vibrating wildly, and the wind was stronger than usual, tearing at their backs. They hit bump after bump. Danny clung tightly to the handlebars so he wouldn't be thrown. His teeth chattered violently, clacking loudly together. Riding Kalyde II was like riding a jackhammer.

What would happen if he fell off the bicycle? Danny gripped the handlebars even tighter and struggled to control his imagination. Keep focusing on Socrates, he repeated to himself.

"Sort of rough!" Murg had a firm grip on the railing around

the padded carrier. " I think it's worse than before because we're traveling farther back in time."

They hit a deep chuckhole and skipped airborne, landing harder than they'd ever landed before.

"I'm not so sure this was a great idea," Murg said.

They hit another bump, then another. It seemed as if the rainbow highway was bucking and weaving, trying to throw them.

"Maybe we're trying to go back too far!" Danny yelled over the wind.

"As long as we don't travel back to Jurassic times, everything will be fine," Murg said.

Danny didn't want to think about dinosaurs. He was refocusing on the Greeks and Socrates when they dropped into a cavernous pit. Danny left his stomach behind. His heart jammed into his throat as the blackness engulfed them. Had they been swallowed by something?

They were racing backwards and upward, then suddenly they were flying out of the pit. They landed bone-jarringly hard before hitting another bump. Danny smacked his head against the handlebars and saw stars. What was he supposed to be thinking about? Dinosaurs? They picked up more speed, the ride becoming even rougher.

"You all right?!" Murg asked.

"My head's spinning!" Colors swirling with darkness danced and cavorted all about him. The wind seemed to manifest shapes that tried to tear him from the magic bicycle. Some appeared to be massive beasts; others were quick and reptilian like dinosaurs.

"Keep concentrating on Socrates!" Murg told him.

They hit a bump awkwardly. Kalyde II spun around. As they landed, they hit another pothole, then began skidding across the rainbow highway.

"We're heading for another pit!" Murg cried. "This one's

huge! No, it's not a pit; it's a break in the rainbow!"

Danny wished they'd leave the faded rainbow highway right now, appearing wherever they were in history. Even dinosaurs would be better than this.

The bridge shattered, colored shards flying in every direction. They abruptly appeared in a prehistoric land, skimming atop and across a swamp. The air was thick and fetid, and they seemed to cut a swath through it. The water appeared polluted, the surface coated with sickly yellow and green growths floating in dark oily slicks. A dozen or so mammoth sauropods with long necks and equally elongated tails stared dumbly as they passed by.

"Those are Brontosaurus!" Murg cried.

"Actually, I think they're Diplodocus," Danny replied, barely containing his excitement. "But don't worry about them, they're herbivores."

"Hey! We're sinking!" Murg cried.

The front and rear tires were slipping into the goo.

"My head hurts! I can't seem to focus!" Danny cried.

"Steer for the shore!"

Kalyde II sank another inch.

A loud splash sounded behind them.

Murg whirled around. "Think lighter! Lighter! Oh, how I hate getting wet! This place stinks! I might never get clean if we fall in."

The swamp water was spouting behind them like a geyser, the rear tire spinning as if they were stuck.

Murg was almost up under Danny's seat to avoid the rising tide.

Danny pedaled furiously and kept thinking they were lighter than air. Fear – thinking that if they got stuck here, anything might happen, they might get stuck for good – pushed Danny into overdrive. Kalyde II surged forward, throwing the pair back as it rocketed across the water. The bike shot between one of the ten-ton beast's legs, then ramped onto solid ground.

They raced into the thick jungle. Danny rode frantically. Large fronds and branches ripping at them. He couldn't believe they'd traveled so far into the past. It was a dream! It was a nightmare! If he could only clear his head, they could get out of here!

"It's okay!" Murg yelled. "You can slow down! Rest!"

They rode out of the jungle and onto a beaten path, finally coming to rest overlooking a patchy fog-enshrouded valley. Below, a massive herd of dinosaurs he didn't recognize thundered across the plains, heading for a river. Something – a group of smaller creatures running on their hind legs – was chasing them, trying to separate some of the younger beasts from the rest of the herd. Wheeling overhead, waiting and watching, were huge reptilian bat-like creatures. Pteranodons? Pterodactyus?

Danny's head was still pounding, though not as bad as before. He examined it, discovering a knot but no bleeding.

"You've got quite a bruise. Are you all right?" Murg asked.

Danny blinked. There were about half the number of dinosaurs running across the valley floor as there had been a minute ago. "A little better. My double vision is leaving. I think the hunters are Deinonychus. The others are Lamberosaurus, or something like that. I did a book report on dinosaurs a couple of years back."

"It's more than I want to know," Murg said.

The ground suddenly shook. The trees swayed, huge leaves thrashing about.

"Let's get out of here!" Murg exclaimed. "Now! That sounds big!"

With earthquake intensity, the ground shook again.

"A T-Rex! Wow! I'd love to see one!" Danny was excited.

"Not this close you don't!" Murg disagreed.

Everything shook this time. Even the air vibrated.

An ear-shattering roar sounded from behind them, almost pushing the magic bicycle off the cliff. Danny had to shake himself to recover, then looked at the path upon which they rested. "It's a game trail!" Danny said, then whirled around. The tops of the trees were·swaying back and forth, then they were pushed aside. As the apatasaurus cleared the trees, it roared again.

"I – I've seen enough," Danny stammered.

"Think Socrates!" Murg encouraged. "Danny? Are you all right?"

Danny was staring dumbfoundedly at the gigantic monster.

Standing almost 50 feet tall, forty feet long and weighing over six tons, the monster's teeth were the size of javelins as they flashed in the hazy light. Its large black eyes seemed to darken as its gaze locked on him. Then he saw a Barosaurus 80 feet long and weighing 50 tons.

Another ground-shaking step galvanized Danny. As he pushed off and started downhill, Kalyde II changed into a mountain bike. The T-Rex saw the movement and pursued, thundering after them.

"Faster! Faster! Think fast!" Murg wailed.

"I'm trying, but something's wrong!"

They hit a bump and sailed airborne, landing softly, then careening down the hill. Danny thought of going faster and faster, but his head hurt even more. He quit pedaling and just thought about speed, but they just weren't going fast enough.

The T-Rex closed. The beast's roar almost blasted Danny off the bicycle.

"You have to believe!" Murg told him.

"I do! No dinosaur can catch the magic bicycle!" Danny cried. He had outraced a Ferrari and flying fish, even ridden atop fog! What was going on? He didn't believe it could catch them!

The T-Rex grew closer and snapped at them. Its teeth clacked together loudly. The tremendous impact shoved Kalyde II ahead even faster. Danny gagged on the dinosaur's fetid breath. It stung his eyes, and he could barely see, but he could feel its intake as the beast readied for another bite.

Chapter Sixteen

Socratic Method

"It's right behind us! Do something!" Murg wailed.

"I don't understand why we're not going faster!" Danny gnashed.

The T-Rex roared, sounding triumphant.

Danny cringed. "Hey! What's that on our tires?!" They appeared thicker and lumpier.

"It looks like tar! That stuff's from the swamp! Quick! Wish the tires clean!" was Murg's reply.

Seeing it clean with his mind's eye, Danny reached down and touched the front tire. The thick, black substance quickly disappeared. His head felt like it was splitting open. He wished they were elsewhere, but nothing happened. As he reached back to touch the back tire, the mammoth reptilian lunged again.

Danny veered down a game trail suddenly, the T-Rex barely missed them.

The reptilian beast gathered itself for another vicious attack.

"DANNY!" Murg wailed.

The back tire cleared. They rocketed forward down the hill, leaving the stunned T-Rex far behind.

"We're as good as gone!" Danny laughed. His joy was cut short as he heard a thunderous roar ahead of him.

"Another one!" Murg cried. A second Tyrannosaur came crashing out of the jungle. "Are we the only thing on the T-Rex menu today?"

"There might only be one place safe!" Danny cried, then steered toward a thick patch of fog hanging over the valley.

The T-Rex tried to cut them off, but they were faster, ramping onto the fog, then bumping across the top of it. The eight-ton beast continued to pursue, its head sticking up through the fog as it snapped futilely after them.

It didn't chase them long. The roar of the first Tyrannosaur challenged the second. It whirled around to face its charging kin. They clashed violently, snapping viciously at each other.

Danny kept riding, heading for a rocky outcropping on a mountain not too far ahead.

A pterodactyl suddenly came flying up through the fog. It seemed as surprised to see them as they were to see it. It whirled away, then gathered its courage and returned. Danny closed his eyes. He saw himself already standing on the outcropping.

Everything shifted. They suddenly appeared atop a rock not far from a cluster of trees. Danny rolled the bicycle under giant bushes.

"Whew! Let's get out of this time. Too many carnivores," Murg sighed.

"My head still hurts."

"Still as bad?" Murg asked.

"No, it's some better. I just need a moment to rest. A moment to focus."

Danny and Murg hid for a while in a leafy thicket, resting and waiting. As the pounding subsided, Danny's head slowly cleared.

Murg wondered if it had something to do with the adrenaline of being chased. "Maybe it's the magic bicycle," Danny replied. "Kalyde can heal. Maybe Kalyde II can, too."

"Hey, it's your imagination. Can you concentrate now?"

"Better, yes."

"Then let's go. This time traveling is dangerous."

Danny rolled Kalyde II out from the trees and dropped down onto the fog. Not wanting to risk another prehistoric encounter, he quickly focused on Socrates and ancient Greece around 401 BC. Almost immediately, a white light engulfed them.

The flash quickly faded, and they burst from the clouds to ride the rainbow highway. It was brilliant and healthy without any tatters, tears or gaps. Vibrant purple surrounded them, and stars twinkled brightly above.

"Much better," Murg said.

Danny pictured Socrates, a short, heavy-set man with unattractive features and dark bulging eyes set too close above a large, rounded nose. Danny imagined what it would be like to speak with the famous philosopher, now in his seventies, who many had called the father of western philosophy. Socrates had been trying to find out what was right and wrong with Man's behavior. He believed that Man's intelligence and moral character came from the soul.

They would be visiting 5th Century BC, the greatest period in Greek history – a time when the Hellenes had learned more than ever before about mathematics, astronomy, philosophy and architecture. Athens was a polis – a city state – not part of a nation but the capital of the Hellenic Empire.

Socrates would be sitting at the Parthenon, relaxed as he casually responded to the odd boy and patch-colored cat on their strange-looking contraption made of wood. The Parthenon had been built atop the 500-foot mount of the Acropolis and was the temple to Athena, the city's patron deity.

With a flash of light, they left the rainbow highway to bounce along a narrow dirt street barely five people wide with mud brick homes on each side. Danny dodged around gawking Hellenes, heading for the Parthenon at the end of the street. The setting sun had left the city in twilight's shadow, but the fading light was still shining on Athena's temple, causing the white marble to radiate an orange-gold hue.

At first, Danny didn't know what the Hellenes were saying, but as he and Murg reached the intersection, he seemed to be able to understand the ancient Greek language. Kalyde II must be translating. Most were pointing and wondering who he was – what he was. Some seemed to think the bicycle might be part of him. He could only imagine what they would say if the bicycle didn't appear to be made from wood.

"They think you're some kind of god," Murg joked.

"Chronos, god of time," Danny responded in kind.

"The god of uncleanliness is more like it," Murg replied, referring to Danny's once white outfit. It was splattered black across the back and mud splotches decorated the front in an abstract tie-dye type pattern. Danny tried wishing it clean but nothing happened.

They were nearing the Parthenon from the north and were now approaching the Agora. Out in front were altars to the Twelve Gods. Inside were their temples and statues to the ten heroes for which the tribes of Attica were named. If he remembered correctly, the Agora also housed the Argyrikopeion – the Hellenes' mint, one-third of the fifty-city council members, and the Old Bouleterion, a court where the ruling class jury of five hundred was chosen by lot.

Danny rode up the Acropolis walkway, passing staring people. Most didn't even move out of the way, so Danny had to weave through them. "Easier than tumbleweeds," he murmured.

"Do you think this will get Socrates in trouble?" Murg asked.

"What more trouble could he get into?" Danny replied. "In about a year, he'll be accused of teaching treasonous politics, corrupting the youth of Athens, not believing in the gods and much more."

"Oh."

"I take it Socrates wasn't a lover of cats."

"Ask me about Egyptians," Murg suggested.

Danny didn't respond. He just kept pedaling.

"Quite a sight," Murg said when they reached the top.

In every direction the polis of Athens stretched for over two miles, stone and mud brick buildings crammed up against each other. Narrow streets looking like dirt trails wandered among the structures. To the north and beyond the olive groves, a great wall had been built against invaders. Just past it were wine vineyards. To the west and southerly they could see islands, including the Isle of Delos. The Aegean Sea was dark now that the sun had almost set.

"What makes you think Socrates is here?" Murg asked.

"I pictured it – imagining that we would arrive here when he was here. He should be alone. His friends Charmides, Critas, Plato and one other, I can't remember his name, should have left already. Or not come here today. Or something."

"You remember more than I would have expected."

"Maybe I'm getting smarter," Danny replied. "There he is!"

Just as Danny had imagined, Socrates was sitting on the steps. A few people had wandered away from what had been a group discussion and were heading inside the Parthenon. Socrates had noticed Danny and Murg approaching and seemed to be waiting for them.

Danny stopped at the base of the steps and said, "Excuse me, Socrates, sir, but I was wondering if you could help me with a problem of the soul."

"While the soul is one of my favorite topics, young man, I don't see how I could help you. I am not a learned man, just a curious one who himself seeks knowledge by speaking with those who are wiser. For an ignorant man learns much when a wise man speaks."

Danny tried to remember what Socrates was like. What would be the best approach? "Perhaps we could share a discourse on the subject, and through this, resolve my problem."

Danny had read that Socrates didn't consider himself a wise man. He'd claimed that he was ignorant of any matter discussed – that he was just seeking knowledge as were those who joined him in discussions. This had been said while defending against the allegation that he had been teaching treasonous thoughts.

"Ah, let us examine such together," Socrates mused aloud.

"He looks and smells like he needs a shower," Murg said.

"They clean themselves with olive oil, then scrap it off," Danny thought back.

"You need one too," Murg told him.

Danny ignored the calico and explained the nature of his problem to Socrates, wanting to know whether it was right to change history by going back and saving his friend and family. He added that he could do so with the help of the gods – that one had agreed to help him.

"You speak very directly, so I must ask, what are you trying to accomplish?" Socrates asked.

"I'm trying to make the right decision."

"Ah. And how would you define right?" Socrates asked.

"I think saving a life, since life is precious, is the right thing to do."

"I want you to try and answer more precisely the question

that I have put to you. You see, my friend, when I asked you before what right was, you didn't tell me enough. You said what you are contemplating doing – saving lives – is a right action. To determine if an action is right, we must first decide what right is."

"Uh, right is doing what's best for the whole," Danny replied, knowing they'd immediately gotten off track.

"Is it? Then Athens enforcing its will upon the others of the Delphan Confederacy was right because Athens had a greater population?"

"That's not what I meant. That sounds like might makes right, and that's certainly not what I meant." Danny mentally groaned. He thought he'd known what he was getting into, but Socrates liked to strip one to his own ignorance, so that the truth could be shown.

"Ah, the thrill of the chase, in this case chasing," Murg thought dryly. "I can see this is going to be fun."

"Then maybe your definition of right needs adjusting. Is right the actions desired by the gods?"

"No – because the gods act in contradictory ways sometimes," Danny replied, remembering the very human qualities attributed to Greek deities.

"Then explain to me what this right characteristic is in itself, so that by fixing my eyes upon it and using it as a pattern I may be able to describe any action, not just the saving of lives, as right, if it corresponds to the pattern, and, wrong, if it doesn't."

"You never answer a question directly, do you?"

"As I have said before, I am an uneducated man seeking knowledge through the discourse of those wiser."

"But I am not wise, either," Danny groaned.

"Then maybe through discourse we may both grow wiser."

"I think this was a bad idea," Murg grumbled.

"I'm trying to do what's morally right," Danny explained.

"Ah, morally right but not necessary legally what is right?" Socrates asked.

Danny nodded.

"Then we need an even tighter definition, a correction to our formula," Socrates said.

"Morally right is doing what's best for the soul?"

"You sound unsure of yourself."

"That's an understatement," Danny replied.

"You speak strangely, young man. Do you believe that any action you take which makes you feel better is right?"

"No, because I could act on emotion. That might feel good but not necessarily be right. I could get angry and kill someone who was irritating me," he emphasized, "but that wouldn't be right."

"So doing right means thinking rationally about something, not reacting based on emotions?"

Danny nodded. If he were knee-jerk reacting he would have already gone back in time and saved Happy, Mom and Sarah. Instead, he was trying to think things through. He was beginning to think he had made a mistake.

"Have we spoken before?" Socrates asked. "No, I don't believe so. I would have remembered you and your strange . . . wagon."

Danny looked around. Many Hellenes were staring at them, but some had started to approach. "I'm a bit short on time," Danny began.

"As are we all," Socrates replied. "So your definition of morally right is thinking rationally about a matter and coming to a conclusion regardless of the emotions involved?"

Danny's head was spinning. "I think that's part of it. I also believe doing right is doing to others what I would want done to me."

"Interesting. Therefore, if you came across a man who enjoyed pain, then it would be right if this man caused you pain?"

"No! That's not what I said. Maybe there is no single truth for what is right! Maybe what's right can be influenced by your situation or your perspective. It's not morally right to kill anyone – the opposite of saving a life – but it's not right to let oneself be killed, either. Killing is looked at differently if it is self defense."

"You twist words grandly. Are you not too young to be a politician? I must warn you to beware, for an honest man may lose his soul in politics."

Danny groaned. "This discourse isn't helping me."

"Then maybe I should call upon my friends to see if they would aid us."

"That's it!"

"I must profess confusion. What is . . . it?"

"I need to speak to Happy, Sarah and Mom about it. Maybe what is right for them is based upon their opinion, not mine."

"If you have the ability to go back and save them, then you have the means to open a discourse with them. But then that would imply that right is a matter of perspective, which can be based on emotions and not rational thinking. A man might be interested in self-preservation, when it might be best if he were sacrificed, a warrior defending a pass, so that others might escape, for example."

"I read somewhere," Danny began, "that on some level we all have the ability to direct our lives based on the choices we make."

"Then it would be possible for us to chose when and where we will die. But we have digressed and moved away from defining what is right."

"Uh, that's all right," Danny said. "If they don't want to be saved, then I think it's wrong to go against their wishes."

"Maybe it would be easier to define what is wrong, than what is right," Socrates began.

"Thanks, anyway," Danny said. "They'll be debating what

is right for the next twenty-four centuries and they still won't come up with an answer. Maybe it's important that I keep asking questions of myself instead of always asking others for answers. To keep challenging myself, re-evaluating as things change."

"Well said. It is not always the answer that is important, but the quest."

"Well, at least I have an idea of how to proceed."

Danny waved goodbye to the Greek philosopher and began pedaling. As he headed down the walkway, he found an easy rhythm, then focused on Benjamin Franklin, 1752 and the day of his famous experiment. Danny recalled the descriptions he'd read and focused on the most accurate paintings.

Franklin was a tall, muscular man with shoulder-length chestnut hair and dark brown eyes that twinkled with curiosity. His nose was a bit aquiline, his chin doubled and his smile both enigmatic and charming. He was a natural philosopher, an assembly clerk, a printer, a postmaster, an inventor and a statesman, among many other things.

Through his eyelids Danny saw the white flash and felt a brief warmth rush across his skin. Then they broke from the clouds to speed along the rainbow.

"Everything looks good," Murg told him. "Or did," the calico suddenly amended. A strange light had suddenly appeared before them. The violet glowing ball bobbed and bounced about as though waiting for them.

"That's odd. We've never seen that before," Murg said. "I suggest avoiding it." Danny steered around it, but it whipped around to follow them. "It's gaining!"

Danny turned around. Sure enough, it was closing in as though it were a heat-seeking missile. Danny tried to picture the bicycle racing faster. They shot ahead. So did the orb, still moving closer and closer.

Suddenly they were engulfed in a bright, lavender light.

Danny gasped, unable to breathe! He visualized the rainbow highway, but they didn't return to it.

Where were they going?

Chapter Seventeen

Founding Father

Just as suddenly, they appeared in what seemed to be an ancient laboratory. The stone-walled room could have been someone's cluttered attic.

The air was musty and filled with pungent scents that made Murg's eyes water. "Where are we? It smells horrible! Someone needs a maid. I have never understood why other animals can't be as neat as a cat."

Besides the sunlight coming from a lone window, the tower room was illuminated by several darkly smoking torches set along the stone walls. Maps and bookshelves crammed with books almost completely covered the walls. Despite the full shelves, a mess of books joined a host of strange ceramic vessels haphazardly arranged on two cluttered tables.

A stuffed owl sat atop several books on the table closest to them. When it blinked, Danny was startled. "Hey, it moved!"

"Oh, Archimedes! What have I done? This certainly isn't what I wanted from my conjuring!"

Danny whirled around to look at the source of the voice.

The man was very old with white hair, a long beard and dark eyes that appeared to be filled with stars. He was dressed in a long dark robe and carried a staff carved with runes.

"Hey, are you . . . " Danny began.

The old man pointed the staff at them, and, in a flash of light, they returned to the rainbow highway.

Danny was stunned for a moment, then said, "Do you think that was Merlin?"

"He fits the description," Murg agreed. "He was another lover of cats."

"But he was just a legend."

"If you say so."

"But legends also say he lived backwards in time! Maybe he could help me."

"Listen, Danny. With a glance, Merlin knew who you are and what you wanted. If he'd thought he could help you, or had wanted to help you, he would have. After all, he was the greatest of all wizards. Now, concentrate on Benjamin Franklin. No one in Camelot that we want to meet can help you with your dilemma."

Having experienced the results of mental wandering while time traveling, Danny kept his thoughts off Merlin and focused on Benjamin Franklin.

The fifteenth of seventeen children born outside Boston, Franklin, the founding father, had been a pious man who believed serving God was doing good to man. His motto had been to make the most of one's abilities and improve oneself to the utmost. If it was good for you and your community, it was a good idea – like the police, fire brigades, colleges and hospitals, even paved streets and trash pick up. Through *Poor Richard's Almanac* and other means, he had drummed up support for his revolutionary ideas, changing the face of America.

Benjamin Franklin had been inspired by Sir Francis Bacon and believed science was a game. When he was 20 years old returning from England, he'd crammed a notebook full of observations on wind, weather, ocean currents and animal life in hopes of improving water travel. He believed that by understanding the physical world one could master one's fate. Human reason was bolstered by the eye of observation.

Danny pictured Franklin standing in a field waiting to conduct his electrical experiment. The Philadelphia skies were stormy, full of towering thunderheads. His 22-year-old son, William, was preparing a kite made of silk and two sticks. They would dangle a key from the string to further their explorations of electricity. From this point on, Franklin's terminology would be the basis of how we now speak about electricity.

Kalyde II raced into the blazing sun once more, leaving the rainbow highway behind.

As they rolled through a sparse cluster of trees, Danny said, "We made it!"

"Going forward in history is much more pleasant than backwards," Murg dryly observed. "Even if we're still in the past."

They heard a sudden gasp to their left. Danny turned in time to see an old man running away, his long-tailed coat trailing behind him.

"We may not have much time," Murg said.

"Why?" Danny asked. He was pulling a clean shirt from his backpack.

"During these pre-revolutionary times, superstition was still stronger than science. And we just suddenly appeared out of thin air. You know your mother used to call you a demon every now and then."

Danny finished putting on his green NO FEAR shirt, then

changed pants. "He may think I'm a witch?"

"A warlock! Not a witch! And you're changing in public. Exposed skin! Shame on you! You must be some kind of evil imp!"

"Murg! That mud had dried. It was getting hard to move!"

"Come on! Let's get going! I see Ben Franklin over there." Murg pointed between a copse of trees and across a grassy meadow.

Benjamin Franklin and his son William were standing near a small barn.

William pointed toward them as they rode across the grassy field. Benjamin Franklin was obviously curious about the boy and his bicycle. If Danny remembered correctly, the bicycle wouldn't be invented for another eighty-seven years by a Scottish blacksmith named Kirkpatrick McMillan.

"Good morning, good sirs," Danny said as he came to a stop nearby. "Are either of you – Mr. Benjamin Franklin?"

"I am, young man. Who are you and how may I be of service?" Ben Franklin asked.

Danny introduced himself and Murg.

After introducing his son, Ben Franklin studied Danny intently and the bicycle even more so. "That is quite an interesting invention you are riding. What is it called?"

"Don't let him examine it too closely," Murg thought. "It might change history."

"A bicycle. A friend made it for me."

"I have never seen its like. Is it a type of mechanical horse?"

"In a sense. It's all done with the legs and pedaling. But it's not the reason I'm here. I'm sorry to bother you, to interrupt your experiment, but this is important."

"You know of my experiment with electricity?" he asked, peering over his spectacles.

"Yes, sir." Danny almost couldn't believe he was talking to Benjamin Franklin, a founding father and a man who had helped shape the history of the United States. It was incredible! If times weren't so urgent, and he hadn't been so afraid of changing history, he would have enjoyed exchanging pleasantries and learning all he could about the great man.

"Maybe you should become a historian," Murg suggested.

Danny ignored her. "I suspect your experiment will be a momentous occasion with far reaching impact."

"It is grand of you to say so."

"Mr. Franklin, I have come a long way to ask you some questions."

"About science?" He sounded pleased. Suddenly, he seemed to catch himself, pulling his rapt attention from Danny and the bicycle. "William, we have tarried. Let's raise the kite into the sky."

William nodded and walked away with the kite, its string trailing back to Ben Franklin.

"My question is about time," Danny said.

"Time, eh?" Franklin asked. He watched William run back and forth. After the second pass, the kite rose skyward.

"Yes, sir, time. It may be more of a philosophical question than a scientific one."

"Then why come to me?"

"Because you are renowned as a wise man with both scientific and religious educations."

"Wise?" Benjamin Franklin looked at Danny over the tops of his spectacles. He appeared amused. "It is true that while a youth, I studied in the seminary, but that was a long time ago. I like to think of myself as a visionary; but I don't think of myself as a wise man, especially in context with say, Jesus Christ and Plato. I am simply an inventor, if the truth be told. But one can invent ideas as well as objects, as Adam Smith has proved."

Danny grew dejected.

"Don't assume he can't help you," Murg thought. "Ask your questions."

"It's actually a hypothetical question, possibly one involving history. What do you think about changing history?"

"Well," Franklin looked thoughtful. "It is good to pass on such thoughts to the young, for they are the future. I believe that we must grasp the present firmly in hand and lead ourselves to a better future. We must be bold enough to recognize what has not worked, so that we won't repeat the mistakes of the past. With human failings, history has a tendency to repeat itself."

"Oh," Danny replied.

"Not quite what you expected," Murg thought.

"I wasn't specific enough," Danny thought back.

"Be careful," Murg cautioned.

"That's not quite what I meant," Danny said. "It's a morality question involving time. If someone dies, and you could somehow go back and prevent it . . ."

"Go back in time?" Franklin asked, looking speculative. He seemed to be studying Danny's clothes more intently than before, from his baseball cap to his t-shirt, his jeans and all the way down to his sneakers.

Danny nodded. " . . . Should you?"

"That is an interesting conundrum. Young master Chase, where are you from?"

Danny hesitated. "Don't tell him!" Murg said.

"You are dressed very strangely." Ben Franklin reached out and fingered Danny's shirt, which read NO FEAR GEAR on the front.

"I might as well be honest. A scientist needs as much information as possible to work with," Danny replied breathlessly. After a deep breath, he said, "I'm from over two hundred years in the future."

Paw over her eyes, Murg groaned.

Ben Franklin's eyes widened. He removed his spectacles and rubbed his eyes.

"This bicycle is special and allows me to travel time," Danny said. "I lost my mother and sister in a car . . . in an accident. I was thinking about saving them, but I'm afraid that I might negatively change time."

"Negatively, you say," Ben Franklin muttered absently, then he knelt, examining the bicycle and running his hand along its shiny metal frame. "Amazing." He examined the chain and gears. "Truly amazing."

"Sir, your experiment today will be amazing," Danny told him. "Don't get distracted. I don't want to change history. In fact, it will be best for all if you'll forget this encounter. You have more important things to do."

"Oh, yes. Of course." As if to emphasize the point, there was a peal of thunder. Ben Franklin looked skyward. "I am not quite sure how to answer your question, young Master Chase, but I will do my best. Ask yourself, is your traveling and possibly changing events beneficial for all concerned? You don't know, correct?"

Danny nodded.

"Is that because you have never done such a thing?"

"Yes."

"Has anyone else in your time done such a thing?" he asked.

Danny shook his head.

"Then, in a sense, this is an experiment?"

"Yes, I guess it is," Danny replied thoughtfully.

"Then you must approach it as such and use your powers of observation." He was thoughtful for a moment, then said, "Instead of changing something large in this so-called past, maybe you should start with something small."

"Something insignificant and recent, maybe?" Danny asked.

Ben Franklin nodded.

"Something that happened in my yesterday?"

"Yes! That would minimize the potential for negative re-sults. You could discover if such a change, if any, would be beneficial," Franklin said.

Lightning flashed, followed by a crack of thunder. Ben Franklin's attention turned skyward.

"I think a special moment is imminent," Murg thought. "We have your answer. We need to test the waters before jumping in."

"Just like you said," Danny thought back. He stuck out his hand. "Thanks for your help, sir. I must be going. I have already distracted you far too long."

"My pleasure, young sir," Ben Franklin said as he shook Danny's hand. "May I ask a question?"

"I may not be able to answer it," Danny said.

"Is the future in good hands?"

Danny thought for a moment, then said, "Our past is in better hands than my future, but we still dream of one nation under God, indivisible with liberty and justice for all."

Ben Franklin smiled. "I like the sound of that." Another crack of thunder made him look skyward. Then he pulled a glass jar from his coat pocket. "Young Master Chase, follow your heart as well as a scientific road map. One without the other, science without morality, might yield disastrous results."

"Truer words were never spoken," Murg thought.

"There he is!" The old man they'd seen earlier had returned with a small crowd. They carried pitchforks, clubs and even a rifle or two. "I told you that Mister Franklin consorted with witches and warlocks. Look at all the strange torture devices he's always conjuring."

"Damn, we've overstayed our welcome!" Murg said.

"I remember reading they burned talking cats at the stake," Danny thought back. "Mr. Franklin, I'm – "

"Don't be sorry. I have enjoyed our discussion. Mr. Dapplemyer has always been jealous of my work. He is constantly spying, hoping to steal something of interest. Now get along."

"Thank you, sir. Goodbye." Danny turned around and

headed for the woods.

"After him! He might disappear just as fast as he appeared!" Dapplemyer cried.

"Well, whether we wanted to or not, I think we've changed history," Murg said.

"Yeah, I don't remember this!"

There was a gunblast, then Danny heard something whiz by his ear. "Hey! They're shooting at us!"

"Get the lead out!" Murg encouraged.

Danny put on a burst of speed and pictured being in the woods. They rocketed forward with a loud whoosh and raced into the forest where he sought the rainbow highway to London 1894.

Chapter Eighteen

The Visionary

On the rainbow bridge, the quest continued as Danny concentrated on H.G. Wells. The famous British author was short with dark wavy hair parted down the middle. Wells had a thin face with high cheekbones and a burly mustache below a round nose. He appeared sickly at times, his poor health due to a lung condition suffered after a schoolyard beating at a young age. Wells was born in 1866 – just thirteen years before H.J. Lawson created the English Safety bicycle. Wells was the underprivileged son of a housekeeper for a country estate and lived frugally, dreaming of being a scientist one day.

Danny had read that Wells was a pessimistic man who saw little hope for man's future. Some of this, Danny thought, could be attributed to his strict and poor childhood, one he would later poke fun at in a comedy he'd written about squiring. The rest probably stemmed from Wells' sickly health.

Wells believed that the cheerless advance of mankind, the growing pile of civilization, was a foolish heaping that one day must fall back and destroy itself. Back then, science was the match Man had just lit, giving Man a glimpse of human comforts and beauty that would one day return to the darkness when the match burned Man.

"Why are we going to see him then?" Murg wondered.

"Because he was a visionary. He was one of the first to write about time, in *The Time Traveller*, then *The Time Machine*, even if they were fictional. Besides, I want another opinion. Both Socrates and Franklin thought highly of Mankind's future. Wells doesn't."

"I see."

Danny was picturing Wells' London address, 12 Mornington Road in the heart of lower middle class London.

Mornington Road stood like a flower atop a long stalk at the end of Tottenham Court Road. To the east were the green glades of Regent Park, a minute or two walk from Wells' home and office. By day the cobblestone streets were bright and crowded, noisy with traffic and hawkers. At night the streets were gas-lit and hazy from coal and woodburning stoves. Trains could be heard roaring by at all hours.

Danny was shooting for the time just after Wells had finished *The Time Machine* and had returned from a retreat in the country. Now he was working on *A Wonderful Visit*, about an angel's visit to earth. Upon her arrival, she'd been struck by an ornithopter and grounded, landing in a churchyard.

The bright white sun blazed around the duo as Danny rode into the off ramp. As they appeared, he concentrated on making the bicycle look old-fashioned and colored it black. There wasn't anything he could do about his clothing. His nondescript whites weren't wearable, and even from the backpack, they had the smell of a skunk.

"1894, here we come," Murg said as they were engulfed by the brilliance.

The warmth spread over them, then they were bouncing along a cobblestone street. "Pardon me!" Danny cried out as he steered around and between several Londoners.

They jumped back with curses and oaths heavy with cockney accents. Although the people were difficult to understand, Danny didn't need a translation.

"Bloomin' idiot!" "Bloody fool!" "Blackguard!"

"What's in a name," Murg began, "some people ask? But have you ever wondered why your family was named Chase?"

"No." Danny couldn't believe the crowd.

The streets were teeming, people escaping their small apartments during the heat of the day. Everything was very close together, and the smells spoke of too many people in too little space.

"There it is, 12 Mornington," Murg said, pointing to a three-story brick building just ahead on their right.

Danny hoped to catch Wells before he left his second-story apartment for his daily walk to Regent Park.

As they rode nearer, the British author stepped from the doorway. Magic was a wonderful thing, Danny thought. "Excuse me, Mister Wells," Danny called out in a respectful voice.

The young man looked over at Danny. A curious expression stretched across his lean face as Wells watched Danny pedal closer. He wasn't the only one watching Danny. Others were curious about his bicycle, still a novelty during this day and age. Kalyde II looked a little like the J.K. Stanley version which had withstood the test of time.

Many along the street nudged one another and pointed directly at Danny. His attire elicited comments, wondering what No Fear meant and what his clothes were made of. Jeans should be known, he thought.

"My name is Danny Chase. Can I speak with you for a moment?"

H.G. Wells eyed him as though examining an eccentric. "Possibly. What is the nature of your inquiry?"

"I'd like to talk to you about *The Time Machine*."

Wells looked startled. "Has it been released early?"

"No, sir. It's kind of hard to explain. Could we go inside and talk?" Danny asked.

"You have an odd accent, young man. Where are you from?"

"America, 1997," Danny whispered.

"Indeed!" Wells responded with astonishment. After a long moment of silence, he said, "You are serious, aren't you?"

Danny nodded.

"How can you prove this?"

Danny went on to explain about his future novel, *A Wonderful Visit*, detailing the plot.

"Incredible!"

"Your time has come," Danny said. "Keep following your imagination and keep writing."

"Come inside," Wells coughed. "Yes, come inside. And bring your bicycle with you. Some blackguard might steal it," Wells finished, then turned around and went back inside.

Carrying the bicycle, Danny followed.

"That is a fine bicycle you have," Wells said. "I have never ridden one myself, though with you being from the future, I expected something . . . more advanced."

Danny smiled and changed Kalyde II into Spacelander mode. This he followed with the latest and most radical and specialized mountain bike, complete with neon colors.

"Amazing! Simply amazing. It transforms, too!" Wells kept looking back at the bicycle until they reached his apartment door.

"This place smells," Murg said. "Underneath the smell of

coal, this place could be rotting."

"Murg, we won't be here long," Danny promised, then sighed.

"I am sorry Isabelle is out," Wells said as he unlocked, then opened the door. "It is not every day we meet someone from the future."

"You believe me?" Danny asked.

"Of course! Especially after seeing your bicycle . . . perform. Besides, don't you believe in the things you write about?" Wells asked.

"How did you know I liked to write?"

"Just a guess," he said, then coughed. "Come in."

Danny entered Wells' small apartment. It had a pair of rooms separated by a folding door. The front room was hot, overly warmed by a coal fire. The bedroom had a double bed, a chest of drawers and a tin bath. Danny remembered water and coal were carried upstairs by servants.

Wells said something, but it was drowned out by a passing train. When the noise faded, the Englishman said, "I'm sorry it's so warm. With my condition, I can't let my apartment get too cool."

"It's all right," Danny said as he wiped the sweat from his brow.

"I suspect there will be better ways to heat a place someday," Wells said. "Probably with electricity."

Danny nodded.

"Have a seat. Would you like some tea?"

"I can't stay long."

"Why?" Wells asked as he sat.

"I'm afraid I might do or say something that would change the future."

"Have you not already changed it by coming back here?" Wells argued.

"Yes," Danny said, thinking back to Franklin and the witch

hunter, "but I'm trying not to change much. You already know so much about the future, I figured I couldn't do much damage."

"Any time any act is observed, it impacts its outcome. But it sounds as if you're a daring young fellow trying to walk the precipice."

"Desperate is more like it."

Wells laughed, then coughed. "So we haven't destroyed ourselves by 1997?"

"Not yet."

"I find this hard to believe. Even now, we are on the verge of destroying ourselves. I assume our killing machines have improved?"

"As you guessed."

"Are you slaves to them yet?" Wells asked.

Danny shook his head.

"Then we are doing better than I would have surmised. How did you get here?"

"That's a long story. In brief, I used alien technology." Danny replied.

"Alien?" he asked.

Danny nodded.

"From the stars? Really?" Wells said as if an idea had dawned. "We haven't created the time machine on our own yet?"

Danny shook his head. He had questions he wanted to ask, but he was in awe of the man. With his scientific knowledge and his somewhat dark perspective, he had revolutionized fiction. Danny could only dream of being so popular some day. Murg poked Danny with a claw, and he jumped.

"Like I said, I don't want to say too much, but I was hoping you could help me with a problem," Danny said. When Wells nodded, Danny proceeded to tell him about the death of his mother, Sarah, and even Happy. Danny rambled, and from

Murg's body language, Danny suspected he'd said more than enough.

"Change time, eh? Yes, I suspect it would. For one, you might still be in Germany instead of in America. Sarah might mature into a grand pianist. Happy, well, I don't know what surfing is, or why anyone would want to do such a thing."

"If you were me, what would you do?" Danny asked.

"I would travel time and ask some of the finest minds instead of coming to a struggling writer with delusions and dreams of grandeur," Wells laughed.

"I've already spoken with Socrates and Ben Franklin."

"And what did they say?"

"It was difficult to get an answer from Socrates," Danny began.

Wells roared with laughter.

"But from our discussion I figured that I should ask the opinions of those I'm thinking of saving. And that asking questions was important. To ask them of oneself and not just seek answers from others – that may be even more important than answers." Wells was nodding as Danny spoke.

"Benjamin Franklin suggested I view it as an experiment and take things slowly, changing little things to see how they affect the future. He also said to do what is best for the greater good. What do you think?"

"I agree with both men, but more so with Franklin. I would also take a scientific approach. It was my first love after all. Personally, I would lean toward changing past events, doing everything I could so that my friend and family would survive."

"Why?"

"Because after death there is nothing. Darkness."

"You don't believe in Heaven?" Danny asked.

"No. We live in a moment of beauty, flaring to brightness, then we die and return to darkness. If there is something afterward, I have seen no proof of it. Religion is designed so man may comfort each other or, in worse cases, control each other. I don't believe in this bloody reincarnation balderdash, either. Danny, although I believe you would be returning them to suffer the ills of society, I suggest it's better than consigning them to nothingness. Yes, indeed, save them."

Danny was thoughtful. "Thank you," he finally said. "I was afraid you'd laugh at me, tell me to go away. I read you were volubly argumentative."

Wells laughed so hard he began coughing. When he'd recovered he said, "Only with those who disagree with me."

Danny smiled. "I should be going. Thanks, again."

"One last question, if I may? Will history look upon me favorably?" Wells asked.

Danny was thoughtful. He wasn't sure where the words came from, but he said, "Only if you're true to yourself."

"Um, Danny . . . I suppose there isn't any chance that you would take me with you, even on a small journey?"

"I don't think that would be wise," Danny said. "Besides, you've already been there in your mind. That's what counts. Thanks, again." With a tip of his baseball cap, Danny turned and left.

When they reached the street, Murg climbed upon the bicycle. "Well, that's three down, one to go. Have you learned anything?"

"Yes and no. Actually, I think I know less than when I started," Danny said as he climbed on Kalyde II.

"Do you mean you're less sure about things?"

"Yes."

"Well, Albert Einstein is next on the agenda. Maybe we'll learn something," Murg replied. "Or not. You know how quests are."

"Futile?" Danny asked.

Murg just chuckled.

Chapter Nineteen

Relativity

With all the photographs available, it was easy for Danny to imagine Albert Einstein. Danny wanted to find him at his venerable New England home, working on his notes. He was sitting on the front porch swing after a morning at the Institute for Advanced Studies at Princeton.

In 1952, Einstein was seventy-two and no longer in the mainstream of physics. He was medium in height and unassuming, although his wildly windswept hair the color of snow helped him stand out in any crowd. His mustache was still dark, as were his eyes. Even in his later years, they still reflected a burning curiosity. Einstein would be casually dressed, unconcerned about his appearance or how the world thought of him.

Through the flashing light of the on-ramp sun, Danny and

Murg appeared on the rainbow highway, racing fifty-eight years forward through time. To match the era, Danny changed Kalyde II into Spacelander mode. "We'll fit right in," Danny said.

"There's always a first time for everything, I suppose," Murg replied.

While Danny focused on Einstein's appearance, he went over what he knew of the legendary man. He'd been born in Germany and had been considered an unruly student and a backward child who had difficulty with mathematics. At least in this, Danny could empathize.

In 1905, after watching pollen grains in liquid, he proposed the existence of atoms based on Brownian Motion Theory. Come 1916, after struggling with Newton's Gravitational Theory, he proposed his Theory of Relativity for objects in motion, where only one system's motion relative to another is detectable. With the world spinning through space, no object was truly motionless. Danny sighed. The example used had been two moving trains running alongside each other.

The Special Theory of Relativity, using light, not objects, was proven when stars beyond the sun were photographed during the eclipse of 1917. Light was shown to bend due to gravity.

Over the years, Einstein changed from an arrogant young man to a serene and humble figure, half comic and half saint, who never understood his celebrity stature. When asked about relativity, he explained that relativity was simple. When a young man sat with a pretty girl for an hour, it seemed as though only minutes had passed. But let him sit on a hot stove for a minute, it seemed much longer than any hour.

In 1933, he escaped Nazi Germany by coming to America. He'd been a man of peace until Hitler's regime had reared its ugly head. Even after World War II, Einstein was worried about the atomic bomb. If one country could construct one, then so could others. With the help of Bertrand Russell, a British philosopher, Einstein anchored conferences focusing on peaceful co-existence – the world living together without fighting.

Danny was interested in his theory that time is an aspect in and of itself. Time might be related to light. Danny wanted to know more. Maybe it had something to do with Einstein's Cosmology concepts; space was a cylinder where time had no beginning nor end. If one traveled long enough, one would come back to that same starting point.

But if that were true, then why was traveling backwards in time a rough ride and traveling forward in time a smooth journey?

With a flash of light, Danny appeared in 1952 in a suburb of Princeton. He checked the addresses and rode to Einstein's house, a classically styled New England home built of brick and surrounded by huge trees and lush bushes. Unlike the yards on each side, Einstein's grounds were in need of trimming.

"He has better things to do with his time," Murg replied.

Danny stopped Kalyde II, the Spacelander, at the end of the concrete walk. "Here we go again." Danny rolled his bicycle to the gate and opened it.

Einstein was sitting on a front porch swing, paper and notebooks surrounding him. He stood when he saw Danny approaching. "Can I help you, young man? You appear a little too young to be one of my former students, but the right mental age for some of my esteemed opponents in the field."

"Uh, I'm neither," Danny said, then introduced himself.

"How can I help you, young Mr. Chase?"

"I'm having some trouble with time."

"So early?" Einstein chuckled. "I thought only those of my age had a problem with time. The best way to deal with time is not to think of the future. I never think of the future. It always comes soon enough"

"I think you might as well explain everything," Murg suggested.

"Do you have a few minutes to spare, sir?"

"Not at my age, but I'm willing to listen. Maybe," he began

with his dark eyes twinkling, " you have a challenge I can solve. You appear to be a young man with a question on your mind. Sit." Einstein motioned to the porch swing, then cleared a space for Danny to sit.

He explained his entire story, from the car accident that had killed Mom and Sarah to helping Kalyde and traveling time. Danny mentioned those he had visited, the questions he'd asked about changing time, and the advice he'd been given.

Albert Einstein listened carefully, only interjecting to ask a few questions. When Danny was finished, Einstein looked at him strangely. "You don't believe me, do you?" Danny asked dejectedly.

"I believe you have suffered a great tragedy. But an extraterrestrial gifting you with a machine that can time travel. Even you must admit that your story sounds fantastic."

Danny nodded. "Sort of like HG Wells' ornithopter. The bike wasn't supposed to time travel, just bend space so I could travel quickly from one point to the next."

"Just?"

"Yeah. Teleporting, you know. I thought I read somewhere you said imagination was more important than knowledge. Were you misquoted?"

Einstein chuckled. "So I did. If one can bend light with gravity, couldn't one do the same with distance? If it is land, there is more to pull and shape. Didn't you tell me that the bicycle couldn't fly?"

Danny nodded. "You said that time is an aspect. If light can be manipulated, why couldn't time?"

"Is time even real?" Einstein asked. "Or just a measurement created by Man to keep track of things? We attribute decay and entropy to time; but even if we weren't measuring time, those things would still happen. And as you probably know, I don't agree with the probability theory for explaining light. Waves and particles. Bah! I do not believe that God plays dice.

Somewhere, there is certainty."

"Tell him that the gift of fantasy is more important than a talent for absorbing positive knowledge," Murg suggested. "That's a paraphrased quote."

Danny was getting a little miffed. "I know you are a great man, but everyone makes mistakes, even geniuses. You didn't trust your math, so you missed discovering the expanding universe. Hubble discovered it instead."

"Ach, that is true."

"Do you think certainty means stability?" Danny asked.

"Listen, young man. Do you have any proof? If so, I may be able to help you."

"I could tell you of the future."

"That would do me little good. In my condition, I don't believe I will experience too much of the future."

"Why don't we take him on a journey?" Murg suggested.

"Would you like to travel with me?" Danny asked. "With Murg and me?"

"I'm afraid I've never been a good traveler and in my current condition . . ."

"You won't even have to pedal. We can just think our way there," Danny replied.

"But there is only one seat," Einstein pointed out, motioning to the bicycle.

"I can change that," Danny said as he moved to the Spacelander. Placing his hands on the bicycle, he thought about a tandem. Imagined it. The Spacelander changed into a two-seater with a carrier on the back for the calico.

"Amazing! How did you do that?" Einstein asked.

"I just imagined what I wanted it to become, then placed my hands on it to help focus my thoughts."

"Thoughts are energy. Didn't you say it is powered by imagination?" Einstein asked as he carefully descended the steps to examine Kalyde II. Danny nodded. "May I?"

"Of course."

Einstein tried several times, but the bicycle never changed shape. "Maybe it only works for you," he said. "Or maybe your imagination is more powerful than mine," he chuckled. "Mine seems to be stuck. These things happen with age, you know."

"But . . ." Danny began, then quoted Einstein, "the important thing is not to stop questioning."

"True. Very true. We must keep an open mind. Who knows where ideas come from. Do they come from memory, an extrapolation or an expansion on something from memory? Or are they a flash of brilliance that has little or no relation to the past?"

"Come on, I'll show you," Danny said. He rolled the bicycle down the walkway and out the gate, then helped Einstein climb aboard Kalyde II. "I just visited HG Wells in London, the year 1894, so let's go back there. That will show you I'm telling the truth." As he focused on Wells, Danny began backpedaling.

"Are you watching where you are going?" Einstein asked.

Danny kept focusing. Kept backpedaling. Why weren't they going anywhere? Then Danny suddenly recalled chasing the Ferrari. When he hadn't believed, the bicycle had slowed down. "You don't believe this will work, do you?"

"I'm trying to keep an open mind. With imagination, anything is possible."

"That didn't exactly sound like a resounding endorsement," Danny murmured.

"Any new theory has its naysayers," Murg commented. "It must be proven."

"But if you don't believe, we won't go anywhere," Danny told Einstein, then realized how childlike he sounded.

The loud honking of a horn and the squealing of tires interrupted their conversation. "A truck!" Danny cried as he applied his brakes. Neither was going to stop in time. Danny changed directions, surging forward, leaving the truck behind as if it were parked.

"I believe this is more of an adventure than I'm ready for," Einstein announced. His eyes were wide and wild.

Danny was growing very angry. He stopped abruptly, then turned around and asked, "Isn't it true, that even by observing an experiment one can have an impact on it?" Einstein agreed. "Then your disbelief is affecting this experiment."

"I'm sorry. I have an open mind; but I require proof, as any good scientist would, to accept something as true."

"You want to go home, right?" Danny asked.

"I am ready if the experiment is ended."

Danny had concluded that Einstein couldn't help him. Maybe only Kalyde could help him. Maybe only he, Danny Chase, could help himself. Socrates had said as much. But before Danny departed, he wanted to give Einstein something to think about.

Danny looked toward Einstein's house, now almost a block away. "Okay. You don't have to believe. But you do need to help me. See yourself at home, standing at the steps that lead to the front porch" Danny kept his eyes on the porch. "Pretend you are already there. Standing there. Are you doing this? Seeing this in your mind?"

"I wish I were home," Einstein agreed.

With his eyes locked on the front porch steps, Danny also wished they were there. Saw them there. Everything suddenly disappeared in a bright flash as though they were having their picture taken, then they reappeared on the sidewalk next to the front porch steps of Einstein's house.

"Amazing! I . . . How did you do that?"

"With imagination and belief," Danny replied as he climbed off Kalyde II.

"That was truly amazing. Unless I passed out, we seemed to skip as though distance had been folded like a piece of paper and we'd punched through it to shorten the distance. Where else can we go?"

"I don't know. As you can see now, it helps if all those who are riding use their imagination to visualize the destination."

"Yes, imagination powers almost all discoveries. Science is nothing more than the refinement of everyday thinking, and imaging is a big part of our lives. It promotes change and advancement."

"I think doubt makes the traveling more difficult," Danny said. "Sort of like hauling along extra weight."

"An excellent description of doubt. It is a powerful force and can close the mind to what could be. I believe you. Yes, I do. Can I see more?"

Danny wracked his mind. What would they have in common? "Have you ever been to Nevada, just north of Las Vegas?"

"Of course, out toward the nuclear testing grounds."

"Let's go there." They rode the bicycle down the sidewalk and out into the street. "Start pedaling, and with your mind's eye, see the road winding through the Nevada desert. Close your eyes if it'll help. I'll steer." They began to pick up speed. "But do more than see it. Feel it. Feel the dry air. The heat. Taste the dust. Hear the silence of the desert."

"I'm thirsty already," Murg mentioned.

"Who said that?" Einstein asked, cracking open a closed eye.

"Keep concentrating," Danny told him.

With a roar of a mighty wind ripping down a tunnel, a white flash engulfed them. The brightness quickly disappeared, and they were riding the rainbow high in the sky. Danny looked over his shoulder. Einstein was shaded in lavender. His hair was bright purple and flapping in the wind, trailing behind them.

"You can open your eyes, sir, but keep focusing on the Nevada desert."

Einstein opened his eyes. "Simply amazing. This is the conduit that shunts you from one point in space to another, shortening the distance?"

"Yes, sir."

"Hmm. Have you always been interested in rainbows?" Einstein asked. Danny nodded. "Have you ever dreamed of riding one before?"

Danny thought back, then nodded. "Yes. Yes, I have. I used to dream of riding on it, or sliding along it to find the pot of gold at the end."

"I see. Then . . . what is that ahead of us, at the end of the rainbow?" Einstein asked, pointing to the bright sun off ramp.

"Our exit."

With a bright flash, they rode into the brilliance, then appeared on a two-lane road of asphalt. The highway looked different than when Danny had ridden it before. It was the early fifties, before the deserted stretch of road had become the alien highway; before Las Vegas had become a modern-day boom town.

Einstein was looking around, observing it all with stunned silence. The land itself didn't appear to have changed much over the years. The road ran in the dry flats between mountains covered with sagebrush and manzanita bushes. "This is Nevada," Einstein finally said. "Young Mr. Chase, you have proven the first of your comments to me, about shorting the distance between two points, I suspect, by folding the distance with your imagination and riding the rainbow along the shunt."

"That's not what I wanted to know, sir."

"Yes, I know. It is not important to you how or why it's happening, just that it is. That is youth talking," he told him. Danny frowned. "Your interest was in time and changing time, correct?" Danny nodded. "Then show me we can travel time."

"Ever been to London?" Danny asked. "To Regent Park?"

"Yes, why?"

"We're going there, but it will be the year 1894. Please don't question, just have an open mind," Danny pleaded.

"Remind him the road will be rough," Murg told Danny.

"Is . . . your cat talking?" Einstein asked.

"A great pleasure to meet you, sir!" Murg extended a paw.

Still a bit overwhelmed, Einstein shook the calico's paw. "Do the cats of the future talk?"

"He's a very special cat, sir," Danny replied. Murg adopted a proud stance as she stretched. "Now, to London?"

"Of course! To London! 1894, you did say?"

"Yes!" Danny began pedaling backwards.

"Are you pedaling backwards because you're going backwards in time?"

"Yes."

"The mind and imagination are such a powerful tool. London, here we come." Einstein sounded like an excited young boy headed out on adventure.

In moments, they were engulfed in the white light. They bounced roughly along the tattered and bumpy rainbow, hitting one or two chuckholes that almost dislodged Einstein. "Why do you think it is so bumpy and faded?" Einstein asked, the wind tearing at his words.

"I don't know," Danny began, then said, "Because the past has been traveled by so many before? It's worn out from heavy travel?"

"As good an answer as any."

They rode backwards into the brilliant off ramp, and with a whoosh appeared in London, coasting along a crowded and narrow street running alongside Regent Park. The turn of the century Londoners were astounded by their presence, jumping out of their way and pointing at them.

Einstein studied the locals' clothing, and cocked an ear, listening to the way they talked, cockney accents filling the air. He sniffed the air and smelled the stench of old downtown London. Smoke and soot hung over the city area. "You have done it, young Mr. Chase. You have indeed done it! Amazing! And you have done it with your mind!"

Although Danny thought the magical bicycle really deserved

the credit, he didn't counter Einstein's statement. They rode along for a while, just letting the wild-haired genius absorb the sights, sounds and smells of old London. Finally, Danny asked, "What do you think about my dilemma?"

"You mean your desire to change time?" Einstein asked. "To save your mother and sister to create a better future for you and your family?" Danny nodded. "Do you believe that things happen for a reason?"

"No," Danny said. "Some things just seem to happen. No rhyme. No reason."

"So you have no control over the events in your life?"

"A lot of times, why?"

"As I said earlier, God does not play dice with the universe."

"What does that mean?" Danny asked.

"That things happen for a reason. If your mother and sister had not died, would you have moved to Texas?"

"Probably not as soon. We weren't scheduled to transfer for another six months or so."

"And if you hadn't moved to Texas, you wouldn't have been there in October – been on the run to meet that extra-terrestrial, Kalle . . ."

"I call him Kalyde."

"Kalyde. And if you hadn't been kind to him, helped him, you wouldn't have been given this magical bicycle. Correct?" Einstein asked. "And you had a choice to help or not to help?"

Danny was quiet for a minute. Murg was smiling smugly.

"Danny, do you believe your life has meaning and purpose?"

"I don't know. I guess."

"Do you believe your actions create reactions? That when you do something, it is as though a pebble has been dropped in a pond? Your actions have rippling effects."

"I can see that. If I helped someone cheat on a test, then we both might get in trouble."

"Or that person might never learn the subject, something

they might need later," Einstein added. "Or, they might advance beyond their means without earning it."

"Easier to say," Murg mentioned, "that if you hit someone, Danny, they might hit you back. Or, they might get their friends and they'd gang up on you. Then you'd get your friends . . ."

"If I had that many . . ."

"You do now," Murg pointed out.

"I get the point. How does this help me with my dilemma?"

"I can't make a decision for you," Einstein told him. "It is a decision you must make based on your beliefs, knowledge and memory. Even your imagination. If you can imagine that your actions will make no impact, then do as you wish. If you are concerned about what might happen, then think it through. Did their deaths serve a higher purpose?"

Danny's mom had always said that a parent's purpose was to be there for their children. "Are you a religious man?" Danny wondered.

"My religion consists of humble admiration of the illimitable superior spirit who reveals himself in slight details that we are unable to perceive with our frail and feeble minds."

"Oh. Well, praying on it hasn't helped."

"But it has made you think about it."

"I still don't know what to do," Danny moaned. "Murg mentions that time, once something has occurred, will try to reassert itself after the change."

"So if you prevent the accident, they might die in another way? And your father or even you, might die with them? As I said, actions create ripples and reactions. Consequences. If you are ready to accept them, do as you wish. If you can imagine your present with them present, then you're already more than halfway there. But remember that wouldn't be if they'd survived."

Danny's head was spinning. If they were alive, they'd be one big happy family living in Germany and he'd still live close to Gretchen. But lost would be his new friends, meeting Kalyde, riding the magical bicycle, his adventure, talking with Murg. Which was more selfish? How could he tell? Danny wasn't surprised his mind was a whirl. He was talking to a genius.

"Two geniuses," Murg added.

"Thanks for trying to help me, sir," Danny said as he checked his watch. "But I'm out of time."

"Out of time?"

"It's way past my bedtime . . . in the future."

They returned to Einstein's present. The ride was much more pleasant this time. "Going forward is always better than backwards," Danny told him as he helped Einstein off the bicycle. He helped the genius walk to his front porch.

"I would be interested in having you come visit again sometime. I will think on what you've told me. What we've experienced. Maybe, in some ways, time is like light," Einstein said thoughtfully.

"Except time isn't linear," Murg commented. "And it has more than one aspect, like light has waves and particles."

"I will think on that. It was a pleasure to meet you both. Come again, please." He shook Danny's hand, then Murg's paw.

"We might, sir. Good day."

Danny began pedaling and thinking about home – his house. He was exhausted and couldn't wait to hit the sack. What was the saying? There was no time like the present. He focused on today – the today he'd left some five hours ago. The white flash of light took him to the rainbow highway.

"If you want to get more sleep," Murg suggested, "you might try getting home an hour or so after you left."

"But Kalyde said we couldn't affect time."

"He was talking about distance travel time. Not time travel. Try it."

Danny focused on his present, trying to return an hour after they'd left, getting home around eight instead of midnight. Through the bright sun waiting for them, they appeared in front of their house. Danny checked his watch. It was spinning backwards, the minutes, then hours melting away until it was eight-fifteen.

"What are you going to do?" Murg asked.

Danny walked the bike toward the garage. He was moving unsteadily, feeling a bit dizzy. "In the morning, I'm going to visit Kalyde and see what he has to say. Maybe he knows something about time travel. I would go tonight, but it's too late."

"Then?"

"Then I'm going to check the history books I read earlier today . . . wow, what a day! . . . and see if my visits changed anything for Socrates, Mr. Franklin, Mr. Wells or Mr. Einstein. I'd hate to find out that Franklin was branded a warlock or something." He rolled the bicycle into the garage and flipped on the light.

"Well, we still have electricity," Murg pointed out. Danny looked around the garage. Everything was as he remembered it. "What if everything is all right?" Murg asked.

"I've been thinking about it, and I've decided I should talk with Happy and see what he thinks. It should be his choice."

"You're not going to change something small, see how things change like Franklin suggested?"

"Some would consider saving Happy's life a small thing." Danny yawned. "And even though he's just a surfer now, he's a good person, and keeping him alive would add to the greater good."

"It will change the natural order of things," Murg said. "Alter the circle of life. Didn't you listen to Einstein? Think it through?"

"Murg!"

"You've spoken to everyone else! I thought it was time for me to put in my dollar's worth. What if the young girl, Tania, still drowns when you save Happy? Are you now judge, jury and executioner, deciding who lives and who doesn't?"

Danny sighed wearily. "I don't know. But I hope Kalyde knows something."

Chapter Twenty

Days Before Yesterday

Although he was tired, Danny rose very early Tuesday, even before the papers arrived. Good thing they'd cut four hours off the present while returning last night. Still, Danny felt time-lagged. His circadian rhythm – which he'd learned about in biology class – must be off.

"Come on, Murg," Danny said to the calico sleeping on the back of the couch. "We won't be going far this time. Just back a couple of weeks, and we won't even be moving." Murg didn't move, so Danny picked her up and carried her to the garage.

Still looking sleepy, Murg unleashed a large yawn. When Danny set her on the bicycle, she said, "You're going to meet Kalyde . . . " she yawned again " . . . in your room before you get home from school on the day he gave you the magic bicycle?"

"Exactly." Danny rolled Kalyde II out of the garage, climbed aboard, then closed his eyes. He visualized his room, focusing on Kalyde's arrival; the Cor-ror-o'lan had the bicycle in tow. Everything set in his mind, Danny began backpedaling.

The darkness converged upon them, and the air ripped like fabric being torn, then they were racing through the tattered and faded rainbow tunnel. It only took moments, then they reappeared in Danny's bedroom. He had to slam on the brakes not to crash into the wall and fly out the window.

"Glad we have amazing brakes," Murg said, then yawned.

"I hear footsteps," Danny whispered. The door opened and Kalyde walked in, guiding the magic bicycle. "Hello Kalyde!"

"Friend Danny!" Kalyde cried.

Danny jumped off Kalyde II.

Kah-laye-dee rushed forward, and they hugged. Then Kalyde noticed Danny's bicycle. He'd made it identical so the Cor-ror-o'lan would notice. "Is that . . . how can that be?"

"I have a lot to tell you," Danny said. He checked the clock. He would get home from school in thirty minutes. "And not much time to explain."

Kalyde sat patiently through Danny's tale but often looked amazed, his wide eyes the size of saucer cups. "That is an incredible story, friend Danny."

"You believe me?"

"Of course. Why wouldn't I? I am sorry to say we know very little about time travel, but with imagination, anything is possible. And as I said, you have a very powerful imagination."

"Well, what should I do?"

"Follow your heart."

That didn't sound like Socrates. "I know what I want to do," Danny began. "What would you do?"

"We Cor-ror-o'lan's are happy with where we are. How

we are. We see no need to change time. If we wish to change, we work in the present to change the future. We have discovered that everything happens for a reason, and that everything has a place. Maybe your mother and sister died so you could change time. Or maybe they died so you would explore time but not change it. That is for you to decide. You must search your own soul. Did any of the wise men give you any useful advice?"

Slowly he replied, "I don't know, yet."

"I'm going to see if my travels changed anything, as Ben Franklin suggested, then, if nothing has, I'm going to ask Happy, then Sarah and my mother what they would like to do. You know, offer a hypothetical situation like I did with Jason. Murg here thinks I should leave things alone. Not interrupt the natural order of things."

"Murg could be a Cor-ror-o'lan," Kalyde replied.

Murg preened, and Danny sighed.

"Danny," Kalyde continued, "you are a good person, I trust you."

"Thanks, Kalyde. That means a lot to me." Danny checked the clock. "We have to go. I don't want to meet myself."

"You will never know you're here until you return here," Kalyde said.

"Now that's confusing," Murg said.

Danny and Kalyde hugged once more, then Danny climbed aboard Kalyde II and they traveled forward in time.

They arrived just after the newspapers were dumped on the curb, and the truck was driving away. "Sorry, Danny, the driver said. "We're running a little late."

"I understand," Danny replied. "I seem to be running short of time all the time."

Before the school bell rang, Danny talked with Christina. He claimed to be working on a time-traveling story about a magic bicycle, then outlined the plot.

"It's a great idea! I love it," Christina told him, her eyes flashing. "Go with it." She touched his hand. "Not only does it sound interesting, but it's probably good for you. You know, sort of a release. I think they call it cathartic."

"It seems to be," Danny said. It also seemed to be driving him crazy.

When asked about saving those who had died, Christina said, "If it's me, don't ask me. Just save me. I can't imagine why someone wouldn't want to live." Her expression suddenly saddened as she thought of something. "Unless someone else had to die so I could live. I – I don't think I could live with that." Then she suddenly smiled. "But nothing's going to happen to me." She looked at the clock. "Hey, the bell's going to ring here soon. I'll see you at lunch!"

"I'll be in the library," Danny replied. "Doing research."

"Go, boy, go!" she laughed.

Her words washed away some of Danny's melancholy.

At lunch, Danny went to the library and skimmed the books on Socrates, Franklin, Wells and Einstein that he'd read before. There was no change in the book about the Father of Western Philosophy, but there were minor alterations in Franklin's history. After his experiment with electricity, there had been charges of witchcraft. They hadn't amounted to much more than bad public opinion.

There was also a reference to him fiddling with the idea of a bicycle – an idea later brought to life by the Scotsman Kirkpatrick McMillan, at least that hadn't changed – much. The same man had invented it, although he gave credit to Franklin for inspiring him.

Danny looked up the bicycle in the encyclopedia. In this time, McMillan had invented the current design of the bicycle. There was no mention of Lawson or Stanley. Yes, he'd changed history. The modern bicycle was attributed to 1839, not 1879. Had he stolen Lawson's and Stanley's claim to fame?

With apprehension, he checked on the histories of HG Wells and Albert Einstein. They seemed unchanged, and Danny breathed a sigh of relief.

As Danny backpedaled through time, the angry winds tore at him. The handlebars threatened to leap from his grasp. Danny recalled Happy's face, his dark wayward hair, his deeply tanned skin, and his shining smile – a beacon of brightness on any bleary day – though Hawaii didn't have many bleary days.

The bicycle suddenly twisted, then bounced airborne. The hard landing almost threw Danny, but he determinedly hung on.

"This is worse than usual," came Murg's telepathic voice. "Even the walls are rippling and bucking. I have concluded that this time travelling may be unhealthy. Or maybe it has something to do with the slight changes we've caused in history. They might be rippling outward, like a pebble dropped in a pool."

"I just wish I was already there!"

The bicycle went into machine gun fast gyrations, then the tunnel shrank on itself, imploding.

As if he'd switched television channels, Danny and Murg were suddenly coasting along a stretch of beach. He was at the bottom of an embankment, the lush mountains and craggy volcanos a magnificent backdrop beyond the roadway atop the nearby ridge. The sandy parking lot was very crowded. Along the shore, a large crowd watched surfers ride the waves and shoot curls.

"I know this place!" Danny cried. It was Happy's favorite beach, called 'The Breakers' by locals. He and Happy came here – had come here – all the time to watch surfers and to even surf themselves. Danny had failed miserably. Happy was a natural. He said the 'o' in Dano helped. The joke was that white boys couldn't surf.

A familiar figure guided Happy's bright red and yellow board toward the shore. "It's Happy!" Danny whispered, overcome with emotion. His heart seemed to swell to bursting, feeling a hundred times larger and making it hard to breathe. He couldn't stop smiling. Danny blinked quickly, trying to clear his blurry vision.

"Just keep cool, like a cat," Murg told him. "You and your family moved yesterday, but tell him you've been delayed a little until later this morning. That way he won't be suspicious. For a surfer-dude, he's fairly observant."

Danny swallowed, took a deep breath, then rolled his bicycle toward Happy.

With his surfboard tucked underneath his arm, Happy was just leaving the water. When he saw Danny, he stopped and smiled. "Aloha!" he yelled as he waved. "This is a surprise! I thought you'd left for Germany already."

"Our stuff is gone, but the base needed Dad for something – something to do with paperwork and orders – so we're here for the rest of the morning," Danny lied. "So I came to visit!" He noticed that Happy was looking at him strangely. "Something wrong?"

"I guess not. You just look . . . I dunno . . . different. Even your voice sounds different."

"You're older, and you've grown!" Murg told him. "This was some fifteen months ago!"

"I think I'm coming down with a cold," Danny said. He couldn't stay here long. Happy might start asking difficult questions, and despite having just done it, Danny hated lying. Now, how was he going to put this? Should he just ask him as he had – would? – Jason? Or mention writing a story as he had with Christina? No, that wouldn't work. He would have to mention it as an idea for a story.

"Where's your suit?" Happy asked. "Don't you want to

surf one more time? Hang ten!" He laughed. "I've been practicing the dead cockroach." Happy set down his board, then
flopped on his back with his feet and hands waving in the air.

"You've already hung twenty," Murg said.

"I don't have much time," Danny said, then glanced at his
watch.

"You don't look like you're feeling well," Happy said. "You
okay?"

"That cold," Danny lied again, then sniffed. He hated this.
"Hey, Happy, if I was drowning, would you rescue me?" Danny
asked, looking out at the crystal blue waters.

"Of course, man! I'd never let my best friend drown. But
that won't happen. You're a good swimmer. Why?"

"Well, I was thinking about trying to surf again, but I keep
thinking that I might hit my head on the board and be knocked
out or something."

"Hey, don't worry, man. I'd be near. Come on! Let's do it!
Don't be afraid!" Happy encouraged him.

"Yeah, I know. But what if you weren't, and I died? If you
could change things, like time travel in HG Wells' *Time Machine,* would you come back and save me?"

"I don't know. Probably. Man, you and your imagination!
Hey, are you working on a story idea?"

Danny smiled. "Happy, you are so sharp."

"Hey, man. Do you want to be saved?" Happy asked jok-
ingly.

That, Danny thought, was the crux of the question.

"Are you sure you're feeling okay? You don't look too good.
Come over here and sit."

"I guess I'm just down about moving," Danny mentioned.
They walked to a cluster of huge boulders at the bottom of the
hill and along the edge of the beach.

The sound of gulls filled the air and the silence between
the two friends. The winds gusted, blowing a little sand over

them.

"If I had the time machine," Danny asked as he sat, "would you want me to come back and save you?"

"Like I said, you and your imagination," Happy laughed, then saw Danny was serious. "You trying to give me a headache?"

Danny shook his head no.

"I don't know. I guess it depends." Happy was perplexed.

"Really? On how old you are or were?"

"Naw. Come to think of it, probably not. It wouldn't be right to go back and change things. Mess with the cosmic order of the universe."

"He is very wise for his age," Murg's thoughts came to Danny. "I wonder if he was a cat in a previous life?"

"W . . . why not?" Danny asked.

"A couple of reasons, I guess. This is really weird. You know, I talked about this a couple of months back when Leila was really sick. She said that everybody dies, it's natural and part of Kahuna's plans. It's just that some people's sunset comes earlier than others. If we knew when we were going to die, we might become consumed by the knowledge, and that might take the fun out of life. Sort of like revealing the end of a mystery novel." Happy laughed. "I can laugh now that's she's healthy."

"In Hawaiian faith, our lives and our deaths are in the hands of Kahuna and Huna," he continued. "I believe there is a master plan. Why go back and rewrite what's already well written? Unless you're a writer of course." He winked. "I vaguely remember a legend where the man's life, Kai'kai, was determined by the circumstances of his death. In our culture, both birth and death are celebrated as part of the cycle. I mean, if I died helping somebody, but if you saved me and they died, then that would be really wrong. Maybe one of the reasons I was alive was to save that person. What do you think?"

Slack-jawed, Danny stared at him.

"I think," Murg offered, "you need to study the history, culture, and religion of a place you're living in instead of reading comics all the time."

Danny ignored him. He couldn't believe his ears. "So I shouldn't save you?" That hadn't sounded very hypothetical.

"I don't think so. Hey, Danny, my friend, don't worry. Nothing's going to happen to me. I promise to be careful. Just for you, no handstands!"

Despite wanting to weep, Danny managed a feeble smile.

Happy suddenly grew serious, his gaze intent and piercing. "Danny, I don't want to know about the future. I want to live every minute, revel in it. I might die tomorrow. That's the way a person should live their life, don't you think? We can't go around being scared of dying all the time."

What about being afraid of living? Danny wondered.

"Nice bicycle," Happy said. "Is that your time machine?"

Danny choked. "When I wish," Danny finally managed.

Happy looked at him strangely, then said, "I feel that way about my surfboard. It seems to suspend time sometimes. Other times, it seems to sling me into the future, the day passing by so fast I can't remember it."

Danny glanced at his watch. "Speaking of time. I'd better get going." Danny wanted to stay longer, but he had a feeling he'd stayed long enough. He'd learned what he'd wanted to know, but it was difficult to believe. Happy didn't want to be saved. Danny couldn't bear it. This would be the last time he'd see his friend.

"At least you have a chance to say goodbye," Murg told him. "We're here, so make the most of it."

"Hey, don't look so sad," Happy said. "We'll see each other again. Best friends can overcome time."

Danny swallowed hard. "You know, you've always been a great friend, Happy. You're fun to be with and you make me see things differently, even better sometimes."

"Hey, bud, don't get so heavy on me," Happy said, clapping a hand on Danny's shoulder. Danny sniffed, and they shook hands. "Everything okay at home? With your mom and dad?"

Danny choked. "For now."

"Man, you can't worry so much about what's going to happen when you move. Or what's going to happen tomorrow. You'll go gray!" Happy told him. He seemed to scrutinize Danny, then a realization suddenly hit him. "Hey, this is going to sound crazy, but you're serious, aren't you? I don't know why I . . . I guess you actually seem older. Sound older. Sadder. I don't like that."

"It's the miles, not the years," Murg thought.

"Danny, I'm going to die, aren't I? And you're asking my permission to save me, aren't you? This isn't hypothetical, is it?" Happy asked, his expression torn between disbelief and belief.

"I've always been a lousy liar," Danny admitted.

Happy was thoughtful. Danny started to say something, but Happy interrupted him. "I don't want to know too much. It's enough to know you'd have been there if you could. If it was meant to be . . . "

"But I'm here now, Happy! I could be there then! Maybe this was meant to be, also!" Danny cried. "We have a second chance!"

Finally Happy said, "I don't know what to say." He took a deep breath. "Danny, you can't keep beating yourself up over it. Kahuna will take care of me."

Danny wanted to scream at him, make him understand. How could Happy be so calm!

"It was good of you to come back and ask. And to say goodbye," Happy told him. "You are my best friend. Even after I'm gone, remember, my spirit will be with you always."

Danny thought for a minute, then said, "You know, I think I have some time to surf, after all."

"Great! Come on!"

Danny climbed off his bicycle. He was surprised Murg didn't say anything, but she didn't. Danny stripped off his shirt, socks and shoes, and surfed like he had never surfed before.

"You are incredible!" Happy told him. "Have you been practicing?"

"Nope! But after riding backwards in time, this is easy."

Happy looked at him strangely, then they laughed heartily.

Then Danny told him about Kalyde and Kalyde II.

"Amazing! You are so lucky! Now you don't have to go to the library to do research for historical novels!"

Danny didn't tell him about Mom or Sarah. He already knew what Happy would say. And as the day seemed to speed along, Happy and Danny played and laughed and had fun, both understood that this was their last day together.

Chapter Twenty-One

Gretchen and Sarah

The morning alarm sounded, and Danny thought he heard Big Jim's van depart. Danny rolled over and groaned. He didn't want to get up to deliver papers or go to school.

Happy's refusal to let Danny save him had thrown him for a loop. As Christina had said, "Who wouldn't want to be saved?" Happy, that's who. And Danny had to respect his wishes.

As Danny lay in a dazed funk, he tried to remember the last two days. He hadn't been with it, sleepwalking through school on Wednesday and Thursday. It seemed the harder he tried to understand things and reconcile events, the more confused he became.

He'd drifted away, caught with one foot in the past and one in the present. Murg said he'd been time traveling too much and had time lag – sort of jet lag but worse.

What day is it? Friday morning? Boy, was he getting confused.

Wednesday he'd thought his luck had changed when Christina agreed to bicycling and to a movie on Thursday. Danny's feet hadn't touched the ground after lunch, his head in the clouds. That only made him more like a zombie. Christina reminded him of Gretchen and Sarah, and Danny missed them both. Could he tell Gretchen about Christina? He decided he should visit Gretchen. Soon.

Wednesday night Danny and Big Jim ate ratburgers, which were really fast food hamburgers. Several times there had been a long uncomfortable silence between them. Eventually, Jim asked if something was wrong. If he could help with something. He claimed he was familiar with good advice from a good book.

Danny didn't feel like talking about it to a stranger, not even a jolly minister who told corny jokes and had a driving code language all his own. But for some reason he opened up. They talked about death. No surprise; Big Jim agreed with Murg about the natural order of things. Murg had acted even more superior than usual after being informed of Big Jim's remarks.

If he'd wanted to go back and save JFK, Danny thought, everyone would probably be all for it.

Thursday he'd gotten in trouble for forgetting some history homework he'd actually finished, so he would lose ten points off the top. He'd also forgotten about an algebra quiz.

Christina had loved riding tandem, and they had ridden well together, functioning as a well-oiled team. Was it something natural? Or magical?

Christina had talked about her art, her family, and lastly, cheerleading. Danny had listened, then told her about Happy – his nightmare about Happy. Christina had hugged him. She'd lost her grandfather last year. She'd said the passage of time had helped her accept the loss, if not understand it. And time would help him accept the loss of Happy, Sarah, and his mother. Christina had also suggested using it in his time-traveling story. It would make a nice twist.

After the movie, they'd ridden back to Christina's house in relative silence. Danny couldn't remember anything about the movie, and that had blown Christina's mind. She had asked Danny to come watch her cheer at Friday's football game. Tonight! Of course he would! That he would remember. As Christina went inside, she wished him a safe trip, reminding him to keep his head on riding and his thoughts on her. That had jolted him. He'd promised he would be there.

Murg, pushing open the door, brought Danny back to the present. "What am I going to do with you? You're in love, young love, but instead of having your head in the clouds, you've got them in yesterday and what-ifs. And your funk is contagious. Hey, I have an idea! Why don't we visit Gretchen this morning and raise my spirits?"

"I was thinking the same thing. We could go, then time travel back so I won't be late for school."

"I'll skip the usual human comment about great minds thinking alike, since it doesn't apply here."

"What do I tell Gretchen about Christina?"

"Everything! She'll be very happy for you."

"You think so?" Danny asked.

Murg nodded.

"Hey, if we leave after we deliver the morning edition," he did a quick calculation, "Gretchen will just be getting out of school for the weekend."

"Let's do it!" Murg said.

"Hey, I can hear you, and we're not on the bicycle!"

"So you can. Amazing!" Murg said. "I love magic. Or maybe you just needed to know we could communicate. Get out of bed! Or I'll use the old fashion method." Murg brandished her claws. "Let's go!"

Danny hopped to his feet and quickly got dressed. He scooped up the calico and jogged downstairs to the bicycle. Murg jumped onto the carrier, and they headed down the driveway.

Immediately after the last morning paper landed, Danny began picturing Gretchen and rural Munich. It was green and hilly, craggy mountains stood majestically in the distant background. The houses and buildings had an old feeling to them, and the architecture was different than any place he'd been – gothic, they called it.

Gretchen's place was in a nice, neat and orderly neighborhood with lots of fountains. He remembered the roads being very narrow, barely wide enough for two cars. The trains had to run along the hillsides.

Most of all, he remembered what Gretchen looked like. Her hair was the color of spun gold, her eyes the blue of the sky, and her skin reminiscent of ivory. No wonder he thought of her when he saw Christina. Was there something wrong with that?

Quite often Gretchen's cheeks were flushed, and she smiled a lot, revealing prominent dimples. She loved to sing, and she and Sarah had sung duets while they hiked.

As Danny rode into the sun, the world silently split asunder, then he was streaking across the rainbow highway. It ended quickly with the burst of light, and he rolled to a stop just outside her house. When Danny saw her walking away from the bus, he quickly changed the bicycle into a tandem. "Hey, babe! Want to go for a ride?!"

"Danny! What're you doing here?!" Her accent was thick with excitement. "And Murg?"

The calico bowed.

"I came to chauffeur you!" Danny said.

"Really? Have you moved back?" Gretchen asked, her eyes alight and dancing. Danny shook his head.

"Oh. Well, how long are you here?"

"Not long, so climb on!" Danny encouraged.

Laughing, she did, holding onto her hat as they took off.

"We have to pedal in time with each other," Danny explained, and soon they were racing down the road.

"How are you doing, my friend?" she asked.

Danny let out a big sigh.

"I thought so. Want to talk about it?"

Danny poured out his heart, rambling on for at least an hour. He told her about everything without letting her interrupt – from the beginning when he'd met Kalyde to getting Kalyde II, traveling back in time, talking with Happy, and getting bounced all around the rainbow highway.

"Why don't you tell her about Christina?" Murg asked.

Danny ignored the calico.

"I'm sorry to hear about Happy." Gretchen replied, taking everything in stride. "Good friends are hard to find, right?" She squeezed his shoulder.

He nodded, and Murg meowed.

"Yes, you are a good friend, too, Murg. This time travel stuff sounds dangerous to me."

"It is," Murg said. "Bumping about. Being chased by dinosaurs and witch hunters."

Danny heard Murg, but if Gretchen did, she said nothing.

"You believe me then?" Danny asked.

"Sure. After all, you're here."

"You want a test ride?"

"Of course, silly!"

Because he'd had good luck with his visits to the beach near Myrtle Beach, Danny pictured them there.

"WOW!" Gretchen yelled as their surroundings split, and they rode into the sun. The clouds quickly gave way to the gleaming highway of colors stretched across the heavens. Gretchen's smile was broad, her eyes filled with wonder. She began to hum, and that reminded Danny of Kalyde, so he joined in. Shortly, they entered the white light and appeared on the beach, rolling across the surface of the shallow water.

"WOW!" was all Gretchen could say.

"And this is different than time travel?" she asked finally.

He nodded.

"Time travel is like being hooked to a runaway train over bad tracks?"

Danny nodded. "Backwards! Do you want me to help you if you're in trouble?"

"You mean if I die, don't you? Danny, I'm not going to die. Not everyone you care for is going to die on you," Gretchen told him.

"But if you did . . ."

She rolled her eyes. "I can't help you solve your dilemma with Sarah. I'd like to see Sarah alive, too, but I don't know about changing history. What if we royally screw up something? What if you die instead? Or both of you?"

"Then let's go see Sarah and ask her – like I did Happy!"

"Oh, no," Murg groaned.

Still, Gretchen didn't respond.

Didn't she hear Murg? Danny wondered.

"Danny, I don't know . . ."

"Please! It won't take long. And we both remember what Sarah looked like. We won't have any trouble getting there. Please!"

"Okay! Okay!" She looked at her watch. "I'd love to see her, too! Just remember, I have to be home soon for dinner!"

"Deal!" Danny told her what to do, how to picture Sarah, then bring her to life. He remembered his sister very clearly. Her strawberry blond hair, dark brown eyes and the patch of freckles that covered her pert nose. She often wore an impish, almost secretive smile as if she knew something funny that you didn't.

This time the trip was much easier. The colors were still muted, and the screaming winds were piercing, but the gaps and holes were fewer, and the ride was smoother, although still hair-raising. For whatever reason, the tandem handled well instead of like a bucking bronco. Gretchen didn't enjoy it, though; she was pale, tight-lipped, and her grip white-knuckled.

Danny concentrated on finding Sarah when she was strolling through the woods by herself. And that's where they found her. She was picking flowers.

Both Murgs puffed and stiffened at the sight of each other. "Oh, no! That's me! I remember this now! I thought I was dreaming!"

"Danny! Gretchen! Murg?" Sarah looked at her Murg. "What're you doing here?"

"Traveling time," Danny said. "We've come from the future." He had decided the best approach was the direct one.

"Danny, you and your imagination! I hope Mom doesn't cut off your supply of comic books. I think you'd go stir-crazy."

"No, really," Gretchen started to explain. She told her today's date. Sarah corrected her, but both persisted vehemently.

"Okay, I'll play along," Sarah laughed. "Why the visit?" She looked strangely at Murg who hadn't approached her. Instead, the Murgs were staring intently at each other.

"This is the Murg from the future. Us, too. Uh, you die in a . . ." Danny began.

Suddenly, Sarah reached out with a hand and put it over his mouth. "This isn't a joke, is it?" Her expression was serious as she looked at her brother for a long time.

Both he and Gretchen shook their heads.

Sarah laughed and sobbed at the same time. "I don't want to know – when."

"I'm sorry," Danny said. He hadn't expected this. "We can help!"

"No, changing the past to save someone you love only

happens in romance novels," Sarah said.

"But this bicycle is magic. I'll show you!"

"Sarah!" came a call sounding like their father. He walked from the woods, surprised to see them. "Oh, hi, Danny. Gretchen. What're you two doing here?" he asked. Gretchen eloquently explained about her parents' new bicycle.

Danny's father from the past came over to examine it. "It's a nice one. And this cat, it could be Murg's twin."

Nobody spoke.

His father patted Danny on the shoulder and gave him a big smile.

Danny had almost forgotten what that was like.

"Son, it's getting late. You'd better ride back to Gretchen's house and head home for dinner. It's a long way, though. If you're tired, I can put the bicycle in the trunk."

"NO!" Gretchen said hastily. "No. We can make it."

"Suit yourself. Let's go, Sarah."

Sarah turned to them as she left. "Talk to Mom before you do anything, okay?" she told him.

Danny nodded, saying, "Let's go home."

"How do we get there?" Gretchen asked.

"Concentrate on your place. Think – there's no place like home. I'll see your house, just like before, but picture us returning only a few minutes after we left. Okay?" Gretchen nodded.

They pedaled out into a clear stretch, then raced along the narrow country road.

"I can't believe she didn't want to know!" Danny said angrily. He didn't understand. Was Jason the only one who wanted to be saved? Who wanted to live? Well, he and Jason anyway, Danny decided.

The world split with a white flash, and they were flying forward across the arching rainbow trail, barely skimming along the colors.

Gretchen smiled sadly. "You know, seeing Sarah, and remembering seeing her at the funeral home, makes me feel . . . I don't know. Weird."

"You don't feel immortal, anymore," Murg said. "Life is precious. Death helps give meaning to life by making us understand how short it can be. Cats believe that death is a call to a higher service, and that life is only a preamble, a place to practice being yourself. Open your senses and immerse yourself in life!"

"Murg," Danny said with exasperation. "I'm trying to concentrate on Gretchen's house." He was focused, but he still couldn't help but wonder what the future was going to be like without Sarah and Mom. The present was already bleak. Would it get worse? And what if something happened to Gretchen? Or Murg?

"Aren't we going a little fast?" asked Murg.

"Huh?" Danny suddenly noticed their incredible pace. Light flashed. The rainbow was gone, replaced by a world they'd never seen before.

"Oh, my God! Where are we?" Gretchen asked.

"When are we?" Murg asked more appropriately.

"What happened to my house?" Gretchen cried as she jumped off the tandem and ran toward the derelict structure that had once been her home. It looked long deserted, the stonework worn and crumbling. Even the boards over the windows were rotted and falling apart. The roof had several holes in it, and most of the shingles were missing. The lawn was mostly dirt and weeds, and the tiered flower beds were long dead.

"We've shot too far into the future," Murg muttered.

"If this is our future," Danny said, "then I want to change the past." Danny climbed off Kalyde II and followed Gretchen, rolling the bicycle along. Murg didn't move.

He stared past the abandoned stretch of homes. Massive gleaming structures stood where Munich's old world architecture had once blended with the new. It was now a high tech city of cold sparkling metal. Many of the buildings appeared to be blown from glass, their mirrored surfaces, reflecting the green-ish-yellow sky. Monorails moved along towering bridges stretching from one building to the next as if an endless silver snake.

"Is that the future Munich?" Danny asked. "Yecch!" He coughed.

"We're really in the future!" Gretchen started to panic. "How did we . . ." She coughed several times.

Danny was also having trouble breathing. "The air's foul. Come on, Gretchen, get back on the bicycle."

"But what year is this?"

Danny glanced again at Munich. The air around it appeared blurred as though heated. Then he looked more carefully; a shimmering dome surrounded it – sealed and protected it. "Come on, Gretchen, I don't like it here," he coughed, "when-ever here is. Let's go home."

Gretchen nodded and climbed back onto the bicycle. She was using her shirt tail to cover her nose and mouth.

"Now, concentrate on your house and front yard like you saw it this morning," Danny said, then coughed. "Now backpedal and we'll be fine." With surprising ease, they fell into a rhythm. "Close your eyes. You're safe on Kalyde II." He pictured Gretchen's house with all the tiered flowered beds in front. The Heinrichs were home. Now!

Suddenly, the future world swallowed them, and they were slinging backwards across the ramshackle highway of colors to-ward the past.

"I wish we'd found a newspaper," Murg said.

"I don't care what the date was."

"Danny? What did you say?"

"There's no place like home," Danny told Gretchen. "Your home." He glanced past her and along the sickly rainbow bridge. Again, it didn't look good, but it looked healthier – brighter – and less tainted then when he and Murg had traveled to the past. Having Gretchen imagine their destination must be helping. Maybe three heads were better than two. Or maybe this rainbow going to the future was less traveled than the one to the past.

They were abruptly engulfed by the white light, then appeared on Schmeisser Street – slowly rolling to a stop in front of Gretchen's house. Everything looked as they both remembered it.

"That was incredible," she said weakly, "but I'm not sure I want to try it again. The ride to the beach was fun but not the time traveling. I don't know how you can stand it." She shivered. "And Munich . . . horrible. But, Danny, please come back and take me riding again soon. I have missed you so much."

"Gretchen! Dinner time!"

"That's my dad! Coming father!" she called back. "We've been gone almost two hours!"

They had mistimed their return. He was probably going to be late for school.

"I guess you should wear a watch or put a clock on the bike," Murg suggested.

"Danny, my dad probably shouldn't see you. Don't worry. I'll keep your secret! I think it's great! Keep riding! 'Bye!" Blond curls bouncing, Gretchen ran to the front door.

"But – "

"You can mention Christina next time. Let's go!" Murg encouraged. "You don't want to be seen by her dad!" The feline poked Danny in the ribs.

As they took off down the street, the bicycle slowly transformed into a single seater. "Home, James!" Danny pictured their house in Ft. Worth. As he did, he really wondered if there was no place like home.

"Gretchen," her father asked as he let go of the front window curtain, "who was that? He looked a lot like Danny Chase."

It had been hard for the colonel to see the boy clearly, but the calico on the back reminded him of Sarah's cat, Murgitroyd.

"It's Peter Smith, Daddy, a friend of mine from school. He just moved here from America. He's in my music class. He's nice and very cute."

Her father frowned. He was dressed in his Air Force uniform and looked very stern. "He sure reminds me a lot of Danny Chase." He shrugged and moved away from the window. "Reminds me I should call David."

"Now that you mention it," Gretchen said, flicking her hair past her shoulders, "he does remind me of Danny. I wonder how he's doing. I miss him."

Gretchen's father watched her walk into the kitchen where her mother was grumbling about burning dinner.

Colonel Heinrich had planned to chide Gretchen for being out so late, but it had slipped his mind. He would have sworn that boy was Danny Chase. Surely Captain Chase would call if they were in town. He'd have to give David a call.

Chapter Twenty-Two

Stolen

Arm in arm, Danny and Christina walked out the front door of the Twin Eagles Junior High School. Danny was smiling. Ever since visiting Gretchen and Sarah, things had gone better than they had all week. He'd remembered his homework and aced a biology pop quiz. At lunch, Christina had also accepted his white rose, a token of their friendship.

If only he didn't feel like he was catching something.

When they reached the cheerleader's bus, Christina squeezed his arm. "Danny, I gotta go. See ya tonight. Don't forget."

"I'll be there," he replied as he watched her board; then he walked to the bicycle racks.

At first, he thought he'd forgotten where he'd left Kalyde

II. Then Danny saw his empty chain, the lock dangling use-lessly. The links had been cut! Somebody had stolen Kalyde II! Oh, no! What was he going to do?

Danny sank to his knees and fought back the tears. His gift from Kalyde – a substitute for Kalyde's company – had been ripped off. And without the bicycle, he wouldn't be able to go to the game tonight! He'd miss seeing Christina perform! And . . . and he wouldn't be able to go back to the past! Talk to his mother! His life would be ruined!

Oh, no! What if the thief discovered that Kalyde II had special properties? That it was magical! What a disaster that would be!

Murg! Murg was smart! She would know what to do!

Danny ran home.

A little over forty minutes later, Danny fumbled with the front door lock, staggered through the house into the kitchen, then stuck his mouth under the faucet. His head followed.

Bouncing, Murg followed her companion, wondering what was going on.

Finally, Danny came up sputtering for air. He was drip-ping, and Murg warily backed out of range. Danny grabbed a towel. "Damn it all, Murg! Somebody stole Kalyde II! I'm still cursed! It's because I haven't changed things! Now it's too late! What am I gonna do!" He stared angrily at the calico. "It's too bad I just can't summon it magically like an enchanted chariot. BAMPH! I think of it being here and it teleports into the kitchen." Danny paused, a look of wonder settling on his face.

"Amazing. A human teenager has an original thought," Murg responded dryly.

"You think all I need to do is concentrate – picture the bicycle standing in front of us?"

Murg nodded. "You really should listen to advice sometimes. What did Socrates say about letting emotions rule your actions?"

"Oh, yeah. Do you really think summoning Kalyde II will work?"

"You have nothing to lose." The calico shrugged, then said, "Only one way to find out! Wish with all your will and imagination that it returns to you. See it coming back to you. It's worth a try. You have quite an imagination, and with that and magic, anything is possible."

"Okay, here goes!" Danny sank to the kitchen floor, leaning back against the cabinets. Then he closed his eyes and began to imagine that the bicycle – sleek, red and gleaming – was returning to him like a rocket, moving swiftly and gracefully around all obstacles.

Spike was laughing so hard that he almost fell off Danny's bicycle while plummeting downhill. He grabbed the handlebars and let out a whoop followed by a holler. This old, battered bicycle was so sweet! He'd never ridden anything that moved so smoothly or so fast. No wonder Chase had beaten them in that race.

Several times Spike had climbed off the bicycle to make sure it wasn't somehow souped-up or supercharged – as stupid as that sounded. He couldn't believe that he could pass cars! It might as well be a motorcycle.

And he could pass cars riding no-handed!

Spike tucked his hands behind his head and leaned back. This was the life! Chase was never going to see this bicycle again. No way! He'd repaint it or something. He could picture it as blue with black trim, grips, and striping. It would really look cool, a dark rocket!

Spike glanced down and his jaw dropped open. He did a doubletake, the bicycle looked a lot like he'd pictured it in his thoughts. He rubbed his eyes. He thought about the dark rocket again, picturing it clearly, then looked down at the bicycle. It was almost exactly as he'd shaped it in his mind's eye! What an incredible machine!

He'd make Chase tell him where he'd gotten it! If he wouldn't tell, he'd pound it out of him! Now that sounded like fun. Spike hoped the wimp wouldn't talk. He owed him for his current injuries. They were keeping him from playing football for the third game in a row! Oh, boy, did he ever owe Chase! Payback would be in spades.

Spike was supposed to join the team and watch the game, but he'd never been a watcher. He was a doer! Watching two already had been pure agony. How were they winning without him? Spike just couldn't understand it. Just lucky, he guessed.

A large gray squirrel with a huge tail ran out into the road, hesitated, then darted back. Spike steered toward it, pretending it was his dad. He pictured squashing it. "You're mine!" Spike ran over it before it could reach the shoulder. "YES!"

Not far ahead, Spike saw a rider. He was stylishly dressed in spandex, an orange and green striped jersey, and a Specialized helmet with a small bill. Spike smiled. No one could outrace him on this thing. No one! Hey, maybe he should take up racing. With this bicycle, winning would be easy.

Spike chuckled. All he needed was a cowcatcher so he could push other riders off the road. Wouldn't that be great! He could picture plowing through a crowd to win it all! A combination of speed and brute power. When he was winning all the time, maybe his father would leave him alone.

Spike laughed, then almost choked when he noticed that Kalyde II had partly transformed again, some sort of protrusion on the front fender. He mentally visualized it again, trying hard to clarify the image. After a few seconds, he looked down. A pointed ram jutted out in front of the front tire. Yeah!

He rapidly closed on the rider, again picturing his dad. Spike steered the cowcatcher into the young man's rear tire, driving the rider off the road. His tire caught something, and the bike bucked, sending the rider flying.

Spike laughed loudly. Incredible didn't even begin to describe this machine! Its shape seemed to conform to his thoughts!

Kalyde II suddenly jerked, sprinting backwards down the road, heading for Danny's house.

"What? What's going on!" Spike lost his balance and was flung forward. His hands shot out but missed the handlebars, and he hit them face-first, knocking him unconscious. Spike slipped from the speeding bicycle and lay unmoving on the road.

Danny had been thinking about what he'd do if the bicycle returned. He'd waste little time, going immediately into the past and talking with his mother. At the least, he'd apologize for being a brat.

A loud thump jolted Danny from his imaginings. He looked around disappointedly. Kalyde II hadn't magically appeared in the kitchen. What was he going to do? Where was Murg? "Murg?"

The calico darted back into the kitchen, nails scratching across the linoleum, then bolted back into the family room. "Come on!"

"Are you . . . Hey! It's here, isn't it?" Danny jumped up and ran to the front door. He yanked it open and found the bicycle standing there. "Hey, it looks different." Danny noted the change in color and the odd addition to the front.

"That looks like a cowcatcher on the front," Murg said.

"How do you know that?"

"A famous cat, Ferdinand, sort of a daredevil type, used to ride on the front of locomotives."

"Oh. But why would somebody want that?"

"To push people off the road."

"I was right! Spike was the one who stole my bicycle!" Danny cried. He cradled Kalyde II, then closed his eyes. He pictured his old red bicycle, harnessing and focusing all his will on the change. When he opened his eyes he was thrilled to see that Kalyde II had returned to normal. He'd been afraid Spike had tainted it.

"All right!" Danny grabbed Murg and gave her a prestige-embarrassing hug and kiss. "Thank you!"

Everything was fine. He could still deliver papers, fulfill his need for speed, go to tonight's football game and see Christina jump and shout! And best, he could still travel back in time to visit his mother! He'd do it right after the football game!

Murg hopped onto the carrier. "Let's shake it down, make sure it's all right!"

"Yeah! You want to come to the game with me?"

"A football game? A bit prehistoric, don't you think, but why not?"

And they were off, racing down the street as though they didn't have a care in the world.

They arrived at the stadium just as Jason was parking his bicycle. "Hi, Danny. Hey, Murg."

"Hay is for horses," Murg thought, then stuck out her tongue.

"I wonder about your cat sometimes," Jason told him.

"Me, too," Danny replied.

"Well," she thought huffily.

"I meant you are a wonder," Danny thought teasingly.

"You feeling all right?" Jason asked.

"Yeah, pretty much. Why?"

"You just look a little pale. Hey, heard the news?" Jason asked.

Danny shook his head.

"You don't have to worry about Spike boy for quite a while. Not that the team hasn't been winning without him anyway, but now it looks like he's out for the season. Lucky us."

"Why?" Danny asked.

"He's in the hospital with a broken collar bone and fractured left wrist. Rocky says he's in real bad shape. Suffered a concussion. And he's delusional."

"What happened?" Danny had a sinking feeling.

"Somebody probably fought back. There's always somebody bigger and tougher. That's what keeps me out of fights. Got the crap beat out of me a couple of years back."

"You really think somebody beat the stuffing out of him?"

"Rocky said that Spike is really out of it. He talks about falling off a rocket, then off a bicycle, then off a race car. Who knows? Maybe he does drugs."

Danny knew what had happened and suddenly felt guilty.

"Stop that," Murg said. "He deserved it. He's a horse thief who was thrown by the horse he stole. If everything thieves stole fought back, there'd be less stealing. Think of it as poetic justice. Ironic, even."

Danny didn't know what to say. He'd been so thrilled about getting the bicycle back that he had never even thought about somebody being on it. But it was obvious. Spike knew there was something special about Kalyde II. Who else knew? Had he told anybody else? Even if no one believed him, Danny foresaw trouble.

What was he going to do?

Chapter Twenty-Three

Friends In Need

As the football game progressed, Danny felt worse and worse. Several times Jason asked him if he was all right, and even Murg began to suggest he should go home. The more Danny thought about the way he felt, the more he wondered if it had something to do with his trip to the future Germany. Had the air been poisonous? Did Gretchen feel as badly as he did? He might have to delay his trip to the past to check on Gretchen.

Determined, Danny managed to make it through the game and greet Christina afterward.

"Hi, Danny! Jason! You made it! And you brought Murg! It's so nice to be remembered," Christina laughed. Then, "Do you feel all right?"

"Not really," Danny said.

"I thought as much," she said, backing up. "You don't look well."

"I told him he looked like death warmed over," Jason said. "But he wouldn't leave."

"I didn't want you to think I'd forgotten – again," Danny said.

"Thanks for remembering. I don't mean to be rude, but I don't want to catch whatever you have," Christina said, sounding apologetic. "You should go home and rest."

"Maybe your opinion will carry more weight than mine," Jason said wryly. "But when I'm the first black Tour de France champion, that'll change."

"Go home, Danny. I'll call you tomorrow and see how you're doing."

"All right," Danny said weakly. He was glad to get away; he needed to check on Gretchen. "I just wanted you to know I was here, and that I thought you performed great."

"Thank you. Too bad we didn't win," she replied, then grabbed him by the shoulders and marched him to the gate. "Jason give me a hand in getting him moving."

"I'll ride home with him."

"You two rode?" Christina asked.

"Of course. Is there a better way to travel?" Jason replied.

"Do you feel well enough to ride?" Christina asked dubiously.

"Yeah," Danny replied. "Riding always makes me feel better."

Christina walked with them to the bicycle racks. Danny put on a good performance, making it look like getting on the bicycle was easy when he was having some trouble standing.

"I'll call you tomorrow," she said and squeezed his hand. "Get better."

Once they'd left Christina and the stadium behind, Jason said, "You sure you can do this, macho man?"

"Yeah, I'm feeling better already."

"Whatever you say, bud." Jason dogged him all the way home.

After they'd split up, Danny said, "Murg, I'm going to visit Gretchen. I need to talk to her. Make sure she's feeling all right. Our visit to the future might be making us sick."

"What makes you think that? I feel fine."

"Just a guess. You never got off the bicycle."

"Well, if you're worried, call her."

"What if it's more urgent?" Danny asked. "I swear I can feel something is wrong with Gretchen."

Murg sighed. "All right. Let's go. As you said, riding makes you feel better. And Kalyde II seems to have healing properties. Let's put them to work."

"I am feeling a little better, and we haven't really used Kalyde II's magic, yet."

"Let's go, then. You know me. I'll never turn down a chance to ride."

They had it down to a fine art by now. They cruised to the frontage road, sprinted for a time, then glided along as they pictured Gretchen's house. Then the world split with a flash. As the clouds disappeared, the rainbow bridge stretched before them.

Riding through the blazing sun, Danny and Murg appeared outside of Munich, rolling down Schmeisser Street. Danny thought that the bicycle needed a local time clock and one appeared. It was almost lunch time.

"How are you feeling?" Murg asked.

"Much better. Lousy instead of horrible. After we check on Gretchen, I guess we'll just have to keep riding."

"It doesn't look like anybody's home." Danny nodded to the open garage. It was empty, and the front door was closed.

"Maybe Gretchen's home by herself. That would be perfect!" Murg said. "We wouldn't have to sneak around. You make too much noise to ever catch your own food."

"Thanks. You really know how to boost a guy's spirits." Danny rolled the bicycle to the bushes on the opposite side of the garage, then climbed over the rail fence. "If she's home, she might be sick."

"It's Saturday here," Murg said.

"That's right. I forgot."

Sounds from a television were coming out the open back door.

Murg peeked into a window. "She's alone, lying on the couch watching TV."

They ran up the porch steps and to the screen door. "Hey, Gretchen! It's me, Danny!" he called out in a loud whisper.

For long moments, Gretchen didn't move. Danny thought she was asleep and started to speak again when she slowly rolled to look at him. Her eyes were distant and glassy, and her face was pale and gaunt. "Danny?" Her voice was faint. "Is it really you?"

"Yes."

"What're you doing here?"

Danny forgot all about his own problems, opened the back door and rushed inside. "Gretchen, do you feel all right?"

"I know, I look terrible." She slumped. "I feel even worse. Not that you look a whole lot better."

"Where is everybody? Somebody should be taking care of you."

"I'll be all right, Danny. Mom's volunteering today at the workshop, and Dad's at soccer practice with Heinz."

Danny's worry grew stronger the longer he watched Gretchen. "You really shouldn't be by yourself." He gently touched her forehead. "You're hot and clammy."

"I've taken something, but I'm burning up. Look at me. I'm sweating."

"That's not good," Danny agreed. He chewed his lip.

"Danny, would you get me a drink of water? Please?" Gretchen asked. "I'm so thirsty."

Danny ran to the kitchen and filled a glass.

Gretchen consumed it without taking a breath, then collapsed again. "Danny, you know what? I think I'm sick from our visit to the future. Remember how bad the air was?" Danny nodded.

"Either it's poisonous, or I was allergic to it. How do you feel? Are you sick, too?"

"I'm feeling better, but I think you're right about our visit into the future." What was he going to do? Again, this was his fault. His curse was stronger than magic!

"Danny," Gretchen sounded scared. "Danny! I . . . I can't see! I CAN'T SEE! Oh, help me, Danny! Please!"

Danny frantically tried to remember where the nearest hospital was located. He looked at Gretchen; she was shaking. Danny started to move toward the phone, then changed his mind. "Come with me!" Danny took her hand and lifted her from the couch. "I'm taking you to the emergency room." Danny helped her to the front door, almost carrying her the last few steps.

"How?"

"On Kalyde II."

"I can't ride a bicycle! I can't see! I'll fall off!"

"No, you won't. It's magic!" He led her outside. Kalyde II was waiting for them at the door, already in tandem form.

Murg hopped onto the back of the Kalyde II. "It seems to be adapting more and more to your thoughts."

"I must really be sick," Gretchen said. "I'm hearing voices."

Danny and Murg exchanged a look, then Danny helped Gretchen onto the bicycle, letting her lean her elbow on the handlebars. He altered the tandem's design, the metal flowing fluidly to his wishes. The handlebars became higher and easier to rest upon.

"Let's go!" Off they went, racing down the road and heading for the nearest hospital.

Murg made a siren noise that startled several natives walking and a few more on mopeds. The trio was quite a sight; a tense, red-haired boy, a sickly-looking young girl, and a feline bellowing at the top of its lungs.

The wind tearing at them, they passed cars as if they were parked. Some honked at them. "Danny, it feels like we're going very fast," Gretchen said.

"We are. But don't worry. You're safe on Kalyde II," Danny said as they rocketed through an intersection, zipping between a pair of trucks. The other side of the intersection dropped off, and they sailed airborne.

Murg caterwauled.

"At least someone is having fun," Gretchen laughed weakly.

Then, they landed softly and raced forward.

"We're almost there! How are you feeling?" Danny asked.

"A little better. I'm beginning to see light."

Danny breathed a sigh of relief. Should he keep riding? Or take her to the hospital. He decided to split the decision. Danny rode by the front of the hospital, memorizing the emergency entrance, then kept going.

"Wasn't that it? Where are you going?" Murg thought.

"We're going to try using some magic to heal Gretchen," Danny said.

"All right!"

"You know, Danny," Gretchen said. "I think I can hear Murg talking to you . . ."

"You do?"

"I – that's unbelievable."

"Any more than traveling into the past or the future?" Murg asked.

"I guess not," Gretchen admitted.

About a mile from the hospital, Danny began mentally picturing the emergency entrance. "Here we go!" he told them.

There was a brief flash, then they coasted to a stop between two ambulances in front of the emergency entrance.

"How are you feeling?" Danny asked.

Gretchen was breathing heavily but said, "Better. But I still don't think I can stand. But I can see! It's blurry, but I can see!"

"We could just keep riding," Danny suggested.

"Danny, I'm scared."

"To the doctor," Danny said. He helped her inside, and Murg followed. The emergency room nurse immediately summoned a doctor and quickly moved Gretchen into an examination room.

While Danny waited, he gave the nurse what information he could about Gretchen. He gave a false name, Hans Becker, for his own identity. Waiting was pure agony. Since he wasn't family, he wasn't allowed to see Gretchen. He and Murg thought that was incredibly unfair. But life seemed to be unfair sometimes.

The nurse informed him that Mrs. Heinrich was on her way and to take the cat outside.

Murg was outraged and contemplated a gesture.

Danny was both relieved and disturbed. Should he stay or go? Mrs. Heinrich mustn't see him. What would he say? How would he answer her questions?

Danny wanted to see Gretchen. He didn't want to leave without saying goodbye. What if . . . what if something happened to her? So many other people he knew had . . . died. Should he stay or go? How could he help? He felt so helpless. Despite Murg's admonishments, Danny chewed his fingernails.

When he was told that Gretchen was resting comfortably, he left, just barely missing Mrs. Heinrich. He saw her from a distance as he climbed aboard Kalyde II. It didn't take them long to get home to Texas. But it seemed a lot longer.

Danny moped around all weekend. Besides Gretchen's illness, he had a terrible fight with Christina Saturday night. Telling her about Gretchen had been a mistake. Christina claimed he thought more about Gretchen than of her. In the end, Christina told him she didn't want to see him anymore.

Jason told him it would blow over, but even he was upset with Danny for canceling their Sunday ride. He claimed that Danny spent too much time by himself – that he needed to pull his head out!

Could things get worse? Danny didn't want to know. He didn't even want to think about it.

The word on Spike wasn't good, either. There were complications. Something about an infection. Danny felt worse and worse. He wished he could talk with Gretchen about it! Or Mom!

Danny constantly wondered how Gretchen was doing. He figured he could picture her and appear by her bed no matter her location. He could leave just as easily with nobody any wiser. He had to see her! Find out how she was doing! He'd thought about speeding into the future, but what if something bad had happened to her? Then he'd have to come back and wait – or make a decision to change things. That gave him an upset stomach and a headache.

After school Monday, he concluded he would go home, pick up Murg, then time travel back to talk with his mother about things.

When he arrived home, Danny found his father's car in the driveway. That was odd. They'd talked last night, and his father hadn't mentioned anything about coming home today. Danny opened the side door to the garage and rolled the bicycle inside.

Murg met him. "Danny, quick – hide the bicycle!"

"Why?" Danny asked, dread sweeping over him.

"Your dad and Gretchen's dad are here," Murg said.

Danny was paralyzed.

"I just finished uncovering your old bicycle. You can say you rode it home," Murg concluded.

Danny quickly turned around and walked Kalyde II to the door. "Go hide in the neighbor's bushes," Danny said as he gave it a shove. The bicycle rolled across the lawn between the houses. "And go invisible!" He was amazed as it faded from sight.

"Danny? Is that you, son? Come in," his father called from the door to the house.

"Coming." As Danny entered the kitchen, he moved to hug his father, but it was obvious he wasn't in the mood.

His arms were crossed. His expression was stern, his stare piercing. "You remember Colonel Heinrich, don't you?"

"Yes, sir. Hello. How is Gretchen?"

"She's stable."

"Stable? Is something wrong?"

"Have a seat, Danny. Gretchen has been very sick, and I thought delirious sometimes, but she's told me everything, and I've told your dad. No one else knows anything about this."

Danny didn't have to fake surprise or worry. "She's been sick? Is she going to be all right?"

"We're not sure. It's an unknown ailment. Now tell us about the Cor-ror-o'lans and about Kalyde II. We figure you got the bicycle from the alien, Kah-ley – Kalyde."

"Tell us what you know, son. It's important," his father said seriously.

Danny squirmed under his stare for a moment, then grew resolute. He wouldn't tell them anything. "About Cororluns and Clyde? I don't understand. What are you talking about?"

"Where's the bicycle, son?"

Danny thought quickly. "In the garage." Danny hated lying, but he wasn't going to tell them anything.

"Listen, Danny," Colonel Heinrich said, "your father and Gretchen both told me about the alien at the haunted house. I know about the magical bicycle, about how you can leap from one place to the next, even time travel, as hard as that is to believe."

"Danny," his father began, "I remember the time I saw two Murgs last June. And you beat me home. It seemed odd then, but with what the Colonel has told me, it makes some sense now."

"And I saw you with Gretchen just the other day," the colonel said. "And the nurse described a young American boy. You fit the description to a tee."

"And people think I have a wild imagination!" Danny replied.

"Danny, I know you and Gretchen time-traveled into the future, and that she became very sick after returning. I have to know more, everything about Kalyde and Kalyde II. You may be sick yourself."

"I feel fine," Danny said, trying to appear nonchalant.

The colonel sighed. "Whatever information you have might help Gretchen. It's important. She's stable but not well. We don't even know if you're infectious."

Danny didn't trust the colonel. They might figure a way to use Kalyde II to contact Kalyde. Try to capture him again. The bicycle might be studied and used for national defense – sometimes known as war. Besides, the bicycle was a gift to him. "I don't understand any of this. Gretchen is sick because she went to the future? I don't get it."

"Don't play dumb, Danny," his father said.

"Danny, my little girl, your friend, needs help. Danny, please tell us what you know. Show us your bicycle! For Gretchen!"

Danny held back his tears of frustration. How could Gretchen have told all his secrets? She'd promised. Danny felt crushed. How could she? She must have really been sick to do such a thing. He hoped so. What if he could help her? If so, he thought determinedly, he would do it on his own terms.

"Danny? Danny? Son? Are you listening."

"Danny, we want you to contact Kalyde."

"I'm very tired, Dad. I think I'll go lay down for a while. Getting into trouble all the time wears me out."

That surprised his father. "But – you should answer Colonel Heinrich's questions! My questions!"

"I would if I could," Danny said, then turned his back to them, heading for the stairs. "But I can already tell you're not going to believe anything if it's not what you want to hear."

"Danny, come back here!"

"Let him go, David," Colonel Heinrich said. "Let's see this bicycle. Danny isn't going anywhere."

The two men stepped into the garage.

"This is it. Same old bicycle. Nothing special about it."

"Gretchen said it could change shapes into a tandem. Maybe it can look like something else, a lawnmower or something. Maybe Danny can make it blend in with something, you know, camouflage. Maybe even make it invisible. Wave your arms about in out of the way places and see if you find something."

"I feel silly. I'm still not sure about this."

"I saw him in Germany. The bike's here somewhere. I know it!"

Danny was lying on his bed, wondering what to do. If his stomach didn't feel as though he'd swallowed an entire bottle of Tabasco, he would've been laughing at their futile search.

What was he going to do? And how could he help Gretchen? Or even himself?

Chapter Twenty-Four

Red-Handed

*D*epressed, Danny lay in the darkness of his room. He hadn't moved from the bed since his father and Colonel Heinrich had given up questioning him, again. His father had stalked off, madder than hell – madder than Danny had ever seen him. The colonel tried to reason, then plead with Danny, claiming he only wanted to help Gretchen. Danny didn't believe him, but there was nagging doubt.

What if Gretchen was still sick? He had to see her – find out what had happened! He was both furious at her and concerned for her. He'd already lost Sarah. Christina had given him the heave-ho. And despite getting him in deep trouble, he wouldn't lose Gretchen, too!

Danny finally decided on a course of action. He would wait

until it was late, then he would summon Kalyde II and visit Gretchen. He would find out the truth. If she were still really ill, then maybe another ride on the magical bicycle would cure her.

The hours crawled by as though paced by inch worms, and Danny dozed fitfully. When he awakened very deep into the night, he listened carefully. He didn't hear anyone downstairs. He hoped they were asleep. Danny crept to the door, listened, then opened it. The house was dark. He started out the door, then changed his mind and closed the door. They might be hiding and waiting, listening for his footfall or the opening of the front door.

Danny went to the window, opened it, and then crawled onto the roof. In minutes he was on the ground behind the house where he summoned Kalyde II. Rolling quietly, it coasted to a stop before Danny. "I hope Murg isn't upset, but we're off to see Gretchen." He sighed. "More trouble, I imagine."

"Danny, look out!" Murg shouted telepathically.

Danny heard a door open and suddenly he was blinded, bathed in the bright light of twin flashlight beams. "HEY!" He covered his face. All he saw was spots before his eyes.

"I told you he had it hidden!" came the colonel's voice. He moved forward and grabbed it. "Got it!"

"Murg," Danny mumbled. "What am I gonna do?" he was confined to his room. The colonel had called somebody, and soon he'd have company. They would question him . . . and . . . and maybe torture him? Surely not. Had he broken any laws? He didn't think so. Then why did he feel like a criminal? He hadn't done anything wrong. "This isn't right."

"I think you should summon Kalyde II and take off. Let's go see Gretchen!" Murg told him.

"How?" Danny asked.

"In your mind, see it standing before you. Have it appear like it teleports in or something, instead of rolling to you."

"Okay, I'll give it a try." Danny closed his eyes, picturing a flash of white, then Kalyde II would suddenly appear. Danny heard a strange noise.

Downstairs, he heard someone yell. "It's gone! How . . . "

Danny opened his eyes. It had worked! Kalyde II stood before him, vibrating ever so slightly. Murg jumped onto the carrier. "Hurry!" As Danny climbed onto Kalyde II, he heard footsteps running up the stairs. "Come on!" Murg urged.

Danny closed his eyes and concentrated on the stretch of frontage road they often traveled. Outside, it sounded as though several car doors slammed. The footsteps grew louder, then his door opened. "There he is! Hey!"

White flashed, and Danny and Murg appeared on the frontage road. "Now we're really in trouble," Danny said. "Oh, well, might as well go for broke!" He began riding. As they picked up speed, he mentally pictured Gretchen, focusing on every detail of her face, her ruddy cheeks, luminous blue eyes and curly golden locks which often hung across her eyes. She was very pretty, Danny suddenly realized. Then the world split with a blinding flash, and the rainbow highway appeared under them.

They raced along the glittering sky bridge, then coasted downhill toward the blazing ball of light. They rushed through it, then appeared in the hospital room. The bicycle skidded across the linoleum floor of the dark room and toward Gretchen's bed! "OH, NO!"

Kalyde II stopped so quickly Danny almost hurtled over the handlebars. Only magic kept him from landing in Gretchen's bed.

"Danny?" Gretchen asked sleepily. "Is it really you this time? Have you come back? Or am I dreaming again?" she asked sadly. Gretchen reached out to touch him and missed. "Dreaming, I guess. And I was going to apologize. I know you're in big trouble. I wished you were here."

Danny felt terrible about what he'd been thinking. It was

obvious that Gretchen was still very sick. Might they figure out where he was going and call the hospital? How much time did he have?

"She still doesn't look well," Murg said, "but better than the last time we saw her." Her face was still drawn, her eyes hollowed and glassy. Danny was thankful there was some color in her cheeks. "Talk to her!" Murg demanded. "That's why you're here."

"Is someone there?"

"Gretchen, uh, hi. It's me, Danny."

"Oh, Danny. It really is you! I'm so sorry. I didn't mean to get you in trouble, believe me! I was just so sick! So delirious! And after the nurse described you, they kept asking questions." She spread her hands in helplessness.

"It's okay," Danny mumbled and took her hand. "Really."

"No, it's not. I swear you've already been here several times, but I guess I was just delirious." She smiled weakly. "You know you saved my life by bringing me to the hospital."

"It was my fault you were sick in the first place."

"That doesn't matter." Gretchen squeezed his hand. "Still friends?"

"Yeah." He couldn't stay mad at Gretchen. He gave her a hug.

"You know," Gretchen began, "I think it was the ride on the magic bicycle that really saved me."

"Then let's go again! Make you feel even better! Truly well!" Murg shouted.

"Did I hear somebody in the hall?" Gretchen asked, suddenly frightened. "Or was that Murg?"

"Murg . . ." Danny began, then he heard heavy footsteps. The colonel might have phoned ahead. The authorities might be coming! "Come on!"

"I can't go like this." Gretchen tugged at her hospital gown.

"We don't have a choice. I'll close my eyes, I promise.

Besides, you'll be in back."

Danny heard someone outside say, "The colonel said to check the room, then post a watch."

"Come on!" Danny whispered. Gretchen was still very weak, and Danny had to help her onto the tandem. "Now, just relax. I'm your tour guide. We are off to some incredible places!" He closed his eyes. Since Danny didn't know when he might get caught, he was going to take her to every place he could think of – every place he wanted to go.

"But we aren't moving."

"Don't worry. The ultimate speed is being there!" Danny thought of Ft. Benjamin Harrison in Indianapolis.

The hospital room flickered – someone opened the door – then it was gone, and they were soaring through the clouds. They parted, and the rainbow bridge appeared. Above, the stars winked at them, and Gretchen smiled broadly. Then she hugged Danny. There was a final burst of white light, and they appeared next to the football field cloaked in darkness.

Danny started pedaling, and they cruised along the road, barely noticing the speed bumps. Kalyde II absorbed them. "Just a connection." Danny pictured Hawaii, his favorites beach with the dark sand. Under the moon, the water sparkled, and the palm trees swayed in the tropical breeze.

Their leap through space was the same, through the clouds, across the bridge and into the brilliant but cool sun at the end of the rainbow. With a flash, they arrived on the black-grained beach. In the moonlight everything had a bluish tint. The water appeared to be made of liquid silver.

Danny headed for the gleaming water. "Danny, where are you going?"

"We can ride atop water!" Leaving the deserted beach behind, they rode out onto the ocean, coasting from crest to crest, riding the gentle swells. The water sparkled as though filled with diamonds. Fish jumped up as if trying to get a better view of them.

"Oh, Danny, this is so beautiful."

Danny continued across the water for a while, then he thought of the mountains where he'd ridden across the fog. Shortly, they were both squealing in delight at they soared across the thick morning mists. The mountain peaks looked like heads poking out to stare up at the rising sun.

"We're flying!" Gretchen laughed.

Danny glanced over his shoulder. Gretchen was looking better, her eyes lively and her face no longer gaunt. Danny smiled at Murg.

Next he pictured Brown County State Park in southern Indiana. Soon they were racing along a winding and curvy road. They banked left, right, then went up and down over and over. There was the smell of fall – decaying leaves and coolness in the air. Danny wished she could see the leaves changing, but the odor was pungent and invigorating.

"Don't stop!" Gretchen cried. "Keep going and going and . . ."

"Exactly what she said," Murg agreed. "Don't stop!"

Gretchen continued getting better and better. They visited the beach in North Carolina, one in Florida and another in San Diego, where they raced across the azure water toward the setting moon. Bright and amber-colored, it sat large atop the horizon.

In Colorado, Danny imagined a change in the bicycle, and Kalyde II became a mountain bike. They raced through the Rockies, screaming down an incredible hill without holding onto anything, their hands in the air as if they were riding a roller coaster. They were laughing so hard and having so much fun tears were rolling down their faces.

Lastly, Danny took her to the arid Nevada desert. The road was deserted, and Danny pedaled fast, thinking even faster. The world was one big blur, the wind rushing by them so fast they could barely breathe. When they slowed, a booming reverberation caught up with them.

"Oh, Danny!" Gretchen hugged him. "Thank you! Thank you! I feel so much better! I feel wonderful! So alive!"

"What else are friends for?"

"Not to get each other into trouble, that's for sure!"

"Yeah." His elation fell away. "What am I going to do about the authorities? About my dad?"

"You'll think of something. You have magic at your disposal – just like Merlin. You know what I think you should do?"

"What?" Danny asked.

"Forget about being in trouble, and go see your mother. Your mom's death is like a ball and chain you've been carrying around. I'm tired of you feeling down and guilty. It wasn't your fault! It isn't your fault that bad things happen to others around you."

"I'm not so sure about that. You and Spike . . ."

"Those were accidents. You might affect other people, but you don't control their fates. They do. And some believe God does. Just worry about your own life, not everyone else's. Mom says some people can't even do that. They'd rather put the blame on somebody else. Besides, we're just kids." She shrugged. "We're not supposed to know everything or worry about anything other than being a good kid. We can wait a while to be good adults." She smirked.

Danny didn't know what to say, but she made more sense than some of the wise men he'd visited.

"Danny, what I'm saying is this. Go make peace with your mom so you can enjoy life. Get on with life. I'd hate for it to stunt your growth or something. You're short enough as it is," she teased. "And do it before something happens to Kalyde II. You've wanted to go back and apologize to your mother since the day of the accident. Before you even could go back in time. Your bicycle is a miracle, a gift from Kalyde and providence, I believe. Use it wisely."

Danny was quiet for a while, the whistling wind the only sound to fill the silence. Finally, Danny said, "What if she doesn't accept my apology?"

Gretchen frowned. "Danny, do you really believe that?"

"I guess not. Will you go with me?"

"No, I probably should be getting back. I think this is something you should do on your own – you and Murg."

"Okay. Have you had enough riding?"

"Never!" Gretchen laughed.

Danny joined her, the joy infectious.

They rode for a while longer before returning to Munich, but they didn't appear at the hospital. They couldn't risk that. Just in case the authorities were waiting at the Heinrich's residence, they arrived a couple of houses down from Gretchen's. The sun was rising, the sky a palette of soft pastels.

"It's going to be a wonderful day," Gretchen said. She made him promise to return soon, if he could, and to write if he couldn't. "I promise to write back, cross my heart and promise to live without sweets if I don't."

Danny laughed. "That should motivate you."

She stuck out her tongue at him.

"Bye. Stay healthy! See you soon!" As Danny began pedaling backward, he thought of their home in Munich, not far away, but a couple of months in the past – Germany in summer.

Chapter Twenty-Five

Redemption

As Danny backpedaled through the mutilated and lackluster rainbow tunnel, he felt something was wrong. He was being sucked backward as though caught in a tremendous current. The bicycle hit violent turbulence, then they struck a rut and launched backwards, disappearing into a gap in the faded purple wall.

They appeared to be standing still within swirling purple-black clouds. Danny's eyes went wide. "Murg! Something's wrong! We're not in Germany! Where are we?" A cold, bone-chilling wind blew across them.

"We've been knocked off the path! We may have been time-traveling too much!"

Danny shivered. "I'm cold. Real cold! I'm . . . I'm already losing feeling in my hands and feet."

"Concentrate on seeing and feeling the rainbow highway underneath you. Quickly! Or we may be lost in time."

They had ridden the highway so many times Danny easily imagined it. Below, the tunnel's colors were faded, a washed out watercolor. Dark ruts, chuckholes and pits were scattered across the arching skyway. The dreary purple wall of the tunnel was full of black jagged holes, from which a multitude of strange eyes watched them. The winds were turbulent, twisting, and biting, trying to cut through him and dislodge him at the same time.

Danny smiled, forcing confidence. A glow would surround them, transport them to the highway.

Just as he'd pictured in his mind's eye, they magically appeared on the faded rainbow skyway once more, racing backward through time.

"Whew, that was close," Murg said, shaking and shivering.

Danny kept one hand on the bars, but stretched as much as he could without risk of being knocked off. "I'm stiff but the chill is fading."

"Now, Danny, concentrate on seeing your mother. Visiting home last summer."

Danny focused on seeing their home in Munich. It was very memorable, made of white stone with a funny roof and Bavarian carvings decorating the trim. There were bushes and flowers blossoming all over and a sprawling garden out back. It had been the beginning of summer, and they had just finished school. The sun was warm and trees, bushes and plants were bright green. Dad would still be at work. Mom at home in the kitchen. Sarah . . .

They appeared in front of the house, slowly rolling to a stop along the street. "You'd better hide!" Murg said. "You don't want to see yourself, or you might try to change something."

"Is that really so bad?" Danny asked.

Murg looked exasperated.

"Oh, all right." Danny hopped off Kalyde II and rolled it to the bushes alongside their house. He tucked it between a blue spruce and a bush.

"I'll do some scouting for you since you have heavy feet," Murg said, then bounded off.

Danny waited. It was too bad he couldn't shapechange like Kalyde or even Kalyde II. Then he could look like someone else. Maybe he could be a census taker and ask questions. Then Danny began wondering if Kalyde II could become something other than a bicycle. Spike had made a change to it that wasn't typical for bicycles.

Danny reached out and touched Kalyde II. It quivered. Danny closed his eyes and pictured a baseball bat. He immediately felt the bicycle shrink away, then a glowing warmth surrounded him. There was a high pitched squeaking as though something were being squashed and compressed. Danny carefully opened his eyes. It had transformed into a baseball bat! Kalyde II could really change shapes.

Danny touched it, closed his eyes, then thought of a magic marker pen. Again there was the swelling warmth, then the squeaking noise. He opened his eyes. It had worked!

Danny slipped the magic marker in his pocket. This was great. He could carry his bicycle with him wherever he traveled. Talk about portable! No more having to worry about it getting stolen. Hey, a watch would be perfect; he could "lock" it to his wrist.

He'd just pulled the marker from his pocket to change it when Murg nudged his feet. "I didn't hear you coming," Danny said.

"Of course, not. Everything is perfect. Sarah's not home and neither am I! I probably sensed something like this happening back then. In fact, I vaguely remember the feeling that I needed to accompany Sarah to her lessons today."

"Because of the sense of time cats have?"

"Exactly. As I said, we exist multi-linearly. Prince, the insipid – though its not his fault, he is a dog after all – is in the back yard. You're crashed upstairs, asleep, and your mom is in the kitchen. Let's go!" Murg headed around to the front door.

Danny stuffed the magic marker in his pocket and followed. When he quietly pushed open the front door, Danny felt sort of weird, as though he were breaking into his own house.

"Quietly," Murg said as he pushed the front door shut. The closing click was louder than imagined.

"David, is that you?" Danny heard his mother ask from the kitchen.

"Oh, no!" Murg said. "Move fast!"

Danny tried to quietly run up the stairs. He made it up several steps, then turned around and started back down as though he were coming from upstairs. His mother came around the corner. Danny rubbed his eyes, then stared with open mouthed amazement. Mom! She was alive! "M . . . M . . . M . . ." Danny stammered.

"Danny, are you all right?" she asked.

Danny began to shake. He was going to break down and cry, he just knew it! Murg spread one claw, then poked Danny in the calf.

"Ow! Oh, M – Mom, I had a terrible dream." Danny moved to his mother. She hugged him. Danny suddenly noticed there was no other feeling like this in the world.

"You had a bad nightmare?" she asked as she stroked his head. "Sit and tell me about it." They sat in the living room on the couch, the same one Danny had been crying on and screaming into for the past few months.

Danny talked about his nightmare, which was really what had happened to him recently. He haltingly told his mother about her and Sarah's accident, their abrupt move to Texas, Spike, and the problems he had with his Dad. Then a bit more composed, he told her about Kalyde, Kalyde II, Spike, time-traveling and his trouble with the authorities.

"You have such an imagination," she laughed and kissed him. "You're going to be a great writer."

"So what should I do?' Danny asked. "About Spike? About Sarah? Should I come back, and save you and Sarah?"

His mother chuckled. "Danny, Danny," she began, then noticed he was dead serious. "No, I don't think so. I don't like the sound of this time traveling. It sounds dangerous. I don't want anything bad to happen to you. But don't worry, I plan to be around for a long time, see you graduate college, get married and have your own kids with wild imaginations."

Danny couldn't tell her that wasn't going to happen; she wouldn't believe him anyway. It seemed that adults had either stifled their imaginations or lost them somewhere. "What about the authorities?"

"Sounds like your problems might go away if you didn't have the bicycle." She smiled. "Then they wouldn't want it, and you wouldn't have all these big decisions to make. You're too young to get gray hairs."

But I have to make them whether I'm old enough or not, Danny thought. "Then I wouldn't be able to save you! And I might insult Kalyde! And I'd lose my friends Jason and Christina."

"Christina? I'm sure Kalyde and Jason would understand. And I don't need to be saved. And who's this Christina? Somebody in real life?"

"But you will! I mean, you might!" Danny amended.

"Danny, we've talked about this before. Pray, and do what your conscience tells you to do. You're a good boy and will grow into a good man one day. What good did the magical bicycle do for you in the dream? Let you go fast? Win? Make friends? You don't need it for that. I have confidence in you. You can do that without a magic bicycle. Create your own magic!"

"Create my own magic?"

"Yes. It sounds to me that the bicycle just allowed you to be yourself. To accept yourself. Are you feeling down about all the moving we do? And only having a few friends instead of many?" she asked.

Danny nodded.

"Oh, Danny. It's not how many friends you have, but if you have good ones. Can you trust them and have fun? Be yourself? One good friend is better than ten fair-weather friends. And popularity isn't as important as being happy. In fact, popularity and fame often bring heavy burdens.

"So don't worry so much about your bicycle. It's just a thing, and people, friends and families, even strangers, are more important than things. I don't want you becoming materialistic." She sighed. "Listen to me. It was just a nightmare, and I'm lecturing on it. I sound like your grandmother."

"Yeah. But Dad – "

"I know your dad really believes in winning, but I don't. Winning isn't everything or the only thing. He loves you, and it's one way he shows it, by encouraging you. Danny, just be true to yourself, be honest and respect others. I think if you do that, good things will happen to you, and the nightmares will go away. Even without a magical bicycle to aid you." She winked, then kissed him on the forehead.

"You really think so?" Danny asked.

His mother nodded solemnly.

"Mom, what am I ever going to do without you?"

"Don't worry, I'll be around for a long time. And even when I'm gone, I'll be around in spirit, watching over you."

Danny fought back the tears. "Mom, I'm sorry for being a jerk sometimes and making you mad."

"Apology accepted. Just remember, even if I get mad at you, I still love you. I'm mad at what you're doing, not who you are."

"I think I'm going to try and sleep a little longer," Danny said and stood. "Thanks, Mom. I think," he choked, then managed, "that I'll sleep better." Relieved but with mixed emotions of joy and a heavy heart, Danny hugged his mother, then walked up the stairs. He headed into the bathroom and closed the door. Murg was waiting there.

To the calico's surprise, Danny transformed the magic marker into Kalyde II.

"You do have quite an imagination. Where to now?" Murg asked.

"The day of the accident. Of their deaths."

"I thought you'd just made peace!"

"I did. Now I want to make sure I didn't cause the accident."

"Fair enough."

Their trip across the rainbow highway was very short, barely glimpsing it before the blinding whiteness engulfed them. They appeared outside the same house but nearly two months into the future. Mom and Sarah were just getting into the car. Danny walk-rolled the bicycle over to the car.

"MOM!" Danny called out. He felt leaden but was determined to do as planned. And he wouldn't get paralyzed as in his nightmare.

"Danny!" his mother snapped. "What are you doing out here? I sent you to your room to think!"

Just as he remembered, she was very angry and getting angrier.

"Obey me, please! To your room! We're already late for Sarah's lesson."

"Okay. I will. I just came to apologize for being such a pain in the neck." Danny leaned in the window and kissed his mother.

She was very surprised.

"Drive carefully, and never . . . never drive mad. Sort of like going to bed mad." He smiled weakly when he really wanted to cry.

His mother sighed heavily. "Apology accepted. We'll discuss this more when I get home. And I won't drive mad, I promise," she said as she started up the car. "Now go inside."

Danny nodded and rode the bicycle up the driveway. He stopped on the sidewalk and watched the car drive away. "I've done what I could," Danny said. "If it was meant to happen and not my fault, then I hope I've done right." He didn't feel quite so restless – so helpless anymore.

"I think it's enough. You've done right," Murg told him. "Now let's go back home to our own time."

"Not quite, yet," Danny said. "There's still something left to do in the past."

Chapter Twenty-Six

Changing Time

*D*anny, Murg and Kalyde II appeared in Danny's Texas bedroom amidst boxes needing to be unpacked.

"When are we?" Murg asked.

Danny glanced at the clock radio. He hadn't arrived home from school yet. And he should have just left, traveling back to the future from the first time he'd traveled backwards to here. Boy, this time traveling stuff was confusing. This would be a tight window of opportunity. He only had a few minutes before he risked meeting himself. Danny walked to the closet door and opened it. Kalyde was there with the magic bicycle. "Kalyde!" Danny shouted. He reached out to his friend and pulled him upright into a hug.

"My friend!" Kalyde laughed. "I have brought you a gift!"

"Uh," Danny stammered as he looked from Kalyde to Kalyde II. "I want to talk to you about that." He sighed heavily. "I can't accept it."

"Why?" Kalyde asked incredulously. He appeared very disappointed, his large eyes sad and his expression hangdog as if he'd just lost his only friend. Even his spiked blue hair seemed to droop.

Danny pointed over his shoulder at Kalyde II. "I've got quite a story to tell you," Danny said.

Kalyde was surprised to see a double of the magical bicycle. "You're back from the future, again?" Kalyde asked.

Danny nodded. The Cor-ror-o'lan listened quietly as Danny told the rest of his tale – of Spike stealing the bicycle, of Gretchen getting sick, and of the authorities learning of Kalyde II.

"I think they want to use it and me to capture you," Danny finished. Downstairs, the front door banged open. He was home!

"Surprising and unexpected, but I understand." Kalyde stroked the bicycle as if it were alive. "I will think of something else! See you soon!" Kalyde touched the bicycle and disappeared in a flash of white.

"HEY!" Danny cried. Suddenly, the whole world went topsy-turvy. The room shaking, the very air vibrating. Danny was knocked off his feet.

"Write yourself a note!" Murg cried.

"What!"

"Write yourself a note! Maybe you can still race in the Oktoberfest 20K! It's important!"

Danny crawled across the floor toward his desk. A notepad and pen had already been shaken to the floor. Danny scrawled a quick note, getting pelted by books as he did so. Behind him, a shelf collapsed.

"Look out!" Murg yelled. A bookcase toppled towards him.

The twisting and lurching suddenly quit. Danny looked around. Nothing was damaged, and the bookcase was still upright, although his room was a mess. He noticed several boxes were missing. No, not missing. Unpacked. He looked at his bookshelves. Yes, unpacked. Then he noticed that Kalyde II, his Kalyde II – the one he'd been riding – was gone. It had worked!

Danny felt elation, then bottom-scraping sadness. There would be no more speed. No more flying across fog. No more time-traveling adventures, and no more visiting Gretchen. He plopped down on his bed. Sometimes getting what he wanted just didn't work out as he'd planned.

"Danny! You'd better get going!" he heard his father yell.

"What?" Danny yelled as he opened his bedroom door.

"The race starts in a few hours!" his father yelled, "and you have to ride there!"

What race? Danny wondered. Could it be the Oktoberfest 20k? Was he still going to race? That was crazy! He didn't have a magical bicycle anymore. He ran down the stairs and into the kitchen.

"Did you fall asleep, again? I'm surprised." His father munched on a muffin as he perused the newspaper. "I would've thought you'd be too excited to sleep. It is your first race, after all."

Danny couldn't believe it! Somehow he'd skipped forward through time. Or was it back? Or was this just some type of strange rippling effect? Well, he couldn't ask Murg or Einstein anymore. He might as well race; he had never raced. Or had he? He remembered racing, although the memory was a bit vague.

"I have something for you," his father said and reached under the table. He handed the helmet to Danny. "We can't have you going to war without some protection."

"Wow! My own helmet!"

"Now, you'd better get going. Go beat Spike and his gang at something you do well. Remember our agreement. You have to get there yourself."

Danny groaned. Without the magical bicycle, he'd be tired before he got there. It was at least twenty miles away.

"Have you changed your mind? I hope not. Get a move on."

Agreeing, Murg meowed and ran for the front door. Danny grabbed some fruit, filled a water bottle, and then followed the feline.

They arrived at the registration booth just in time. The starting and sign-up area was a zoo, just like Danny remembered, but worse because he hadn't gotten there as early as before.

A nice lady told him to hurry, that they were going to start in a few minutes. She quickly gave him his number and told him to line up. Danny looked around. The place was jammed; a crowded festival in the streets with everyone ready to dance on two wheels instead of legs. Flags, ropes, signs, and people were everywhere along the packed street curbs and beyond.

Danny couldn't see any openings close to the front or the middle, so he rolled his bicycle to the back of the pack. Danny looked for Jason and Spike, or anybody else he knew, even the bald-headed guy, but didn't see them. He looked to Murg who shrugged, then meowed encouragement.

Most of the riders were stretching and making last minute adjustments. Danny didn't need to. He'd just ridden twenty miles, and he could ride some more. Wasn't that smart? But so what? At least he was here! And he was going to race for real this time! No sandbagging. No holding back. Danny smiled. He wasn't tired at all.

All he had to do was beat Spike and the others. He hoped that the extra miles wouldn't hurt him – that he wouldn't wear down near the end. He prayed the Chase curse wouldn't strike again.

Danny suddenly wondered if the same riders would fall in

front of him as they had before in the last race – the one that hadn't happened. Probably not. And if they did, it wouldn't cause him to wreck because he wouldn't be that close to the front-runners anyway! Then Danny had a second thought. Murg had mentioned something about time trying to reassert itself, keeping a similar course as before like a river. He'd be wary, just in case.

Soon after Danny settled in, the gun sounded, signaling the start. The mass slowly moved forward like an undulating caterpillar. Danny had to wait for space to clear. What a bummer; he might already be far behind Spike and the others.

Danny checked the crowd. He didn't see Christina, either. Well, she probably wouldn't be impressed. He wondered how losing was going to affect his future. He'd miss her unless he could think of some other way to get to know her.

Murg poked him. Danny was startled. Finally, those ahead and the riders around him were pushing off and moving away. Danny sighed and finally shoved off, coasting as he fit his sneakers into his toe clips. All he could do was his best. Then he caught a glimpse of Christina out of the corner of his eye. She wasn't even watching him. But then, why would she?

Danny pedaled along slowly at first, following those in the front of him. For the first two kilometers, he felt hemmed in – almost claustrophobic – so he didn't press the issue. He had to be patient and wait for things to spread out. After the third kilometer, he began to work his way forward. Murg mewed her approval. Several bikers watched with curiosity as they passed. Others just smiled at the boy and his cat.

Danny was surprised to find that he wasn't fatigued at all. He wished he could ride faster. He didn't want to lose. He didn't want to get pounded any more. And he didn't want to bring Spike lunch money! Danny began to press forward after the fifth marker. He didn't want to lose Jason and Christina as friends, but they weren't his friends, yet. And might not be, he thought sadly.

Well, Danny decided as he began to weave between riders, he would just have to make his own magic. He hunkered down across the handlebars and forced himself to work the up stroke as well as the down stroke. His old bicycle rode along smoothly. When Kalyde had repaired his bicycle, he must have made it better than before. It rode soundlessly without a clink or rattle.

Danny missed Murg's conversation but encouragement still came in a variety of meows and murrs. When they were cut off and almost crashed, she hissed. Danny was glad he'd practiced dodging tumbleweeds. Or had he? He still seemed to have the skills.

For the next few kilometers Danny tried to keep a consistent and even pace – just as he'd seen while watching the Tour de France. He focused on each rider ahead of him and saw himself passing them. Each was a new and distinct challenge, one at a time like leap frog.

Danny still didn't see Spike or any of the others. He was beginning to worry. He just wished he could see the finish line, and for a moment, he did and smiled wistfully.

At the eleventh mark, he began to grow thirsty. A series of small, rolling hills during the twelfth kilometer made his legs tingle. A little later, they began to grow a bit heavy. Danny still passed riders. He tried not to slacken his pace, to ignore his fatigue, but he found himself gliding more than he should. Still no sign of Spike, Rocky, Hank or Jason.

Somewhere around kilometer fifteen, his breathing began to labor. His legs felt as though they were thick. He could tell he was definitely slowing down. That extra twenty miles had been too much. A couple of riders, a bearded guy and a woman with a long pony tail passed him.

"I'm losing it!" Danny muttered. He wasn't just losing it. He was going to lose. And he hadn't even seen Rocky, who was the slowest of the riders. They were probably long gone.

If only his father had given him a ride, so he wouldn't have had to bicycle those extra twenty miles. He'd be kicking butt!

Danny was complaining and thinking of giving up when he passed marker sixteen. Then he saw Rocky. All thoughts of quitting suddenly disappeared. Danny pedaled faster, envisioning himself passing Rocky who was moving slower, his clothing drenched in sweat. Danny raced up behind him. He wasn't feeling as tired as before. Murg meowed, encouraging him.

Rocky turned around, his eyes wide, face red and mouth open. "No! No," he gasped, "way, Jose'!"

Danny finally found a second wind. Or was it his third? He had a tangible goal to shoot for – somebody important to pass. He was going to beat at least one of the bullies. And if Rocky was here, he suspected Hank was nearby. Go for two, Danny told himself. Without glancing back and while ignoring Rocky's curses, Danny set his sights on Hank. Danny found him not far ahead.

Seeing Hank's back, Danny lost all thought of fatigue. Somewhere well past the seventeenth marker and along an incline, Danny caught him. Hank glanced nervously over the top of his glasses. They hung off kilter and were heavily fogged. A grim determination came across Hank's flushed face, and he pedaled harder. Faster. Then Hank stood on the pedals and ran.

Danny smiled calmly. They had a ways to go. Besides, he'd raced a Ferrari and won. They raced each other up the hill. Danny tried to pretend there was a tail wind pushing him. He wished he had someone to draft, but they were passing riders who looked at them as though they were crazy. They were kicking early!

"You're a loser, Chase!" Hank gasped.

Danny didn't look at him, but his mouth became a tight line. He slowly passed Hank and pulled away.

Murg turned her backside and flicked her tail at Hank as

they crested the hill.

It's all downhill from here, Danny thought – and hoped.

"Spike!" Hank screamed, coasting so he could cup his hands to yell. "Chase is coming!"

That only made Danny more determined. "Hey, Murg," Danny gasped, "I'm doing pretty good with this old thing!" Maybe he wasn't such a bad bicycler after all. All the time he'd spent riding on Kalyde II had improved his conditioning. Or had he been training as much? Yes, he was sure he had been but without the magical bicycle. Having two memories was confusing. Well, he was out to prove the first race – the one that hadn't happened – hadn't been all imagination and magic. Maybe, just maybe, he could create his own magic.

Danny didn't want to be a loser. If he won, then he'd win the bet and freedom from some hassling. Jason would be his friend again. Christina would like him. And his dad would be happy. Everything would be wonderful. And if pigs had wings they'd fly, he remembered his mother saying.

Danny passed the eighteen marker. He wiped sweat from his eyes and tried to push harder. He didn't seem to go much faster, but he wasn't tired any longer. He felt loose, coasting on his second wind. He hoped he didn't need a third.

Then Danny saw Spike. The mammoth boy was glancing over his shoulder, watching Danny advance nearer and nearer.

Danny closed his eyes and imagined gaining on Spike. When Danny opened his eyes, he just looked ahead, not even glancing at Spike. Catch him. I've caught him. Now pass him. Bye, bye, Spike, Danny thought.

"For you, wimpoid!" Spike yelled and spat.

The spittle slapped Danny's cheek. He didn't even look at Spike; Danny refused to give him the pleasure. Out of the corner of his eye, Danny saw that he was passing Spike. It was slow but sure. If it was the last thing he did, Danny was going to beat Spike!

Spike suddenly steered his bicycle into Danny's, clipping his rear tire.

Danny's bike skipped sideways, almost throwing him off. Danny tightened his grip on the handlebars and regained control.

Laughing, Spike passed him.

Danny worked to catch up, slowly, inch by inch, he gained on his foe.

When they were almost wheel to wheel again, Spike swerved into his path, cutting him off.

Danny dropped back, put on a burst of speed and caught him. "Some of your own medicine!" Danny cried as he bumped Spike's bike.

Spike roared as he regained control. He came swinging back toward Danny.

Danny steered into him, and their bikes clashed.

Spike took a wild swing at Danny who ducked.

Murg took advantage of the close proximity and swiped at Spike's leg.

"Ouch! Hey! You – "

Danny steered away. Just as he was readying himself for another clash, he noticed Spike's angry red face. His eyes were wide and his gaze irrational.

Danny remembered Socrates talking about reason and not letting one's emotions dictate life. Use your head, Danny thought. Murg would have said the same if she could talk. And if this were an experiment, Danny would have been able to calculate beforehand that Spike's weight gave him an advantage.

"I'm gonna knock you off that bicycle!" Spike shouted.

The largest of the Bash brothers swerved wildly in Danny's direction. With a smile, Danny tapped the brakes, slipping behind Spike's bicycle. Their wheels barely missed. Spike had braced for impact, but since there was none, he went careening off the road onto the shoulder, kicking up dust and gravel.

Danny put on a burst of speed, pulling ahead.

As Spike steered onto the road, he yelled, "Chase, you sucker! If you beat me, I'm going to beat the crap out of you when this is over!"

Danny ignored him and slowly pulled away.

Murg again showed her behind and flipped her tail.

Danny suddenly laughed, then held it in check. Not yet. But – he was winning! Without the magical bicycle, he was winning! He could do it! HE COULD DO IT! BE A WINNER! This time he didn't need to sandbag or hold back. He was going for it, and it felt good! So good! He was making his own magic!

Around the nineteenth marker and with the finish line in distant sight, Danny spotted Jason. His friend was pedaling smoothly and easily. Danny thought that Jason was the natural, not vice versa. Here I come, buddy! He didn't have to beat Jason to win the bet, but he wanted to show him. Prove himself and gain some respect.

Danny focused on Jason's red jersey and pretended it was growing larger and larger. Soon he was right behind number 116.

Jason glanced over his back. "Hey, hey! It's Chase! All right! Gonna give me a race, are ya, man? Good! Come on!" He stood on his bicycle and sprinted.

Danny did the same. For a moment he felt a cramp but ignored the pain and pushed through it. Not much farther, he thought.

Danny weaved right.

Jason swerved left to pass a biker who was also straining.

Anyone with any energy left was sprinting. They didn't gain much ground on anybody else, but Danny slowly gained on Jason, edging forward inch by inch.

"Yee-haw!" Jason yelled. His smile was hard pressed.

Murg wailed like a siren.

Danny pulled even with Jason's back tire. He kept pushing closer, now even with his pedals. There was less than half a kilometer to go. Soon, they were even, their breathing and heartbeats in time with each other. The finish banner above the line was readable.

"I can do it!" Danny gasped. His chest was afire. His legs were filled with hot and cold spikes. Danny again weaved right and Jason left to pass two racing riders. They were almost at the line, less than 200 yards to go. The riders they passed glanced at them and put forth an extra effort.

Danny recognized them. These were the guys who had fallen last race – the race that hadn't happened. Would they fall again? Danny tried to give them a wide berth but not lose speed.

Out of the corner of his eye, he saw Christina and Cynthia cheering. He wished Sarah, Gretchen, and his mother were here watching.

The two riders abruptly came crashing together as though magnetized, then bounced outward in both directions. Danny collided with one. Jason ran into the other rider. In a tangle of flesh, metal, and chains, they crashed, spinning and tumbling across the asphalt.

Everything happened so fast that the only things Danny remembered were Murg's alarmed howling, then the jamming pain in his shoulder. Even his neck hurt. Danny rolled over and over, twisting with something heavy attached to his legs. Then he stopped, although his head was still spinning. His legs hurt, and his bicycle was sitting atop him. He pulled his feet from the clips and looked around. People were running at them.

Groaning, Danny stood unsteadily. The finish line wasn't far away. Where was Murg?

The calico was gingerly walking toward him. Danny grabbed his bicycle, then gently picked up Murg and set her on the carrier. Somebody cheered as Danny painfully climbed back on his bicycle.

Where was Jason? Danny suddenly wondered. He glanced

back. Jason was under a pile of bicycles and screaming hoarsely, tears rolling down his face. A bone was sticking out of his right arm like a white spike.

"I've got to help my friend," Danny said. "Jump, Murg!"

The calico slithered off the bicycle just before Danny dropped it. Riders passed as he moved to help Jason and untangle the accident.

"Sucker!" Spike yelled as he sailed by.

Danny ignored him.

With pain and confusion in his eyes, Jason watched Danny carefully lift the bicycles off him. His mouth formed the word 'why', then others were there, helping him aid Jason. A woman said, "Let me through. I'm a nurse!" More gathered around.

"Finish, man!" Jason yelled hoarsely and nodded toward the line. "I'll be okay."

Danny limped to his bike and climbed aboard. He waited for Murg, then glided to the finish line, pedaling only twice.

He still managed to beat Hank and Rocky.

Spike was laughing at him when Danny came to a stop. "Wimp! Turkey! You're gonna be buying me lunch the rest of the year or making hide payments."

Danny just shrugged and walked over to the curb where he dropped his damaged bicycle and sat. He was a loser! And he hurt all over. He'd scraped his chin and bled from the mouth. His right knee was lacerated along with his elbow and hand. They throbbed in time with his shoulder. His neck was stiff, too. A fine way to finish my first and probably last race, Danny thought.

A woman asked him to walk to the first aid tent to be examined. With her help, he made it. Another woman cleaned his wounds. As she was putting on the bandages, Christina visited him. She looked serious.

"Hi, Danny. I'm Christina Mornay."

"I know that name. You're an artist."

Christina blushed. "I just want to say that I think what you did was pretty cool. Even heroic." She smiled.

Danny felt better already.

"And so did Cynthia. Jason said thanks, too. As you saw, he has a broken arm. They're taking him to the hospital, but before he left, he told me to tell you that if you lost to Spike because of him, he'd buy lunch for Spike the rest of the year!"

Danny smiled. "Really?"

"Yeah! Hey, you gonna be okay?"

"I think so." He looked down at himself, then out the tent flap at his bicycle. "My bike's not in too good of shape, though."

"I'm sorry. It looks horrible."

"Me too, I've got to ride it home."

"No! Really?" she asked.

Danny nodded.

"You rode it here?"

"I had to if I wanted to race."

"Hey, my mom will probably take you home. Want a ride?"

"Definitely," Danny said with a broad smile.

"How come you ride with a cat?"

"She used to ride with my sister before she died, and now Murg won't take no for an answer. It's either take her along or look like this all the time," Danny said, holding up his bandaged arms.

Christina laughed. "I love cats. Hey, I'm having a party," she began as they walked out to his bicycle.

Chapter Twenty-Seven

Second Chances

"**Y**ou what?" Danny's father exclaimed shortly after Danny had explained what had happened in the race. His expression was one of total disbelief.

"I stopped to help my friend. The accident was terrible. His arm was broken, and he was screaming."

His father rolled his eyes. "But you were winning. Winning! And you just quit! Spike beat you! Damn it! That's part of your problem, Danny. You don't stick to things. You don't care enough about winning." He began to pace.

Danny was silent, thinking about what his mom had told him. She should see us now, Danny thought sadly.

"I don't know what I'm going to do with you. Sometimes I really wonder if you're my son. We aren't interested in the same things at all." Frustrated, his father dropped into a chair, sighed in exasperation, then closed his eyes.

Danny started to speak, nothing came out, so he tried again. "Mom said that people are more important than things."

His father looked at him sharply.

But Danny managed to continue. "And that winning and being popular don't matter very much if you're not happy being yourself. That family, friends, and helping people were important." Danny tried to go on but couldn't. The words seemed to enlarge, wedging in his throat.

His father continued to stare.

Not being able to stand it, Danny looked down at the floor.

Finally, his father looked away with a distantly thoughtful expression, then he broke the silence and said, "That does sound like your mother, doesn't it?"

Danny nodded.

"Well, there's certainly no question that you're her son."

"Why can't we just get along like we used to?" Danny asked.

"Things have changed. Well, I'll just have to adjust, but I don't think I can take your mom's place." He was quiet for a minute, then said, "How badly are you hurt? Should I take you to a doctor?"

"I don't think so. I just need to keep the wounds clean and take some aspirin or something. I'll have to toss papers with the other arm."

"All right. Let me know if you change your mind. Now tell me about your friend – Jackson, was it?"

"Jason," Danny corrected, then told him what he remembered about Jason from the other time when they'd been friends. The time that was no longer. Danny mentioned that Jason didn't have any brothers and that he was also new at school.

"I enjoyed having brothers, somebody to do things with. Tell me, son, before the accident, you said you were winning."

Danny nodded, somewhat proud of himself.

"How did it feel?"

"Exhilarating. I haven't felt anything like it. I was tired, but I wasn't, you know. It's kind of hard to explain. I was full of fire, I guess. I was imagining winning, and I felt... proud. I thought you'd be proud of me, too. But – "

"Really? You enjoyed it, then?"

"Yes."

"Good. Then I think you should keep riding and see if you can win the next one," he suggested.

Danny was shocked.

"When is the next one," he asked Danny.

"Thanksgiving. In Denton. The Turkey Trot."

"Thanksgiving? So soon. Then you'd better start training, that is, if you're interested."

"Yes!"

"But we can't have your grades stay the way they are if you're going to race. As long as you improve your grades and keep them up, at least B's," his father said sternly, "you can keep racing."

"Deal!" Danny jumped off the couch and into his father's arms. "Thanks, Dad."

His father hugged him back. "Danny, I'm sorry. I don't promise anything except I'll try to do much better. I just get mad – and frustrated so easily. I miss them so much."

"I miss them, too. Every minute," Danny agreed. "I'll try to do better, too. It's a long race, isn't it?"

"Yes. Yes, it is," he replied, his eyes shining. "Now, let's take a look at your bicycle. It may need some repair work."

"We'll do it together, Dad."

Tired, aching but happy, Danny dragged himself up the steps and to his bedroom. He collapsed on his bed as though there wasn't a single bone in his body. They'd spent hours repairing his bicycle, talking and having a good time.

Murg came strolling into his room and sat staring at him. "Murg! What a day! Who would have thought that by not winning the race I still won."

Murg purred.

"Now I can start all over again without my moods getting in the way with Jason and Christina. At least I hope so."

Murg meowed encouragement

"I guess making peace with the past and letting it lie is important."

Murg caterwauled.

Danny closed his eyes and sent a heartfelt thanks out into the world. "Thanks, Mom! Thanks, Kalyde!"

"You know, my friend," Danny said sadly. "I miss talking to you and having you talk back."

Murg strolled over to the closet door and rubbed against it. "And I'll miss being able to zip over and see Gretchen. We were rainbow riders!" Murg sat for a moment, gave Danny an irritated look and began scratching the doors. "The speed was very cool, too," he said wistfully. "Oh, well, you can't have everything, I guess."

Frustrated, Murg caterwauled, then ran and jumped on Danny before returning to the closet door and sitting in front of it.

"What? Oh? What's in the closet?" Danny rolled out of bed and limped to the closet. "You want me to check it?" Danny asked and Murg nodded. "Okay."

Danny pulled it open and gasped. "Kalyde II! And there's a note on it!" Danny snatched it from the handlebars.

Murg jumped onto the bicycle's carrier. "What's it say?"

Danny smiled. "It's from Kah-laye-dee!"

Murg just rolled her eyes.

"It says that if I return the bicycle he will be shamed. On Cor-ror-o'lan, any gifts returned are deemed improper and insulting. He asks me to keep Xenden – I guess that's the name of the bicycle – but to promise not to do any more time traveling. He trusts me! This way a part of him will always be with us. Yes!" Danny heard his voice echo – and suddenly became subdued.

"That's right," Murg said with quiet exasperation, "or your dad will hear you."

"Sorry. Yes. Yes. Yes. Yes." Danny was so happy that he grabbed Murg and began dancing. He didn't ache any more. "Thanks, Kalyde," he whispered. Danny closed his eyes, touched the bicycle and visualized it as a watch. Swelling warmth was accompanied by a squeaking as if something were being compressed.

Danny opened his eyes. "It still works." Danny put his watch in the drawer, then strapped Kalyde II to his wrist. "Murg, we're going to be smarter about using Kalyde this time. Sneakier and more careful."

"Ah wisdom – at last. You're on a roll. Roll with it," Murg told him.

Danny went downstairs to the kitchen telephone. He dialed Christina's number. "Hello? Christina? Hi, this is Danny Chase! I know this is unexpected, but – uh, I was wondering if you'd go riding with me. I know where I can get a tandem. Yeah, two seats. Uh, yes, now. No, if I'm riding with you I'm sure I won't be tired anymore. You will! Cool! I'll be there in about an hour! Oh, yeah, I need directions." He jotted them down. He wasn't supposed to have been there, yet. "Yes, Murg will be coming." Danny looked at the calico.

Murg winked back at him.

"Dad, I'm going riding," Danny said quietly.

"Again? So soon?" he asked without looking up.

Danny didn't say anything.

"Getting an early start on training, eh?" He looked up. "You sure you're ready?"

Danny nodded. "I want to test it. Make sure it's okay."

"Fine, son. Just be sure you're back in time to deliver

tonight's papers."

"Okay."

Outside in the garage, Danny and Murg climbed onto the bicycle and headed for the woods. They found a well-concealed spot, and he locked his bicycle to a tree, then took off his watch. "You know, riding is going to heal my wounds."

"That's a good thing," Murg allowed.

"But I'll have to keep wearing the bandages. Like I said, we're going to be smarter about this – this time," Danny repeated.

"I will help wherever and whenever I can. I'm fond of the bicycle, and you too!"

Danny set the watch on the ground, then thought of Kalyde II becoming a bicycle. With a dazzling glow that enveloped them in warmth, Kalyde II expanded, changing shape and color as it became a bicycle once again. With a smile, he set Murg on the carrier, then climbed aboard.

"Hang on!" Danny shouted. He pedaled faster and faster, racing down the street and heading for Christina's house. If Jason was in the hospital, Danny would suggest visiting him.

All in all, he somehow thought that Sarah and his mother would be satisfied with things, if not happy . . .

Then the wind and speed wrapped around him to carry his cares away and fire his imagination, again.

Vampire Hunters
Selection from Chapter One
"The Initiation"

"Ahhh . . ." the front door opened slowly, allowing a faint light to be cast across the porch. Scooter jumped a foot and almost screamed. Startled, he darted behind the bushes near the gate, then peered around the corner and through the gate. At first, Chandler's shadow was crisp, his slender form distinctly outlined against the interior light, but the backlit darkness couldn't totally conceal his pale complexion. His face and arms had a gleaming quality that reminded Scooter of earlier, when the house had radiated an eerie luminescence. Dressed in navy clothing, Chandler appeared disembodied, his bald head and bare arms floating along as though unattached.

Scooter was amazed. Was he really black? Afro-American? How could anyone tell? Because his parents had been black? Marcus Chandler was white, whiter than sun-bleached bones.

Scooter took a breath, crossed his fingers, then jumped in front of the infamous director. With quivering hands, Scooter snapped picture after picture, the flash illuminating the night as though lightning from a storm.

"AWWWW!" Chandler screamed, his hands going to his face, covering his eyes. In the flashing white light, Scooter could see Chandler's gaunt face. It had been transformed into something horrible, contorted and twisted as if he were in sheer agony.

His flesh appeared to take on an even brighter, unholy illumination. His eyes were amazingly bright, blazing red embers within deep black pits.

"Who's there! Damn you! Damn the press! Why won't you ever leave me alone!" Chandler suddenly swung at Scooter, who stumbled backwards to avoid the blow. Almost dropping the camera, Scooter turned and ran toward the Armadillos.

"You're dead meat!" Chandler cried as he blindly pursued the young redhead.

"Hear me! Dead meat! You're not in California anymore! You're in TEXAS! Hear me! Texas! And you're trespassing on my property!"

Kristie and Russell looked at each other with fear in their eyes, their thoughts the same: Run! Straining at his collar, Flash barked. As Scooter raced past them, not even pausing as he tossed Garrett the camera, the golden Lab jerked free and joined his friend in flight. Russell and Kristie bolted together, following in Scooter's wake.

"Nothing to worry about," Garrett told them.

"Race to the wheels . . ." CJ yelled.

"Yeah!" BJ said. Holding their hats, the brothers fled. Jo was just a few slow steps behind.

Garrett knelt to pick up the fallen photo, then stood, looking from the gray slate to Chandler. As Garrett watched, the infamous director sprinted through the grass, unerringly heading toward the truck they were hiding behind as if guided by radar, Racquel's fingernails dug painfully into his arm.

Garrett's sneer was short-lived, his expression slowly becoming doubtful. He wasn't afraid of anything . . . unless this guy was really a vampire. Could that be? Impossible. But . . . he looked like a vampire! And the way he moved . . . "Come on, Racquel," Garrett breathed, scared for the first time in a long time. As Chandler hurtled the fence, Garrett grabbed Racquel and ran as fast as he could, dragging her along with him.

"Please! So help me, I'll never do this again!" Russell gasped as he ran, holding his arms in front of his face for protection from the ripping branches. He could barely see Scooter and Flash ahead of him, darting in and out of the trees with surprising agility.

Despite his awkwardness, nobody could outrun the Scooter. He would get to the bicycles first. But what about the rest of them? If he was caught and his dad found out . . . Russell sprinted as if slavering Dobermans were breathing down his heels.

Huffing and grunting, Jo ran as fast as she could, rumbling through the woods. She wanted to be far away from here. Jo liked to believe she was like her three brothers – one tough *gringa*. But now, all she wanted was to cruise the backyards on her Harley, the wind in her face blowing away the fear and sweat. Something grabbed at her feet. Jo stumbled. Unable to recover, she fell forward.

Nearby, Kristie came to a halt. Was that a scream? She strained to listen, but couldn't hear anything besides the thundering of her heart and the gasping of her ragged breath. She couldn't see anything either. What if something had happened to one of them? She was unexplainably afraid for Scooter. Should she use her flashlight? Or would it give her away? She wished she had never come along – wished she were elsewhere.

Unable to control her fear, Kristie fled. The boys would take care of themselves. Boys always did. In the distance, she heard a dog bark and wondered about Scooter. She said a heartfelt prayer for him as she ran.

"Man, oh man, oh man . . ." Scooter breathed, sprinting all out and easily outdistancing the others. He barely noticed Flash running smoothly alongside. Scooter ran through a low branch that nearly decapitated him and he didn't even slow down.

He had only one thought in mind. ESCAPE! Unless he was lost, the chain link fence should be coming up soon. Then he'd be at the deserted house, on his bicycle and long gone.

Scooter thought he heard the crack of a stick behind him. Worried about his friends, Scooter glanced over his shoulder. "Russell?" As he turned around, something bit into Scooter's leg and he somersaulted head over heels, his world abruptly crashing to black. Flash began barking wildly.

"Where's Russell?" Racquel asked Garrett.

"He'll be fine," Garrett replied. She looked doubtful, so he kissed her on the cheek and said, "Probably ahead of us. He left before we did. Trust me, Babe." Racquel didn't smile, so he said, "Come on, or I'm gonna leave ya." Racquel hesitated only a moment before following.

Still running, Russell thought he heard something fall, then the silence was heavy as the rapidly thickening fog muffled all sound. The mists were pervasive and almost waist deep in some places. He couldn't see where he was running and worried he might step in a hole.

Somewhere, Flash began barking. Russell paused, struck by the feeling that something had happened to Scooter. Should he look for him? He heard a soft swishing noise. Then a slow intake of breath, followed by a much sharper gasp. Russell's fear threw him into overdrive. Hoping Scooter would forgive him for being a coward and a deserter, Russell sprinted toward the abandoned cabin.

Elsewhere in the woods, BJ grabbed CJ by the arm. "The bicycles are this way."

"No way, bud. Your sense of direction sucks," CJ disagreed, but BJ dragged him along anyway. They quickly moved toward a thicket where a colossal oak had fallen long ago. It was draped so heavily in fog it might have been poured like soup. A gentle breeze wafted through, and the mists around the tree shifted as though the downed colossus were going to arise.

"We're lost!" CJ cried. "And I lost my glasses! Hey, I thought I saw something," he said as he pointed ahead.

"Right, son of Helen Keller. Ya don't even have . . ." BJ started, then he too saw the cloud of dark fog. It drifted toward them, gathering and assuming a human form. Its arms stretched forward, claws reaching for them. "Let's get out of here!" They ran, stumbling along, missing trees but tripping over rocks, stumps and fire ant mounds. All around the fog continued to grow thicker and thicker, entrapping the duo within its misty borders.

"Wish you hadn't dropped the flashlight," BJ said.

"Moan and groan. Moan and groan," CJ retorted. "It won't do us any good anyway." They had come to a line of buried pickups that stretched left and right. The row was truncated at four trucks as though the rest of the world didn't exist.

"We're going in a circle!" BJ cursed.

"I told you!"

As though a breeze touched the mists, they suddenly billowed and roiled. Something appeared to slide out from between the upended trucks. The boys reversed direction, bolting into the woods with fear driving them on.

After a seemingly endless time of flight, the brothers finally paused near an old rusted pickup sitting in the woods by itself. They bent over with hands on their knees, their breathing harsh and raspy. Cold sweat ran down their faces and their shirts were soaked. They hoped to have outraced whatever was pursuing them. "I'm exhausted," CJ gasped. "I swear either he's fast, or two things are chasing us!" BJ simply nodded, unable to speak.

Something suddenly appeared in the fog, quickly moving in and out of the tall grasses. As it grew closer, for a moment, BJ thought he recognized the figure. "Dad?" he whispered incredulously.

There was the sharp snapping of a stick behind the brothers. "COME ON!" CJ cried. BJ looked for the familiar figure – one that couldn't have been there – and found nothing in the mists. He must have been imagining things. Hoping Dad would come back. Footfalls were heavy behind them. "COME ON!" CJ cried again, grabbing his brother this time. "I see him! He's here! Chandler's here!"

The Mochrie brothers fled at a dead run.

Shortly, BJ and CJ arrived at a creek bed where the fog was even worse, heavier and opaque. CJ paused, but BJ said, "Keep going this way."

"I can't. I'm beat!"

"You won't believe what I thought I saw . . ." BJ began. He thought he saw something out of the corner of his eye. "I ain't puttin' up with this any more!" He shakily pulled out the .38. "Show yourself!" he wanted to say, "Dad!" but did not. He might be imagining things – his fear and wishes combining together.

Both were sure they heard the quiet, mocking laughter this time. BJ hesitated, unnerved and unsure of where to fire. The laughter came from every direction. "That old guy is everywhere!" CJ whispered desperately.

"Like a vampire!"

The brothers looked at each other and ran again. CJ was behind his brother when something suddenly grabbed him, lifting him off his feet. "Got you!" Chandler cried.

CJ couldn't breathe! Couldn't scream!

"CJ?" BJ called as he skidded to a stop. Where was he? Damn the fog! "What's wrong, bro? BRO! COME ON! THAT VAMPIRE'S COMIN'! He's on our right!"

To his right and not far away, the white mists whirled and roiled. A cold breeze rippled past him as something dark took shape within the fog. Eyes of red flame held him frozen for a moment, then BJ raised his .38 and fired again and again, the blast ripping the night and echoing along the lake. The .38 clicked empty and BJ turned and ran. That hadn't been his dad! He was just imagining things! Wishing he was here to save them!

CJ heard his brother flee. He jerked back a bit and managed to gasp, "BJ! Don't . . ."

"You're going to pay!" Chandler shouted at CJ. The angry moviemaker leaned forward, his pale face twisted with anger and his eyes blood red and blazing. "And how! You'll wish you had never come here!"

Panic surged through CJ. He tried to escape, but could not. The fog seemed to thicken, then darkness encroached from all sides.

California Ghosting
Selection from Chapter One
"Ghostly Hitchhikers"

Blasing didn't respond. He recognized when simply saying anything could provoke a confrontation. Blasing saw something out of the corner of his eye. "LOOK OUT!"

Angela looked back to the road and slammed on the brakes. An old man and his mule were in the road! Angela cringed, awaiting the bone-crushing thump and the sight of bodies flying.

Instead, the pack animal and its master passed through the hood, then the windshield. The ethereal prospector smiled a toothless grin and doffed his dusty cap as he sliced through the interior of the 4-Runner. The ghostly mule was less accepting, its eyes wide with panic. Suddenly, the rank smells of old sweat, dust and unwashed mule overwhelmed them.

After the 4-Runner squealed to a stop, Blasing whirled around, eyes popping wide. "What the hell was that?" He pointed at the grayed and somewhat translucent miner dressed in worn clothing. As if desert mirages, distorted background shapes could be seen through the spirit. The ghost was obviously angry, cursing and tugging on his mule's bit, trying to convince it to move. The pale beast was amazingly overloaded with transparent boxes and bags bound together as if caught in a large spider's web.

"Is that a ghost?" Blasing whispered incredulously. "Ms.

Starborne, I . . . ." His lips worked silently.

Angela watched Blasing struggle with the concept of wandering spirits, his handsome face a mask of stunned confusion and his eyes unsettled. He ran a hand through his hair, then his dark gaze met her unwavering stare; he seemed to have composed himself quickly. "I don't believe in ghosts." He didn't sound convinced.

"You will," Angela said cryptically, no longer looking at Blasing but feeling the weight of his stare. "Maybe he's . . . wandered away." According to Peter, this wasn't supposed to happen.

"Wandered away? From where?"

"I'll ask," Angela said, trying to sound casual as she began rolling down her window. Her heart was pounding, her palms were damp, and the urge for a cigarette was strong.

"Isn't that dangerous?" Blasing asked. The near accident was not a big deal, but she was acting as if this were an ordinary, everyday experience.

"It might be."

The ghost spat, wiped his mouth. "Lillybell! Dang it ya floppy-eared varmint. If I had my stick ya wouldn't be actin' like this!" The mule appeared offended, setting its ears back in preparation for the forthcoming struggle.

Angela cleared her throat, starting to speak, but was stopped by the ghostly prospector. "This is your fault, purdy lady. Why I oughtta . . ." He began stalking toward the car.

The mule snorted, then nosed its master, almost knocking him off his feet. The miner staggered, then whirled quickly, yanking off his hat and slapping his unruly companion. "Think you're cute, do ya?" Lillybell bared her teeth, then began hee-hawing and rocking back and forth. Madder than a hornet, the prospector threw down his hat and began hopping back and forth.

"You know, I've never heard of a ghost being this far away

from the resort," Angela said tightly. Then she realized she'd let important information slip.

"You mean the Ghostal Shores Resort really is haunted?" Blasing asked. "Not just a gimmick like Disneyland?"

"This makes no sense at all," Angela continued uneasily, trying to ignore Blasing's hot stare. "Spirits are supposed to be tied to a person or a place, not wandering around looking for food and lodging."

"Ghostly hitchhikers. Right."

"Believe it," Angela replied.

"I wish I'd stayed in Tahoe instead of letting you drag me here. All I have to deal with there are drunks, jealous boyfriends and confused teenagers in hormonal overdrive."

Angela's eyes flashed, then narrowed; she bit back a retort, along with a childish urge to stick out her tongue.

It was probably wise to drive away, but Angela found herself morbidly fascinated. The old miner had moved behind his mule and was leaning against its rear, grunting loudly and pushing as hard as he could. The mule took two quick steps forward, then another sideways. The prospector fell on his face, partly disappearing into the ground.

Angela almost laughed but didn't, sensing the miner might turn his wrath on her. "Are you going to Ghostal Shores?" Angela didn't recognize him, so he certainly wasn't from the resort.

The miner didn't reply, instead he hauled himself to his feet and began digging into a pack. "Ya win, ya ornery beast." He gave Lillybell a sugar cube. "Lady, will ya kindly get your newfangled whatchamacallit out of the way? The first carriage that went by really shook up Lillybell, but you scared the hell outta her!"

Angela's anger swelled; she started to say something about walking in the middle of the road, then realized it was pointless. When you were dead, you didn't care about getting run over.

"I said get the hell outta here!" He began to walk menacingly toward them. "Nobody messes with JP Johnson!"

"Ms. Starborne . . ." Blasing began.

Without another word, Angela stomped on the gas pedal and the 4-Runner raced away.

Otter Creek Press, Inc.
P. O. Box 416
Doctors Inlet, FL 32030-0416

Telephone: (904) 264-0465
Toll Free: (800) 326-4809
Email: OtterPress@aol.com

You May Order

Retail price: $13.95 (U.S.); $15.95 (Canada)
Please include $4.00 per copy for tax, shipping & handling

Copies _____   Amount Enclosed _____

Name of Book _____

Name _____

Address _____

City _____ State _____ Zip _____

Otter Creek Press, Inc., accepts money orders and checks.

About the Author

William Hill

William Hill is a native of Indianapolis, Indiana, and first learned to read through comic books and adventure and science fiction novels.

Although not a military brat, he has lived in Kansas (Shawnee Mission), Tennessee (Nashville and Bristol – setting of *Dawn of the Vampire*), and Texas (Denton, Dallas, Richardson, and Cedar Creek – setting of *Vampire's Kiss* and *Vampire Hunt*). He has "serious" degrees in Economics from Vanderbilt University and an MBA from the University of North Texas.

Since realizing that the corporate world stifled creative thought and discouraged personal imagination, Bill has been employed as an alchemist in South Lake Tahoe and an EMT/Ski Patroller at a North Lake Tahoe resort.

Although his first writing love is magic-oriented fantasy, Hill's first and second novels – *Dawn of the Vampire* and *Vampire's Kiss* – were supernatural thrillers published by Pinnacle.

Bill and his lovely and supportive wife, Kat, currently reside in Lake Tahoe, Nevada. **Bill intends to write imaginative fiction and fantasy until dirt is shoveled upon his coffin.**